MAINLINE CHRISTIANS AND U.S. PUBLIC POLICY

Selected Titles in ABC-CLIO's
CONTEMPORARY
WORLD ISSUES
Series

For a complete list of titles in this series, please visit
www.abc-clio.com.

Books in the Contemporary World Issues series address vital issues in today's society such as genetic engineering, pollution, and biodiversity. Written by professional writers, scholars, and nonacademic experts, these books are authoritative, clearly written, up-to-date, and objective. They provide a good starting point for research by high school and college students, scholars, and general readers as well as by legislators, businesspeople, activists, and others.

Each book, carefully organized and easy to use, contains an overview of the subject, a detailed chronology, biographical sketches, facts and data and/or documents and other primary-source material, a directory of organizations and agencies, annotated lists of print and nonprint resources, and an index.

Readers of books in the Contemporary World Issues series will find the information they need in order to have a better understanding of the social, political, environmental, and economic issues facing the world today.

MAINLINE CHRISTIANS AND U.S. PUBLIC POLICY

A Reference Handbook

Glenn H. Utter

CONTEMPORARY WORLD ISSUES

A B C CLIO

Santa Barbara, California
Denver, Colorado
Oxford, England

Library of Congress Cataloging-in-Publication Data
Utter, Glenn H.
   Mainline Christians and U.S. public policy : a reference handbook / Glenn H. Utter.
      p.   cm. — (Contemporary world issues)
   Includes bibliographical references and index.
   ISBN-13: 978-1-59884-000-1 (hard copy : alk. paper)
   ISBN-13: 978-1-59884-001-8 (ebook)
   1. Christianity—United States. 2. Christianity and politics—United States. I. Title.
   BR515.U88 2007
   261.80973—dc22

                                                                      2007014509

12   11   10   09   08   07   1   2   3   4   5   6   7   8   9   10

ABC-CLIO, Inc.
130 Cremona Drive, P.O. Box 1911
Santa Barbara, California 93116-1911

This book is also available on the World Wide Web as an ebook. Visit www.abc-clio.com for details.

This book is printed on acid-free paper ∞

Manufactured in the United States of America

Contents

Preface

This reference work offers an overview of eight major mainline Protestant denominations along with the Catholic Church in the United States and the value positions they promote in the public arena, emphasizing the differences as well as similarities among them. The book presents these churches' historical development from colonial times to the present; the dominant values held by the leadership, clergy, and lay members; their social missions; and their efforts to influence public opinion and public policy on several social, economic, and political issues. An examination of the conversations, disagreements, and interest conflicts within each denomination provides insight into how value positions and the relationship between the denominations and the larger world have developed.

The first chapter offers a brief historical sketch of each denomination as well as a description of its organizational structure. Of particular interest is how members of the church may voice their views. In these religious groups, members' views often are strongly held and frequently relate to deep matters of faith in God, assumptions about the purpose of human life, and intensely held moral convictions about acceptable behavior. Therefore, not surprisingly, religious denominations historically have experienced divisions as well as strenuous efforts to bring about collaboration and union among groups that share common beliefs and concerns. As with any organization, Robert Michels's "iron law of oligarchy"—any organization, no matter how democratically structured, tends to be governed by a relatively small elite; the law is exemplified by the quote, "Who says organization says oligarchy"—confronts those in the mainline denominations who wish to express their concerns to the overall church. However, in recent decades an interesting phenomenon within mainline denominations has occurred that at least partially moderates the effects of Michels's law: dissident members have formed so-called renewal movements in order to create an effective voice in discussions of Christian doctrine, traditions, and policy.

Chapter 2 examines in greater detail various public policy questions on which the nine denominations treated here have taken public stands. The dominant value concerns of these churches become clearer as they are expressed in concrete issues such as capital punishment, embryonic stem-cell research, the war in Iraq, and abortion. There tends to be overall agreement among the denominations on many of these issues, but at times interesting distinctions become evident. Often European countries are contrasted with the United States regarding the level of religious belief and commitment among citizens. Chapter 3 provides a brief examination of the historical development of religious institutions and their present status in six European countries: England, France, Germany, Italy, Poland, and Sweden. With the exception of Poland, these countries, from which many U.S. mainline churches originated, have far lower rates of religious participation than the United States.

Chapter 4 presents a chronology of events related to the nine U.S. mainline denominations, beginning with the colonial period and ending with the most recent events affecting the status of these churches. Such historical events as the American Civil War, the two world wars, the Great Depression, and the Vietnam conflict often initiated debates and influenced the activities of the denominations. Chapter 5 offers biographical sketches of individuals associated with the mainline denominations, including historical figures such as Reinhold Niebuhr and Harry Emerson Fosdick, who contributed significantly to developing the character and values of mainline Christianity, and recent denomination leaders as well as more controversial persons, such as Daniel Berrigan, John Shelby Spong, and Joan Chittister, who have urged their denominations and the general public to take ever-greater steps toward modification of traditionally held values.

Chapter 6 presents data derived from recent studies of religious behavior in the United States, including membership trends and the attitudes of mainline clergy toward various types of political behavior. Importantly, all the mainline denominations treated here, with the exception of the Catholic Church, have experienced declining membership in recent decades. In addition to data summaries, the chapter provides selected documents that present the positions denominational and ecumenical organizations and members have taken on public policy questions. They defend their views in the context of often passionate expressions of value convictions. Chapter 7 lists selected organizations associated with mainline denominations. These organizations either operate in close concert with the denominations to further the goals of the church in the wider society, or strive to alter the doctrinal direction and policy stances of the denomination. Finally, Chapter 8 includes an annotated bibliography of selected print and nonprint resources that the reader may consult for further investigation of these institutions that have played, and continue to play, an important role in American social and political systems.

I wish to thank the Reverend Gerald Haglund, a Conservative Congregational Christian Conference chaplain, and my colleagues at Lamar University, John W. Storey, chair of the history department and James L. True, Jack Brooks chair of government and public service in the political science department, all of whom are good friends, for the stimulating conversations that helped me to understand more clearly the place of religion in public life. In addition, I want to express my sincere appreciation to Brenda Nichols, dean of the College of Arts and Sciences, Cruse Melvin, associate dean of the College of Arts and Sciences, and Stephen Doblin, provost and vice president for academic affairs at Lamar University, for the generous support they provided in helping me complete this writing project. Of course I accept full responsibility for any errors of fact or judgment.

1

Background and History

Although there are a multitude of Christian denominations in the United States, this study concentrates on the larger groups that are commonly categorized as mainline. Mainline denominations generally include those churches that can trace their history back several generations, usually at least to the nineteenth century. They can be distinguished from those Christian groups that tend to hold conservative or fundamentalist beliefs and associated values, which are usually referred to as evangelical. Evangelicals or fundamentalists tend to accept the inerrancy of the Bible. The scriptures are considered a correct and complete guide to living as a Christian because its authors received inspiration directly from God and therefore at least the original writings contain no errors of history, science, or rules of conduct.

In contrast, the mainline denominations accept the Bible as divinely inspired, but do not necessarily regard scripture as devoid of error or cultural influence. Therefore, mainline denominations more willingly debate contemporary issues such as evolution, same-gender marriage, and the ordination of homosexuals. Mainline denominations traditionally have placed greater emphasis on the "social gospel," holding that Christians have the responsibility of improving the physical condition of human beings in addition to concerning themselves with the status of others' souls. Mainline denominations may be less emphatic regarding other Christian beliefs, such as the deity, virgin birth, the bodily resurrection of Jesus, and the second coming of Jesus as prophesied in the Book of Revelation. Nonetheless, as the preamble to the National Council of Churches of Christ in the USA states, the member denominations—including all of the mainline Protestant churches that are treated in this book—"in response to the gospel as revealed in the Scriptures, confess Jesus Christ, the incarnate Word of God, as Savior and Lord" (NCC 1996).

Mainline Denominations

This volume will focus on nine mainline denominations: the Episcopal Church, Presbyterian Church (U.S.A.), Evangelical Lutheran Church in America, Christian Church (Disciples of Christ), American Baptist Churches in the USA, United Church of Christ, Reformed Church in America, United Methodist Church, and Catholic Church. With the exception of the Catholic Church, these denominations, in contrast to what can be categorized as fundamentalist, or evangelical, denominations, have all experienced a decline in membership over at least the last decade. While the Catholic Church has increased the numbers of members, from 46.6 million in 1965 to 65.3 million in 2002, its proportion of the U.S. population has actually decreased slightly, from 24 percent in 1965 to 23 percent in 2002 (Steinfels 2004, 29). The increased membership in the Catholic Church has been attributed to a great extent to the arrival of large numbers of immigrants from countries in which a substantial proportion of the population are Catholic adherents.

Although much discussion has occurred in recent years regarding the increased participation of evangelical denominations in politics, the mainline churches have a long tradition of involvement in various public policy issues and have attempted to achieve objectives closely associated with their values, which are in turn related to the basic religious beliefs of the organizations. These churches have acted on the conviction that their members have a basic responsibility for caring for their fellow human beings, that there exists a fundamental brotherhood and sisterhood (or at least neighborhood) of humankind. They have established extensive bureaucratic organizations to carry out these responsibilities, and many have founded offices in Washington DC to have some influence on national policy. For instance, the national office of the United States Conference of Catholic Bishops is located in the nation's capital. In 1948 eight Lutheran bodies established the Lutheran Council to represent them in Washington. In 1946 the northern Presbyterians established a part-time representative in the capital. The National Council of Churches, an organization of which several of the mainline denominations are members, established a Washington office in the early 1950s and took part in the political effort to gain passage of the Civil Right Act of 1964.

The following sections present introductory profiles of the nine denominations, each of which has a unique historical development and an organizational structure that resulted from the union of differing factions within the same tradition of beliefs and values.

The Episcopal Church

The word "episcopal" derives from the Greek *episcopos*, which means overseer, or bishop, and hence the Episcopal Church specifically acknowledges the importance and authority of bishops within the organizational structure (Wall 2000, 48). The church believes that a continuous line of church leaders, called the apostolic succession, exists from Jesus's original apostles to the present. Apostolic succession is represented in rites of ordination and consecration of bishops, priests, and deacons by the laying on of hands by a bishop (ibid., 10). Konolige and Konolige (1978, 5) refer to Episcopalians as "Episcocrats"—the traditional aristocrats of the United States. The Episcopal Church has its beginnings in the colonial era as the Church of England's (Anglican) representative in the New World. The Puritans in Massachusetts had left England for the New World in part to separate themselves from the Church of England, so the Anglican Church did not have a great presence in New England. Its greatest support developed in the royal colonies of Maryland, Virginia, North Carolina, and South Carolina (Konolige and Konolige 1978, 43). Only with the presence of royal authority did the church extend its presence in the colonies. Konolige and Konolige (1978, 50) note that Anglicanism appealed to those who preferred to have religion play a less dominant and burdensome role in their lives. Unlike the Puritans and other Christian groups, Anglicans were more tolerant of such behavior as drinking alcohol, dancing, and various other social practices that Puritans considered to be vices.

With the American Revolution, Anglican adherents faced the decision of whether to remain loyal to Great Britain and the Church of England or to support a break not only with England but also with its church. Many Anglican priests left their parishes under coercion, and as many as 70,000 church members left the colonies during or immediately following the conflict (ibid., 55). The outcome of the revolution necessitated such a break with the formal structure of the Church of England, and hence the Protestant Episcopal Church in America was born. In subsequent generations, Episcopalians came to prominence in American society, politics, and finance, and many of the more distinguished American citizens were members of the Episcopal Church. Four of the first five presidents were at least nominally associated with the Episcopal Church, which is not surprising because these four presidents (George Washington, Thomas Jefferson, James Madison, and James Monroe) were from Virginia, the state with the greatest allegiance to the Anglican tradition. From the time of Washington to the present, eleven presidents have been affiliated with the Episcopal Church, the greatest number of any denomination. Many other noted Americans were associated with the Episcopal Church. As Konolige and Konolige (1978, 41) state, "Episcopalianism was a large part of the bond that pulled together the great capitalists of the age—the Morgans, Harrimans, Whitneys, Astors, Vanderbilts, Stillmans, Fricks, and the thousands of lesser lights—into a social, political, and business aristocracy that ran America in, and like, their private clubs."

The Episcopal Church membership tended to be conservative in personal conduct and in politics, but theologically more liberal, with less emphasis placed on doctrinal purity and virtuous conduct. In more recent years Episcopalians tended to display greater tolerance toward modes of behavior traditionally condemned by Christians. Presaging the 2003 selection of V. Gene Robinson, an actively gay priest, as a bishop, in 1997 New York Bishop Paul Moore, Jr., ordained a lesbian woman, Ellen Marie Barrett, as a priest, an action that at the time precipitated a great deal of controversy within the church. Some of the Episcopal clergy, bishops James Pike and John Shelby Spong prominent among them, added to the dissension within the church by questioning some of the foundational beliefs of Christians, including the virgin birth, the resurrection of Jesus, and the notion of original sin (see, for instance, Spong 2005).

Within the contemporary Episcopal Church, the principal governing body, the General Convention, meets every three years. The first General Convention met in 1785 in Philadelphia, and the seventy-fifth General Convention met in Columbus, Ohio, in the summer of 2006. The church has established a bicameral convention, composed of a House of Bishops and a House of Deputies. In the House of Bishops, approximately 300 bishops, active and retired, with at least one bishop from each diocese, meet to consider proposed resolutions and legislation. The presiding bishop, selected by the House of Bishops for a nine-year term, chairs the House of Bishops. Each of the dioceses, foreign and domestic, select eight deputies (four laypersons and four others who can be a combination of priests and deacons) as members of the House of Deputies. The House of Deputies considers and votes on legislation independently of the House of Bishops. The president of the House of Deputies, elected by the General Convention, chairs that chamber. The presiding bishop and the president of the House of Deputies establish a number of committees that consider and revise legislative items for presentation to the convention. Similar to the U.S. Congress, legislation must pass both houses in identical language (Straub 2006). The General Convention elects twenty members to the Executive Council—four bishops, four priests or deacons, and twelve laypersons—and the provincial synods elect eighteen additional members. Between meetings of the General Convention, the Executive Council meets once in each of the church's nine provinces to implement the policies adopted by the General Convention.

In addition to the more than 7,200 local parishes, dioceses, and the General Convention, the Episcopal Church is composed of many groups and organizations that engage in the mission of the church, including organizations involved in communication, news publication, and education (eleven seminaries, eight colleges, one university, and over a thousand schools and early childhood education programs). Individual dioceses support social service and health organizations, including homes for the elderly and youth, hospitals, and centers for the homeless (Mead, Hill, and Atwood 2005, 108). The church also supports groups concerned with multicultural programs, racial relations, the environment, economic matters, and the promotion and maintenance of peace.

Presbyterian Church (U.S.A.) (PCUSA)

As with the Episcopal Church, one measure of the political influence of the Presbyterians is the number of presidents who have been affiliated with the denomination: ten presidents have been members of the church. The process of establishing the current Presbyterian organization, the Presbyterian Church (U.S.A.), which took place from 1983 to1987, represented the most recent unification in a general trend of factional divisions and reunifications within the Presbyterian denomination in the United States. The PCUSA resulted from the union of the United Presbyterian Church in the United States (UPCUSA) and the Presbyterian Church in the United States (PCUS). The denomination has a current membership of nearly 3.5 million.

Presbyterianism began in North America in the first decade of the eighteenth century with the establishment of the first presbytery—a court composed of ministers and lay elders—in 1706 (Hart and Noll 1999, 197). The presbytery formed a synod in 1716. In 1788 the church established the Presbyterian General Assembly, which remains the major decision-making body within the denomination. The church leadership tended to oppose the Second Great Awakening, a general religious revival in the United States that occurred from 1800 to 1803, because of the high emotionalism of the revival as well as the lack of emphasis on theological correctness. Many lay members left the church, joining in the creation of the Disciples of Christ and other groups, including the Cumberland Presbyterian Church. In the 1830s the denomination divided over such issues as theology and slavery, forming Old School and New School assemblies. In 1857, as the Civil War approached, New School Presbyterians divided into northern and southern groups, and the Old School followed suit with the secession of the southern states from the union. The southern branch of the Old School became the Presbyterian Church in the Confederate States of America, and following the war the northern wing took the name Presbyterian Church in the United States. In 1870 the northern old and new groups rejoined forces to become the Presbyterian Church in the United States of America (ibid., 197).

Various pressures on organized religious belief in the late nineteenth and early twentieth centuries, including urbanization, industrialization, scientific developments such as Darwinian evolution, and a general secularization in society, encouraged additional divisions among Presbyterians. Many within the denomination attempted to accommodate traditional religious beliefs with these various modernizing currents. Called liberals or modernists, these members supported higher criticism of scripture, regarding the

Bible not as the revealed and inerrant word of God but as a text to be examined using objective scientific and historical methods. The modernists accepted the compatibility of evolutionary theory and religious belief and associated God's revelations with a progressive view of history (ibid., 103). They viewed historical events as a progression toward the establishment of God's kingdom on earth. The church was to be a guide to ethical action and the improvement of humankind, which amounted to advocacy of the social gospel, the belief that the Christian's duty involved ameliorating the social evils attributed to industrialization and urbanization.

More conservative Presbyterians expressed an alternative worldview to that of the liberals, claiming that instead of offering opportunities for progress, the future would bring moral and spiritual decline that would result in the horrible events of the end times prophesied in the Book of Revelation, ultimately ending in Christ's millennial reign on earth. Conservatives in the PCUSA insisted on adherence to traditional Christian doctrine, including the inerrancy of scripture, the virgin birth, and the substitutionary atonement and bodily resurrection of Jesus as the measure of a true Christian. However, the liberals succeeded in making tolerance of opposing views the standard to be followed. In 1936, after the general assembly of the PCUSA suspended J. Gresham Machen from the ministry for establishing the Independent Board for Presbyterian Foreign Missions, Machen founded the Presbyterian Church of America, later renamed the Orthodox Presbyterian Church (OPC). Shortly thereafter, Carl McIntire, a former student of Machen's, left the OPC to establish the Bible Presbyterian Church.

In 1958 the PCUSA and the United Presbyterian Church of North America joined to form the United Presbyterian Church in the United States of America (UPCUSA). Although the Presbyterian Church in the United States, also known as the Southern Presbyterian Church, refused at the time to join the new organization, in 1973 conservative members of the PCUS left the denomination to form the Presbyterian Church in America, thus leading to the union of the UPCUSA and the PCUS to form the Presbyterian Church (U.S.A.) in 1983 (ibid., 198).

The PCUSA organizational structure includes the General Assembly, which meets yearly and acts as the final authority in the church. However, any amendment to the church's constitution requires ratification by the presbyteries, which are the regional church organizations. The stated clerk, elected by the General Assembly, acts as the chief executive officer of the church. Each year the General Assembly selects a moderator to preside over meetings of the group. The moderator also serves as the representative of the church between meetings of the General Assembly. In 1988 the PCUSA established its national headquarters in Louisville, Kentucky. The church's publishing house, Westminster John Knox Press, is also located in Louisville. Sixty-eight colleges maintain relations with the PCUSA, and the church maintains eleven seminaries and six secondary schools (Mead, Hill, and Atwood 2005, 143).

The PCUSA conducts mission activities in several areas. The church supports the Worldwide Ministries Division as well as International Health Ministries, Presbyterian Disaster Assistance, and Interfaith Relations. Within the United States, the church has the National Ministries Division, Multicultural Ministries, Racial Ethnic Ministries, and Presbyterian Border Ministry. The PCUSA focuses on advocacy in several areas, including criminal justice, environmental justice, social witness, women's advocacy, and U.S. foreign policy. The church maintains formal relations with the United Nations and has an office in Washington DC (PCUSA 2006).

Evangelical Lutheran Church in America (ELCA)

The Evangelical Lutheran Church in America (ELCA) is the largest Lutheran denomination in the United States, with just under 5 million members reported in 2006 (*Houston Chronicle* 2006, F3). Although various smaller Lutheran groups make up less than 2 percent of the total number of Lutherans (Noll 2003, 3), the Lutheran Church–Missouri Synod (LCMS) constitutes the next largest alternative Lutheran body, which, along with the Wisconsin Evangelical Lutheran Synod, constitutes approximately 38 percent of Lutherans in the United States (ibid., 4). The ELCA membership thus represents approximately 60 percent of all Lutherans in the United States. However, like other mainline denominations, the ELCA has experienced declining membership in recent years (down just over 2 percent from 1990 to 2000), and the organization achieved its majority status among Lutheran churches not from attracting new members but from the union of various smaller Lutheran bodies. Presiding Bishop Mark Hanson in late 2006 acknowledged that the ELCA had lost 80,000 baptized members in 2005 and 275,000 in the last five years. Hanson advised church members to resist explaining away such declines in terms of demographic trends and instead emphasize the mission of the church to spread the Christian message (Hanson 2007).

Lutherans first gained a presence in North America in the early seventeenth century, when Scandinavian, Dutch, and German settlers came to the New World. They tended to congregate in the Hudson River region, an area that ultimately became the states of New York and New Jersey (ELCA 2006). In the decade following the ratification of the U.S. Constitution, there were approximately 250 Lutheran congregations in Pennsylvania and smaller numbers of Lutherans in other states (Noll 2003, 5). In the next seventy years, the number of congregations grew to more than 2,000 (ibid., 9). Immigrant Lutherans continued to look to their home countries as a major source of pastors, and they often conducted church services in their native language.

As Lutheran groups from different European countries became more integrated into American society, they began the process of merging with one another. The first such significant merger occurred in 1917 when three Norwegian synods combined to establish the Norwegian Lutheran Church of America, and in 1918 three German synods formed the United Lutheran Church in America (ULCA). World War I became a significant spur to cooperation among Lutheran groups who joined forces to provide assistance to U.S. military personnel. In 1917 the National Lutheran Commission (NLC) was established for that purpose. An estimated 60,000 Lutherans became involved in this effort, forming the Lutheran Brotherhood as a separate organization to assist the commission (ELCA 2006, 2). Until 1930 the NLC concentrated it efforts on providing assistance outside the United States, but in that year the organization initiated domestic programs. Also in 1930, three German Lutheran groups combined to form the American Lutheran Church (ALC). After the Second World War, the efforts at unification continued. In 1960 the ALC, an essentially German group, merged with Danish and Norwegian Lutheran groups, maintaining the name American Lutheran Church, and in 1962 the ULCA, German, Slovak, Icelandic, Swedish, Finnish, and

Danish groups joined together as the Lutheran Church in America (LCA) (ELCA 2006).

In 1976 more moderate LCMS members, including 300 congregations and 110,000 lay members, joined to form the Association of Evangelical Lutheran Churches (AELC). In 1979 representatives from the ALC, LCA, and AELC met to form the Committee on Lutheran Unity, and in September 1982 all three Lutheran groups held simultaneous conventions, voting to move toward unification. The conventions approved a proposal to establish the Commission for a New Lutheran Church to deal with the details of the merger. In August 1986 all three groups again met simultaneously and voted to accept the new constitution for a unified Lutheran church, the ELCA, which became the fourth largest Protestant group in the United States.

The Churchwide Assembly, which meets once every four years, acts as the central decision-making body of the ELCA. Approximately 600 lay members, including equal numbers of men and women, and 400 clergy have voting rights at the assembly. The assembly elects a presiding bishop—who serves as the denomination's chief pastor and chief executive officer—and a secretary. It also elects a thirty-seven-member church council, which constitutes a board of directors and serves as the organization's legislative authority between meetings of the assembly (Mead, Hill, and Atwood 2005, 120). The geographical organization of the ELCA includes sixty-five synods in the United States and the Caribbean area. A bishop, elected by the voting members of the synod assembly for a six-year renewable term, governs each synod. Units of the denomination include evangelical outreach and congregational mission; global mission, including missionaries and relief and development; multicultural ministries, including antiracism training; higher education and schools; and Women of the ELCA (ELCA 2005). The publishing outlet for the ELCA is Augsburg Fortress, headquartered in Minneapolis. The ELCA publishes *The Lutheran*, a monthly magazine containing church news and articles about current issues within and outside the denomination. The Department for Ecumenical Affairs engages in interfaith communications and the pursuit of communion with other Christian denominations. The ELCA maintains relations with the Lutheran World Federation, the World Council of Churches, and the National Council of Churches of Christ in the USA.

Christian Church (Disciples of Christ) (CCDC)

The Christian Church (Disciples of Christ) (CCDC) grew out of the Second Great Awakening in the first decade of the nineteenth century and a distinctly American aversion to extra-biblical creeds and the hierarchical structure of many existing denominations. When Barton W. Stone, a Presbyterian minister in Kentucky, held a revival meeting at Cane Ridge in 1801, Presbyterian authorities, disturbed by the indifference toward church doctrine and the emotional behavior of the participants, criticized the event. Stone and five colleagues at first organized a separate presbytery, but in 1804 they disbanded the new organization and established the foundation of what would ultimately become the CCDC on the principles of the Bible as the sole source of authority, the recognition of no organization above the congregation, and the goal of ultimately uniting all Christian believers (Cummins 2003, 3). A contemporary of Stone, Thomas Campbell, immigrated to North America from Ireland in 1807. Originally a Presbyterian minister, Campbell objected to the authority of the Presbyterian establishment and organized the Christian Association of Washington, Pennsylvania. In 1809 Campbell issued his *Declaration and Address,* which contained two basic messages: the essential principles of the New Testament and the objective of Christian unity (ibid., 4). Thomas Campbell's son Alexander also immigrated to the United States and joined his father in the new religious movement. In 1811 the Christian Association became the Brush Run Church, which joined the Redstone Association of Baptists. However, by 1816 Campbell's declarations of grace over law and the New Testament over the Old Testament led to the organization's ouster from the Baptist alliance. Campbell's group joined with another Baptist organization, the Mahoning Baptist Association (ibid., 5), but when the Baptist association dissolved in 1830, the Brush Run Church became an independent organization of Disciples.

In the 1830s Christians and Disciples gradually unified into one movement, and by 1860 the organization had spread widely throughout the United States, with 2,100 congregations and a membership of 200,000 (ibid., 7). Unlike the Presbyterians, who fragmented their organization over the issue of slavery, the Campbell-Stone movement sought to avoid division by declaring the issue to be a matter of opinion rather than of faith (ibid., 8). From the end of the Civil War to the First World War, the movement concentrated on publishing journals, engaging in missionary work, establishing educational institutions, and cooperating with other Christian organizations (for instance, the Disciples became charter members of the Federal Council of Churches in 1908). Following the First World War, controversy erupted among the Disciples over the appropriate interpretation of the Bible, which resulted in the dominance of a theological approach that emphasized more historical investigation of the scriptures and sensitivity to current cultural changes.

Following the Second World War, the Disciples struggled with questions about the overall organizational structure of the group. In the late 1950s the denomination commissioned a panel of scholars to examine organizational guidelines, and in 1960 the church's International Convention established the Commission on Brotherhood Restructure to create a more effective organizational plan to combine the various groups within the Disciples. In 1968 an organization assembly approved the Provisional Design for the Christian Church (Disciples of Christ), transforming the group into an official denomination. In 1997 the groups removed the word "provisional" from the organizational document, but the denomination chose not to prepare a formal constitution (ibid., 15). The CCDC has a current membership of less than one million. Like other mainline denominations, the CCDC lost membership in the 1990s (approximately a 20 percent decline). The CCDC has had influence in government on the federal level, with three of its members being elected president (James A. Garfield, Lyndon B. Johnson, and Ronald Reagan).

Congregations of the CCDC are divided into thirty-five regions. Each region provides various services to the members and ministers of local congregations. The General Assembly, the central representative body, meets once every two years. The Administrative Committee, composed of forty-four voting members, meets twice each year. The general minister and president serves as the general pastor of the denomination, is the chief executive officer responsible for administering the various activities of the church, and is the principal representative of the denomination in ecumenical discussions (CCDC 2006a). The CCDC's publishing outlet, Christian Board of Publication, has its headquarters in St. Louis. The CCDC supports twenty-one colleges and universities, and the National Benevolent Association manages eighty-three operations (Mead, Hill, and Atwood 2005, 251–252). The CCDC's Division of Overseas Ministries supports more than 200 missionaries and others serving in fifty countries. They provide such services as education, health care, refugee assistance, and community development (CCDC 2006b).

American Baptist Churches in the USA (ABC)

Unlike the more conservative and fundamentalist Southern Baptist Convention (SBC), which is the largest Protestant denomination in the United States with more than 16 million members, the American Baptist Churches in the USA (ABC) has a membership of just under 2 million. The denomination's membership declined more than 5 percent between 1990 and 2000. The ABC is a member of the National Council of Churches and generally takes more liberal stands on social issues than does the SBC. The two denominations are alike in their adherence to "believers' baptism," which involves the rejection of infant baptism in favor of limiting this sacrament to those mature enough to express their belief, acceptance of the individual's direct relationship with God, and preference for autonomous local congregations.

The Baptist movement originated in English Congregationalism, which rejected the tradition of individuals entering the Christian church through baptism as children. Rather, membership in the church should be a voluntary individual decision (ABC 2006). The first Baptist churches formed among English-speaking people in Holland because authorities in that country were more tolerant of alternative Christian beliefs than the authorities in England. In 1612 Thomas Helwys, a leader in the movement, returned to England to begin the first Baptist church. Baptists gained a foothold in North America when Roger Williams, then an orthodox Puritan, arrived in Massachusetts in 1631 and soon alienated the Puritan establishment when he claimed that the civil authority should not require residents to adhere to those elements of the Ten Commandments relevant to the relationship between human beings and God (Reichley 2002, 65). In 1636 Williams and a group of followers left the Bay Colony, ultimately settling what would become Rhode Island. The colony allowed freedom of worship, inviting other groups, including Baptists, to settle there. The first

Baptist church in North America was established in Providence. Williams himself became a Baptist but soon left because he disagreed with the radical individualism of the movement.

The Baptist movement continued to expand during the seventeenth century, and in 1707 adherents established the Philadelphia Baptist Association, which included five congregations in Pennsylvania and New Jersey. Baptist groups continued to form and grow throughout the eighteenth century, and by 1790 there were approximately 60,000 members and 560 ministers in 750 churches (ABC 2006). The Second Great Awakening of the first decade of the nineteenth century added greatly to the membership of Baptist churches, and by 1850 they had become the second-largest Protestant denomination in the United States, second only to the Methodists. Reichley (2002, 171) notes that politically, Baptists and many of their leaders in the early nineteenth century, due to their socioeconomic position and support for egalitarian values, tended to support the Jeffersonian Democratic-Republic Party. Baptists also supported a strict separation of church and state. Following the 1787 Constitutional Convention, John Leland, a Virginia Baptist pastor, intended to oppose the new Constitution but withdrew his opposition when James Madison assured him that religious liberty would be guaranteed through ratification of a constitutional amendment. Therefore, present-day Baptists assert that their denomination exercised significant influence on the adoption of the First Amendment guaranteeing religious liberty. The Baptist movement divided in 1845 when the Baptist Home Mission Society rejected a Georgia Baptist affiliate's nomination of a slaveholding minister to become a missionary. In response, Baptists in nine southern states established the Southern Baptist Convention (Reichley 2002, 181–182). The northern Baptists organized as the American Baptist Missionary Union, and in 1907 they established the Northern Baptist Convention. In 1950 the Northern Baptist Convention reorganized, becoming the American Baptist Convention. In 1972 the organization assumed its present name, the American Baptist Churches in the USA.

At the 1972 convention, members restructured the denomination to increase the representation of member groups, establishing a 200-member general board. The effort to provide for greater coordination notwithstanding, the ABC remains committed to the primacy of the local churches in pursuing the Christian mission (ABC 1974). Under the leadership of the general secretary, various

ABC bodies, including the general council of chief executives, the staff of the national program boards, and the chief executives of the thirty-four ABC regions, coordinate the activities of the denomination (Mead, Hill, and Atwood 2005, 189). Each region provides support for individual congregations, including Christian education resources, leadership development, camping programs, and educational opportunities for pastors. The ABC operates twenty children's homes, seventy-seven retirement homes and communities, twenty-seven hospitals and nursing homes, nine theological seminaries, and sixteen colleges and universities. Judson Press serves as the denomination's publishing outlet (ibid., 189).

United Church of Christ (UCC)

In 1957 the unification of four denominations—the Congregational Churches, the Christian Church, the Evangelical Synod, and the Reformed Church in the U.S.—resulted in the United Church of Christ (UCC). The Congregational churches and the Christian Church had merged in 1931 to form Congregational Christian Churches, and the Evangelical Synod and the Reformed Church combined in 1934 to form the Evangelical and Reformed Church. The unification notwithstanding, the four denominations continue to maintain their separate identities (Mead, Hill, and Atwood 2005, 146). The UCC has a membership of approximately 1.7 million; the denomination lost nearly 15 percent of its membership from 1990 to 2000.

The Congregational Churches traditionally have opposed centralized institutional authority. However, throughout the nineteenth century Congregationalists recognized the necessity of some organizational structure. In 1808 the Congregational Andover Theological Seminary was established. Congregational clergy in New England voted to denounce the War of 1812, and ministers presented antiwar sermons. In 1852 the Congregational Churches formed a national organization. In 1853 the Congregational Church in Butler, New York, demonstrating a progressive bent, ordained and called to ministry a woman, Antoinette Brown. In 1867 the Christian Church began to ordain women, becoming the first denomination to do so (UCC 2006a). In 1869 the German Reformed Church, which had taken its name in 1793, abandoned the word German and became the Reformed Church in the United States (Mead, Hill, and Atwood 2005, 128). James O'Kelley, a Methodist who believed that Methodism had become too hierarchical, began the Christian Church in Virginia in the late eighteenth century. At the same time, in Vermont, Abner Jones, a Baptist, established the First Free Christian Church. As other churches were founded, the minimally organized group of organizations became known as the Christian Connection. Other organizers, including Barton W. Stone and Alexander Campbell, hailed as the original founders of the present Christian Church (Disciples of Christ), contributed to the establishment of the Christian movement. In 1844 Christian congregations in the South established a separate Southern Christian Association when the New England Convention of Christians approved a resolution condemning slavery. The two groups did not reunite until 1890 when a new General Convention was established. The Evangelical Synod was formed out of the various groups of Germans, adherents of the Lutheran and Reformed traditions, who came to the United States in the 1830s and 1840s. Several Evangelical groups merged during the second half of the nineteenth century. In 1872 three denominations united to establish what would come to be called the Evangelical Synod of North America. Two prominent theologians, brothers H. Richard Niebuhr and Reinhold Niebuhr, were associated with the Evangelical Synod (UCC 2006b). The General Synod of the Reformed Church approved unification in 1932, and the Evangelical Synod General Convention did so one year later.

In 1937 a study group composed of representatives from the Congregational Christian and Evangelical and Reformed churches began to investigate the feasibility of union. In 1942 the General Synod of the Evangelical and Reformed Church and the General Council of the Congregational Christian Churches registered their support for a unification proposal. However, final merger would take several more years because some members of the Congregational Christian Churches opposed union (UCC 2006c). In 1954 a joint meeting of the Congregational Christian Executive Committee and the Evangelical and Reformed General Council approved a unification plan, the Basis of Union, and in 1957 both groups met at a General Synod in Cleveland, Ohio, to approve the final unification as the United Church of Christ. Those who still opposed the union organized as the National Association of Congregational Christian Churches, which has a current membership of 70,000, and the Conservative Congregational Christian Conference, which has a membership of 40,000.

The UCC has a highly decentralized organizational structure. Its constitution states that "The autonomy of the local church is inherent and modifiable only by its own action" (Mead, Hill, and Atwood 2005, 147). Local churches are grouped geographically into associations. The associations assume the responsibilities of ordaining and installing clergy, assisting churches in need, and accepting new churches into the denomination. Ministers and elected lay delegates compose each association. Associations within a larger geographical area compose a conference, which coordinates the activities of local churches and associations within the conference and the work of any organizations that may have been established. The General Synod meets once every two years. Members include delegates from the conferences, the denomination's Convenanted Ministries, and other groups within the denomination. As John Thomas, general minister and president, has emphasized, "The General Synod speaks to and not for our local churches" (Smallwood 2005). The General Synod elects an Executive Council, which acts for the synod between the biennial meetings. The General Synod also elects the general minister and president, who serves a four-year term and may be reelected for two additional terms (ibid.). Other elected offices include the executive ministers of Local Church Ministries, Wider Church Ministries, and Justice and Witness Ministries. Among its functions, the Executive Council makes recommendations for action to the General Synod. In the area of education, the UCC is associated with twenty-nine colleges and universities (Mead, Hill, and Atwood 2005, 147–148).

Reformed Church in America (RCA)

Members of the Reformed Church in America (RCA) can trace their denomination's origin back to 1628 and the arrival of an ordained minister from the Netherlands in the Dutch settlement of New Amsterdam. Although the English acquired the settlement in 1664, renaming it New York, several Dutch Reformed congregations had been established and ultimately (in 1764) adopted the English language. The original Reformed congregation established in 1628, now the Collegiate Reformed Church, continues as an active congregation in New York City. During the Revolutionary War church members were divided between loyalists and supporters of independence. Following the war some members split from the church and others moved to Canada and joined the Presbyterian Church of Canada (RCA 2006). In 1819 the church incorporated as the Reformed Protestant Dutch Church, but in 1867 the denomination changed its name to the Reformed Church in America. In the early years of the United States the RCA cooperated with other denominations to become involved in missionary work, both in other nations, such as China and India, and among Native Americans. In 1857 the RCA reorganized its Board of Foreign Missions, becoming independent of other religious groups. During the mid-nineteenth century the RCA continued to grow, prompted by continued immigration from the Netherlands. The Reformed Dutch Church, like other Protestant denominations, continued to experience divisions over issues of doctrine and church authority, and in 1857 some members left to form the Christian Reformed Church (CRC), a denomination that currently has a membership of approximately 195,000 (Mead, Hill, and Atwood 2005, 133). In 1882, others left the church to join the CRC. These defections notwithstanding, the RCA continued to grow, moving westward and gaining adherents among Dutch settlers.

After the Second World War the RCA assisted Dutch immigrants who left Europe to settle in Canada. In the United States, in the first decade after the war, the RCA devoted resources to establishing 120 new congregations to adjust to the shift in population toward urban and suburban areas. Many of these new congregations were for the first time composed of largely non-Dutch people who did not originate in the Dutch Reformed tradition. In the 1970s the organization worked to form congregations among Asians, Hispanics, Native Americans, and African Americans. In 1972 the RCA approved the ordination of women as elders and deacons, and in 1973 the denomination ordained the first woman minister (RCA 2006).

The RCA organizational structure at the local level consists of individual church congregations. Churches in a geographical area are then grouped into a classis. Above the forty-six classes (plural for classis) the church is organized into eight regional synods, each composed of equal numbers of ministers and elders, which meet once or twice each year. The central representative group is the General Synod, which meets annually to consider denominational policy. Between meetings of the General Synod, the General Synod Council fulfills the policies the synod has

enacted. Among its duties, the council oversees the overall operation of the RCA and its congregations and associated institutions.
The denomination, presently composed of approximately 290,000
members, has its greatest presence in New York, Michigan, New
Jersey, Iowa, Illinois, and California. Robert H. Schuller's Crystal
Cathedral in Garden Grove, California, is affiliated with the RCA.
The denomination has taken part in the ecumenical movement
and has entered into full communion with the other mainline
churches, including the Evangelical Lutheran Church in Amer-
ica, the Presbyterian Church (U.S.A.), and the United Church of
Christ. The RCA is a member of the World Alliance of Reformed
Churches, the World Council of Churches, and the National Coun-
cil of Churches of Christ and has also joined the newly established
Christian Churches Together.

United Methodist Church (UMC)

As with other Protestant denominations, the United Methodist
Church (UMC) evolved through mergers of several church groups.
In 1939 the Methodist Episcopal Church; the Methodist Episcopal Church, South; and the Methodist Protestant Church united
to form the Methodist Church. In 1968 the Methodist Church
merged with the Evangelical United Brethren to form the present
United Methodist Church. Methodism began with two brothers,
John and Charles Wesley, who initiated careers as missionaries for
the Church of England. After having brief and unsuccessful stays
in North America in the 1830s, each returned to England, had
life-changing religious experiences, and led a renewal movement
within the Church of England. John Wesley sent other preachers to
America—most notably Francis Asbury—to facilitate the growth
of Methodism. In 1773 ten preachers held the first Methodist conference in the colonies. Still associated with the Anglican Church,
they emphasized strong discipline in the organization. During the
American Revolution, Methodist leaders tended to side with the
loyalists, and John Wesley himself publicized his opposition to
the revolutionary movement. Following independence the Methodists in the United States moved toward independence from the
Anglican Church.

In 1784 Methodist preachers met in Baltimore to form the
Methodist Episcopal Church in America. In subsequent years
the group established a General Conference to meet every fourth

year (the first was held in 1792), wrote a constitution, and in 1789 established a publishing operation, the Methodist Book Concern (UMC 2004a). In 1800 followers of Philip William Otterbein and Martin Boehm established the Church of the United Brethren, the members of which were almost exclusively German speaking. In 1803 Jacob Albright established the Evangelical Association, another German-speaking church. The Methodist churches greatly increased their membership during the Second Great Awakening of the first decade of the nineteenth century. From 1773 to 1816 Methodist churches had increased from 1,160 to more than 214,000 members (Allen 1998, 30). The Methodist Episcopal Church experienced defections during the early years. African Americans, experiencing discrimination, left to form separate organizations. In 1816 disaffected African Americans established the African Methodist Episcopal Church, and in 1821 another group of African Americans formed the African Methodist Episcopal Zion Church. In 1830 a group of 5,000 ministers and laypeople, dissatisfied with the lack of lay representation and the refusal of the organization to provide for the election of district superintendents, formed the Methodist Protestant Church. Anticipating the breakup of the Union, the greatest split in the Methodist movement occurred when the 1844 General Conference voted to suspend a Southern bishop and slaveholder for refusing to free his slaves. Southern representatives quickly devised a plan of separation that led to the formation of the Methodist Episcopal Church, South. During the half-century following the end of the Civil War, Methodist churches, including the Methodist Episcopal Church; the Methodist Episcopal Church, South; the United Brethren; and the Evangelicals experienced large membership growth. The Methodist Episcopal Church achieved a 400 percent increase in membership. Clergy and lay members debated various issues within the churches in the late nineteenth and early twentieth centuries, including the granting of representation to women and the ordination of women, and experienced the general rise to prominence of liberal theology and the Social Gospel movement.

After the First World War a movement began toward unification of the Methodist denominations. The Evangelical Association, which in 1894 had split into two groups, reunited in 1922 as the Evangelical Church. In 1939 the Methodist Episcopal Church; the Methodist Episcopal Church, South; and the Methodist Protestant Church united as the Methodist Church, thus forming a denomination of 7.7 million members (UMC 2004b). In 1946, after twenty years of planning, the Evangelical Church and the United Brethren Church merged to form the Evangelical United Brethren Church. The final move toward union occurred in 1968 when the Methodist Church and the Evangelical United Brethren, themselves the product of past unions, merged to establish the UMC.

The basic organizational structure of the UMC includes six types of conferences. The General Conference, which meets once every four years, acts as the central policy-making body of the denomination. It is composed of approximately 900 delegates, half lay members and half clergy. The second type of conference, the Jurisdictional Conference, also meets once every four years. There are five jurisdictional conferences (Northeastern, Southeastern, North Central, South Central, and Western). An equal number of clergy and laypersons serve as delegates (Allen 1998, 63). Each jurisdictional conference elects and assigns bishops, draws episcopal area boundaries, and implements General Conference policies. The Annual Conference, composed of clergy and laypersons representing congregations, votes on constitutional amendments and elects delegates to the General and Jurisdictional conferences. The bishop of the episcopal area presides during the conference. Each geographical district of the denomination may hold a District Conference, composed of members selected at the Annual Conference. This conference administers the various programs and ministries of the district. The fifth type of conference is the Charge Conference, composed of the council members of one or more local churches. Usually meeting annually, this conference supervises the activities of the local church. Finally, all local members may attend the Church Conference, which is held by individual congregations and deals with subjects relevant to each local church. In addition to these six types of conferences, regions outside the United States hold Central conferences, which have bishops and administrative officers of their own (ibid., 64).

Members of the Council of Bishops serve as the administrative leaders of the UMC. Members include fifty active bishops in the United States; eighteen bishops from Europe, Asia, and Africa; and more than ninety retired bishops. The president of the council, elected by the bishops, serves a two-year term and presides over meetings but does not exercise any additional authority within the council. An executive secretary serves as the chief operating officer for the council (UMC 2006a). Council members attend the

General Conference but are not voting delegates (UMC 2006b). The Judicial Council, composed of five clergy and four laypersons, receives appeals of decisions made by the General Conference or any District, Annual, Central, or Jurisdictional Conference, or a bishop.

The UMC engages in various social service activities, supporting, directing, or operating 225 retirement homes and extended care establishments, 70 hospital and health-care facilities, 50 child-care institutions, and 30 operations for those with disabilities. The UMC engages in various educational ministries, including support for eight two-year colleges, eighty-two four-year colleges, ten universities, and thirteen schools of theology (Mead, Hill, and Atwood 2005, 233). The denomination's Board of Global Ministries supports, directly or through cooperation with other denominations, mission work in thirty-eight countries in Africa; twenty countries in Asia; seven countries in the Middle East; thirty-two countries in Europe; twenty countries in the Caribbean; seven countries in the Pacific; and eighteen countries in North, South, and Central America (Allen 1998, 68–71).

Catholic Church

Like the mainline Protestant churches, the Catholic Church in recent years has experienced dissent within the denomination, especially since the Second Vatican Council. Pope John XXIII called this council, which met in Rome three months each year from 1962 to 1965. The council addressed the general concern for the church's stance toward the modern world. Among the issues confronted were the ordination of women as priests, birth control, whether to allow priests to marry, and the status of divorced church members. Such issues have divided more liberal and more conservative clergy and laypeople (Szasz 2004, 60). In addition to substantive issues, the Second Vatican Council provided for certain democratizing elements within an otherwise hierarchical organizational structure, including the establishment of regional and national episcopal conferences. In the United States, bishops established what came to be called the United States Conference of Catholic Bishops (USCCB), which became an outspoken advocate for reform and social action on such issues as the U.S. economy, nuclear weapons, and AIDS (Varacalli 2006, 12). In addition to conferences of bishops, the actions of the Second Vatican Council also gave rise to the formation of priests' senates to represent clergy before their bishops, sisters' councils to represent sisters and nuns, and parish pastoral councils to voice the sentiments of church members before the local priest. How these new organizations ultimately would affect the hierarchical authority structure was unclear: whether restructuring would result in a more congregational type of authority in which local parishes make decisions for themselves, or a more modest sharing of authority between the clergy and laity on the one hand and the higher levels of the hierarchy on the other (ibid., 13).

The Catholic Church, with a membership of approximately 65 million, is the single largest religious denomination in the United States (Mead, Hill, and Atwood 2005, 94). Unlike the mainline Protestant denominations, the Catholic Church from 1990 to 2000 experienced steady growth, increasing adherents by approximately 16 percent. Researchers have attributed this membership increase largely to the immigration of great numbers of people from Catholic countries. Despite the increase in membership, church attendance among Catholics fell in recent decades. In 2000 an estimated 40 percent of Catholics attended mass at least weekly, a much lower figure from fifty years before (Reichley 2002, 322).

At the same time membership increased, the number of priests and nuns declined. Reichley (2002, 321) reports that the number of Catholic priests fell from 58,600 in 1966 to 45,200 in 2001, and the number of nuns declined from 180,000 in 1965 to 79,400 in 1999. In the late 1990s the number of men studying for the priesthood had fallen to less than 15 percent of the 1960 number. Reichley also notes that by 1999 the median age of nuns had increased to 69 and that just 6 percent of nuns were less than fifty years of age (ibid.). The decline in the number of priests and nuns has led to what Steinfels (2004, 11) terms a crucial transformation within the Catholic Church: the passage of leadership from the clergy to laypeople, a shift that conflicts with the traditional emphasis on maintaining a system of centralized authority. The Catholic Church in the United States, as of 2004, had 11 cardinals, 45 archbishops (including 7 cardinals), 336 bishops, and approximately 46,000 priests. The church is organized into 34 archdioceses and 151 dioceses (Mead, Hill, and Atwood 2005, 95). Within the dioceses are approximately 18,500 parishes (Steinfels 2004, 4). Bishops oversee the dioceses and archbishops govern the larger dioceses, or archdioceses. The Catholic Church is unique among the mainline denominations in that the worldwide organizational structure has situated at its peak one person, the pope, the Bishop of Rome, also known as the vicar of Christ, who is acknowledged as Christ's major representative on earth and hence has authority over all bishops, priests, and lay members of the church.

From the early days of colonization, many non-Catholic settlers objected to the presence of Catholics in the New World. For instance, Massachusetts Bay passed so-called anti-priest laws, making the church illegal in the colony. Any priest, missionary, or other person associated with the Catholic Church was to be considered a threat to the peace (O'Toole 2004, 41). During the first half of the eighteenth century, anti-Catholic and anti-immigrant themes tended to dominate in the nativist movement, represented by the Know-Nothing group. The associated American party, begun in the 1850s, entered electoral politics, nominating former president Millard Filmore as its presidential candidate in 1856. Anti-Catholic sentiment notwithstanding, the number of Catholics in the United States continued to increase, assisted by immigration from countries such as Ireland where the Catholic faith predominated. O'Toole (ibid., 43) notes that immigration through the port of Boston increased from 2,000 in 1820 to 120,000 in 1850, with nearly half of the new arrivals coming from Ireland. One measure of the concern that non-Catholics had regarding the Catholic Church is that just one Catholic has been elected president. When John Kennedy campaigned for the presidency in 1960, he understood that it was necessary to assure voters that he would make decisions independent of the Catholic hierarchy. Speaking to the Greater Houston Ministerial Association, he stated that "I believe in an America where the separation of church and state is absolute—where no Catholic prelate would tell the president (should he be Catholic) how to act. I do not speak for my church on public matters—and the church does not speak for me" (Dionne 2006, B11).

Although the hierarchy of the Catholic Church in the United States has changed considerably since the Second Vatican Council, the top of the leadership structure—the bishops—remains solidly within the tradition of the church. The pope in Rome appoints each of the bishops independently of any official input from the local church leaders or laypersons, and they serve until they are seventy-five years old. Steinfels (2004, 307) notes that this method of selection can leave the bishops separated from the overall changes that are occurring in the denomination, and they may fail to represent adequately the views of laypeople and priests. Of the more than 45,000 priests, approximately 30,000 serve in dioceses and 15,000 are affiliated with specific orders, such as the Benedictines, Dominicans, Franciscans, and Jesuits (Archdiocesan Archives 2006). There are more than 13,000 permanent deacons, men who have been ordained for ministry but who are not priests. The bishops have the authority to designate those in the church administration below them, and they appoint priests. Given the declining number of priests, the recruitment of pastors to serve parishes has become especially difficult.

The United States Conference of Catholic Bishops, which resulted from a combination in 2001 of the National Conference of Catholic Bishops and the United States Catholic Conference, oversees the administration of the Catholic Church and often takes public stands on various economic and social issues. The conference is incorporated in Washington DC. Offices associated with the USCCB include the Catholic Campaign for Human Development, Catholic News Service, Ecumenical and Interreligious Affairs, Government Liaison, Hispanic Affairs, Pro-Life Activities, and Social Development and World Peace (USCCB 2006).

The Catholic Church maintains approximately 7,000 elementary schools, 1,300 high schools, and 238 colleges and universities and employs 175,000 educators, out of which 164,000 are lay teachers (Archdiocesan Archives 2006). The church supports 597 hospitals and 483 health-care centers, and Catholic social service agencies help those in need with food, clothing, housing, and disaster assistance. Social service agencies provide a variety of other assistance, including adoption services, foster care, pregnancy care, and programs to prevent and treat drug and alcohol abuse.

National Council of Churches of Christ in the USA (NCC)

All eight of the mainline Protestant denominations discussed previously have joined with the National Council of Churches (NCC) in the effort to develop ecumenical cooperation among varied Christian churches and organizations. The preamble to the organization's constitution states that member groups "confess Jesus Christ, the incarnate Word of God, as Savior and Lord" and "covenant with one another to manifest ever more fully the unity of the Church" (NCC 1996). Member denominations include Protestant, Anglican, Orthodox, Evangelical, and African American churches representing 100,000 local congregations and 45 million people (NCC 2006). The General Assembly serves as the major policy-making body of the organization. Between the annual meetings of the General Assembly, the governing board meets frequently to execute policies determined by the assembly. The organization's officers include a president, a general secretary, and four vice presidents, all of whom are elected by the General Assembly. Established in 1950, the NCC replaced several ecumenical organizations, including the Federal Council of Churches, which had served as the major U.S. ecumenical organization since 1908. The NCC maintains five program commissions: Communication, Education and Leadership, Faith and Order, Interfaith Relations, and Justice and Advocacy. These commissions pursue objectives in such areas as peace and justice, poverty, racism, the environment, education, and the production of religious television programming (ibid.). Various nonmember denominations, including the Catholic Church, cooperate with the NCC in performing service functions. The NCC maintains an office in Washington DC to promote the organization's moral and ethical positions on public policy issues. Mainline denominations engage in ecumenical interaction through the NCC as well as through bilateral and multilateral discussions in order to create greater opportunities for cooperation and possible unification.

Whether through the NCC, cooperative activities among churches, or individual initiatives, these nine denominations, informed by closely related religious and moral convictions, pursue often similar goals to ameliorate perceived social, economic, and political ills. However, within the denominations, dissenting groups have formed that object to the direction the denominations have taken on various policy questions and that either are attempting to alter or "renew" the denominations or are moving toward separation.

Renewal Movements

The liberal-conservative controversy so prominent in the late nineteenth century continues today in the mainline denominations, which amounts to one crucial element in the so-called culture war between those holding more liberal social and political beliefs and perspectives and those adhering to more conservative ones. The cultural divide occurs not only between mainline denominations and more conservative, fundamentalist, or evangelical denominations but also within the mainline denominations themselves. Whereas mainline denominations have sought to increase the interaction among them, dissidents within denominations have developed groups that raise objections to such goals or contemplate separation from the home denomination. Dissidents face a dilemma: should they remain within the existing structure of a mainline denomination, or should they secede, joining another denomination or creating a new one? Many have decided to follow the first option. More conservative, evangelical elements within these denominations have expressed their dissatisfaction with the path their denominations have been following and have established various organizations to represent their views within the church. Wishing not to surrender completely all influence in their home denominations, they have created what are called "renewal movements."

Within the Episcopal Church some of those dissatisfied with the church hierarchy established the American Anglican Council (AAC), which advocates the church's return to a recognition of and commitment to biblical authority and the orthodox beliefs of the Anglican Communion. The group believes that the Episcopal Church has made compromises with contemporary culture by allowing false teachings to influence the church's stands on moral and theological questions. The AAC began in 1995 when a small group of Episcopal bishops, scholars, laypersons, and other church officials met to express their concern that the church's leadership had strayed from the historical Christian faith based on scripture. Recognizing that the Episcopal Church had lost membership in recent decades, this group emphasized its membership in the 77-million-member Anglican Communion. At a subsequent meeting in 1996 a larger group of concerned Episcopal Church members developed a more detailed expression of their beliefs and initiated an organizational structure. The group elected a board of trustees and subsequently incorporated as the American Anglican Council. In 2003 the AAC expressed its strong opposition to the selection of V. Gene Robinson, an openly gay priest, as the bishop of the New Hampshire Diocese. Other Episcopal and

Anglican organizations have been established to provide a voice for those opposing the leadership of the Episcopal Church. Forward in Faith North America proclaims that it defends the historic Christian faith and scripture and opposes any attempts to stray from those values. Ekklesia, an international group of Anglicans with headquarters in Carrollton, Texas, professes adherence to scriptural authority, the historic creeds of the Christian faith, and the sacraments as instituted by Jesus (Ekklesia 2006).

In 1988 seventy-three ministers and elders of the Presbyterian Church (U.S.A.) met in Dallas, Texas, to issue a call for renewal in the denomination. More than a thousand Presbyterians met the following year to continue the call for renewal and to create Presbyterians for Renewal (PFR). The organization remains active in the PCUSA, objecting particularly to efforts by more liberal members to alter traditional doctrine and to approve the ordination of actively gay pastors (PFR 2006). Recently PFR has challenged a report from the Theological Task Force on Peace, Unity and Purity of the Church (LeBlanc 2006, 8).

Within the Evangelical Lutheran Church in America, the Word Alone Network (WAN) began in 1996 as an electronic discussion group to express concern over the proposal to join with the Episcopal Church in full communion. The proposal included sharing ordained clergy and adopting the Episcopal notion of apostolic succession through bishops who retain the exclusive authority to ordain ministers. The 1997 ELCA Churchwide Assembly narrowly defeated the concordat, but in 1999 the assembly adopted the interchurch agreement, titled Called to Common Mission, with minor revisions. Mark Chavez, executive director of the WAN, has claimed that the ELCA is engaged in idolatry, placing trust in something other than God (ibid., 6). Concerned about proposals to change ELCA policy on homosexuality and the ordination of gay pastors, the 2004 annual convention of the WAN adopted a resolution affirming biblical teaching on sexual relations and marriage and opposing any revision in the church's interpretation of biblical standards. At the 2005 annual convention, participants approved a resolution initiating the establishment of an association of churches in the ELCA that adheres to a common confession of faith. In 2006 the WAN reported having 230 member churches and approximately 6,000 individual members and more than 1,000 pastoral members (WAN 2006). More than 105 congregations have left the ELCA to join Lutheran Congregations in

Mission for Christ (LCMC), an alternative denominational structure formed by those who decided they could no longer remain with the ELCA. The LCMC adopted a constitution in March 2001 (LCMC 2006).

Within the United Methodist Church, a renewal movement in effect began with the establishment of the denomination in the 1960s, when Charles W. Keysor, a Methodist pastor, began publication of *Good News*, a magazine for evangelicals within the church. The organization Good News, which resulted as an outgrowth of the magazine, continues as a renewal movement in the UMC. James Heidinger, president of Good News, has expressed satisfaction that evangelicals were successful in establishing their influence within the UMC. For instance, since 2000, representation at the General Conference has been based on the number of members in a region, a policy that has increased the voice of the more conservative southern region. Different groups in the UMC have disagreed over the ordination of homosexuals, but so far denominational decisions have maintained the more traditional biblical interpretation of sexual relations.

Members of the American Baptist Churches USA have created dissenting groups within the organization. Bill Nicoson, executive director of American Baptist Evangelicals (ABE), believes that evangelicals within mainline churches may conclude that separation is the best option (LeBlanc 2006, 7). In the ABC, the Pacific Southwest region began the process of withdrawing from the denomination over the issue of homosexuality. In September 2005 the region's board of directors, representing more than 300 of the denomination's 5,800 congregations, voted to begin the process of separation. Although the ABC's official policy holds that "the practice of homosexuality is incompatible with Christian teaching" (Moll 2005, 23), the denomination allows "gay-affirming" congregations to maintain their affiliation. ABE leaders announced plans to create a new association that could include as many as 2,000 churches (ibid., 23).

The mission statement of the Institute on Religion and Democracy (IRD) declares that the organization is committed to renewing democratic society through an ecumenical alliance of Christians in the United States who assent to biblical and historic Christian teaching. The organization, which was established in 1981, regards churches as a vital element in civil society (IRD 2006). However, according to the IRD, mainline denominations have "thrown themselves into multiple, often leftist crusades—radical forms of feminism, environmentalism, pacifism, multi-culturalism, revolutionary socialism, sexual liberation and so forth," all of which supposedly have harmed the church and society (ibid.). To remedy the situation, the organization claims, churches must return to the traditional concerns of Christianity (ibid.). Committees associated with specific denominations are affiliated with the IRD. Presbyterian Action has focused on the PCUSA's stand on marriage, homosexuality, and a proposed amendment to the U.S. Constitution defining marriage as the union of one man and one woman. Episcopal Action has concentrated on a leadership group in the Episcopal Church that the committee considers unrepresentative of the lay membership of the church. UMAction, the United Methodist committee, works to bring about "scripture based" reform in the denomination.

Within the Catholic Church, members concerned about the sexual abuse scandal formed organizations such as Voice of the Faithful (VOTF) in order to hold the church leaders responsible for the scandal and to increase the voice of lay members in the functioning of the denomination. VOTF wants to ensure that church leaders respond to the needs of the victims of abuse. One goal of the organization has been to establish a fund to allow donors to contribute to ministries and programs with the assurance that the money will not be used for "secret settlements, legal fees, and public relations" (Post 2002).

Mainline Christian Denominations and Public Policy

By 2006 the electoral and public policy victories conservative religious groups had achieved began to energize those who were uncomfortable with the emphasis on such issues as abortion and same-gender marriage at the expense of what were considered more pressing concerns, including poverty, affordable health care, and global warming. Many moderate and liberal Christians who opposed the Bush administration's policies, such as the Iraq war and budget cuts for social welfare programs, began to organize, forming such groups as Faith in Public Life, Catholic Alliance for the Common Good, Faithful America, and Network of Spiritual

Progressives (Murphy and Cooperman 2006). Some believe that the so-called religious left is ready to reassert the political influence it wielded during the civil rights era of the 1950s and 1960s, and that members of mainline denominations are a potentially significant element in the reemergence of a progressive religious movement. However, observers question whether organizational success can be matched by increasing numbers of adherents, given that mainline denominations generally have been losing members in recent decades and have faced difficult internal conflicts.

The mainline denominations confront a variety of challenges to their role as influencers of U.S. public policy. While they generally have representational structures—including regular conventions—that allow grassroots members to be heard at the highest levels of the denominations, as well as organizational resources that facilitate communication with the larger society and planned activities to further their mission, disagreements involving deep religious beliefs and values can reduce the ability to convey to the larger society the stands of the denominations on particular issues. Most recently, strong disagreements over sexual matters have created serious divisions within many of the denominations. Chapter 2 examines in greater detail specific public policy issues on which many of the denominations have taken a public stand and identifies the factors that tend to contribute to, or limit, the prospect for success.

References

Allen, Charles L. 1998. *Meet the Methodists: An Introduction to the United Methodist Church*. Nashville, TN: Abingdon.

American Baptist Churches in the USA (ABC). 1974. "American Baptist Policy Statement on Primacy of the Local Church." http://www.abc-usa.org/Resources/resol/primacy.htm.

American Baptist Churches in the USA (ABC). 2006. "The Origins and Development of Baptist Thought and Practice." http://www.abc-usa.org/whoweare/ourhistory/history.aspx.

Archdiocesan Archives. 2006. "The U.S. Catholic Church: Historical Background." http://www.archstl.org/archives/about/cathhist.htm.

Christian Church (Disciples of Christ) (CCDC). 2006a. "Office of the General Minister and President." http://www.disciples.org/ogmp/.

Christian Church (Disciples of Christ) (CCDC). 2006b. General Ministries home page: http://www.disciples.org/internal/genmin.htm.

Cummins, D. Duane. 2003. *A Handbook for Today's Disciples in the Christian Church (Disciples of Christ)*. St. Louis, MO: Chalice.

Dionne, E. J., Jr. 2006. "Clarifying Separation of Catholic Church and Statesmen," *Houston Chronicle* (March 4): B11.

Ekklesia. 2006. The Ekklesia Society home page. http://www.ekk.org/news.php.

Evangelical Lutheran Church in America (ELCA). 2005. "Churchwide Units." http://www.elca.org/churchwide.html.

Evangelical Lutheran Church in America (ELCA). 2006. "Roots of the Evangelical Lutheran Church in America." http://elca.org/communication/roots.html.

Hanson, Mark S. 2007. "Tackling Membership Decline." *The Lutheran* (January): 58.

Hart, D. G., and Mark A. Noll. 1999. *Dictionary of the Presbyterian and Reformed Tradition in America*. Downers Grove, IL: InterVarsity.

Houston Chronicle. 2006 "Membership of ELCA Dips." (August 5): F3.

Institute on Religion and Democracy (IRD). 2006. "Mission Statement." http://www.ird-renew.org/site/pp.asp?c=fvKVLfMVIsG&b=356299.

Konolige, Kit, and Frederica Konolige. 1978. *The Power of Their Glory, America's Ruling Class: The Episcopalians*. New York: Wyden.

LeBlanc, Douglas. 2006. "Evangelicals in the Mainline: Should They Stay or Should They Go?" *Christian Research Journal* 29 (1): 6–8.

Lutheran Congregations in Mission for Christ (LCMC). 2006. "A Historical View of LCMC." http://www.lcmc.net/historical_view.htm.

Mead, Frank S., Samuel S. Hill, and Craig D. Atwood. 2005. *Handbook of Denominations in the United States*. 12th ed. Nashville, TN: Abingdon.

Moll, Rob. 2005. "American Baptist Exodus: Scripture, Homosexuality Divide Another Venerable Denomination." *Christianity Today* 49 (November): 23.

Murphy, Caryle, and Alan Cooperman. 2006. "Seeking to Reclaim the Moral High Ground: Religious Liberals Are Gaining New Visibility in American Politics." *Washington Post National Weekly Edition* (May 29–June 4): 12.

National Council of Churches (NCC). 1996. "Constitution and Bylaws." http://ncccusa.org/pdfs/nccconstitution.pdf.

National Council of Churches (NCC). 2006. "NCC at a Glance: Who Belongs, What We Do, How We Work Together." http://.ncccusa.org/about/about_ncc.htm.

Noll, Mark. 2003. "American Lutherans Yesterday and Today." In Richard Cimino, ed., *Lutherans Today: American Lutheran Identity in the 21st Century*. Grand Rapids, MI: William B. Eerdmans.

O'Toole, James M. 2004. "Catholics I: Majority Faith with a Minority Mindset." In Andrew Walsh and Mark Silk, eds., *Religion and Public Life in New England: Steady Habits, Changing Slowly*. Lanham, MD: Rowman and Littlefield.

Post, Jim. 2002. "Voice of the Faithful in the Future." http://www.voiceofthefaithful.org/Who_We_Are/future.html.

Presbyterian Church (USA). 2006. "U.S. and World Mission." http://pcusa.org/navigation/mission.htm.

Presbyterians for Renewal (PFR). 2006. "The History of PFR." http://www.pfrenewal.org/home/index.php?option=com_content&task=view&id=55&itemid=70.

Reformed Church in America (RCA). 2006. "Brief Outline of RCA History." http://rca.org/NETCOMMUNITY/Page.aspx?&pid=2181&srcid=2183.

Reichley, A. James. 2002. *Faith in Politics*. Washington DC: Brookings Institution Press.

Smallwood, Irvin. 2005. "General Synod Overwhelmingly Calls for 'Full Marriage Equality.'" http://news.ucc.org/index.php?option=com_content&task=view&id=243&Itemid=54.

Spong, John Shelby. 2005. *The Sins of Scripture: Exposing the Bible's Texts of Hate to Reveal the God of Love*. New York: Harper Collins.

Steinfels, Peter. 2004. *A People Adrift: The Crisis of the Roman Catholic Church in America*. New York: Simon and Schuster.

Straub, Gregory. 2006. "Introduction to General Convention." http://www.episcopalchurch.org/53785_9883_ENG_HTM.htm.

Szasz, Ferenc Morton. 2004. "How Religion Created an Infrastructure for the Mountain West." In Jan Shipps and Mark Silk, eds., *Religion and Public Life in the Mountain West: Sacred Landscapes in Transition*. Lanham, MD: Rowman and Littlefield.

United Church of Christ (UCC). 2006a. "The Christian Churches." http://ucc.org/aboutus/shortcourse/chrchu.html.

United Church of Christ (UCC). 2006b. "German Evangelical Synod." http://ucc.org/aboutus/shortcourse/gerevasyn.html.

United Church of Christ (UCC). 2006c. "The Evangelical and Reformed Church." http://ucc.org/aboutus/shortcourse/evaref.html.

United Methodist Church (UMC). 2004a. "The Churches Grow, 1817–1843." http://archives.umc.org/interior.asp?mid=1209.

United Methodist Church (UMC). 2004b. "World War and More Change, 1914–1939." http://archives.umc.org/interior.asp?mid=1219.

United Methodist Church. 2006a. "Introduction to the Council of Bishops." http://archives.umc.org/interior.asp?ptid=21&mid=5856.

United Methodist Church. 2006b. "Council of Bishops Frequently Asked Questions." http://archives.umc.org/interior.asp?ptid=21&mid=5860.

United States Conference of Catholic Bishops (USCCB). 2006. "USCCB Departments and Associated Offices." http://www.usccb.org/depts.htm.

Varacalli, Joseph A. 2006. *The Catholic Experience in America*. Westport, CT: Greenwood.

Wall, John N. 2000. *A Dictionary for Episcopalians*. Revised ed. Cambridge, MA: Cowley.

Word Alone Network (WAN). 2006. http://wordalone.org/who.shtml.

2

Problems, Controversies, and Solutions

Mainline Christian churches obviously do not exist in a vacuum. While they have internal debates and conflicts, these denominations also act in various ways in the larger society, attempting to influence, and at times being influenced by, current trends in the secular world. Among the public policy issues on which mainline churches have expressed a position, or at least have had internal debates, are abortion, immigration, stem-cell research, the death penalty, same-gender marriage, faith-based funding, U.S. foreign policy, welfare policy, and the government's role in economic and social matters. In order to have an impact on questions of policy, the churches must reach some level of agreement among the denominational leaders, clergy, lay leaders, and lay members. As with any interest group, the larger the membership of the group, the more likely that the organization will have its voice heard in the larger decision-making arena. The nine denominations that are under consideration here vary greatly in membership. The Catholic Church, the largest single denomination, has an estimated membership of more than 65 million. Other denominations have much smaller memberships. The United Methodist Church has a current membership of 8.3 million; the Evangelical Lutheran Church in America, 5.2 million; the Presbyterian Church (U.S.A.), 3.4 million; the Episcopal Church, 2.3 million; the American Baptist Churches in the USA, 1.4 million; the United Church of Christ, 1.3 million; the Christian Church (Disciples of Christ), 820,000; and the

Reformed Church in America, 289,000. The nature of the public policy area can also affect the probability of success. Generally, domestic issues are subject to greater influence than are foreign policy issues, the latter tending to be informed by considerations of power politics more than ethical concerns and are matters about which the general population remains less informed.

Sheer numbers of adherents by themselves do not necessarily present an accurate measure of the influence a denomination has on public policy. As noted in Chapter 1, the Episcopal Church traditionally exercised far greater influence on public policy than the numbers of its lay membership might suggest. At least three other factors affect the influence that a given denomination might have. First, the intensity with which the membership holds the beliefs and values of the church may contribute to the denomination's impact on the policy-making process. Associated with intensity is the extent to which the membership is in agreement with the clergy about the social, economic, and political objectives of the church. If the membership is deeply divided, the church leadership cannot be as persuasive in the public arena. Finally, the prestige that the leadership and individual members enjoy in the larger community can add to the church's influence. One measure of that prestige is the number of members who are serving as public officials as well as the number of members who are engaged in prestigious professions.

Sexuality Issues within Denominations

Controversies within a denomination can diminish its potential influence in the public arena. For instance, in the Catholic Church revelations of sexual abuse by priests of young boys over several years and reported attempts by church leaders to cover up the scandal have occupied much of the attention and resources of the church. The sexual abuse scandal surfaced in January 2002 when the *Boston Globe* began reporting on priests in the Boston area who had been charged with sexually molesting minors. Reportedly, the church hierarchy had avoided taking steps to end the abuse and had actually reassigned to other parishes those priests against whom complaints had been made, thus allowing them to continue the criminal behavior. The abuse scandals as well as the reports of homosexuality among priests appeared to have had an effect on church attendance and donations to the church. Gallup poll data indicate that by the end of 2002 Catholic Church attendance had suffered a 7 percent decline (Steinfels 2004, 41). The abuse scandal did not create, but did accelerate, trends such as the decline in church attendance, a reduction in the number of those choosing to enter the priesthood, and an increased willingness of church members to question the decisions of the denominational leadership. Bishops were castigated for failing to act quickly to assist the victims of abuse or to prevent additional young people from becoming victims of abuse. Reports published in January 2003 indicated that over the last sixty years, 4,268 people had charged 1,205 priests with abuse (ibid., 45).

The case of Father John Geoghan placed in relief the dissatisfaction that lay members had with the Catholic Church hierarchy. Although the archdiocese had been aware of Geoghan's misdeeds, in 1984 Bernard Cardinal Law approved the priest as pastor of St. Julia's parish, where he continued to molest children (Dreher 2002, 27). Following complaints, Geoghan went into treatment once more, after which he returned to the parish and continued to molest children. In 1993 Geoghan assumed the chaplaincy of a nursing home but reportedly continued to sexually abuse children. In 1998 Pope John Paul II finally defrocked Geoghan, and the Catholic Church was forced to pay millions of dollars to settle civil suits related to his criminal conduct. In 2002 Geoghan was convicted of child molestation charges and in 2003 was killed by another inmate while serving his prison sentence.

Although lawsuits concerning the sexual misdeeds of clergy began in 1985, when a Louisiana priest was convicted of molesting several boys in the Diocese of Lafayette, the church leadership failed to respond quickly to claims of sexual abuse. Following the Louisiana case, Reverend Thomas Doyle, a canon lawyer, coauthored a report warning that other cases would likely come to the surface, that the bishops needed to act quickly, and that traditional methods of treating child molesters did not achieve satisfactory results. The bishops failed to act on the recommendations (ibid., 28). The ultimate costs of settling lawsuits proved staggering, with an estimated $1 billion paid to plaintiffs since 1950 (*Houston Chronicle* 2005a). In 2003 the Archdiocese of Boston reached a legal settlement with 552 people, agreeing to pay $85 million, and the Diocese of Orange, California, agreed to pay $100 million to 90 abuse victims. In July 2005 the Diocese of Covington, Kentucky, paid $120 million to hundreds of victims (*Houston Chronicle* 2005b). The Diocese of Portland, Oregon, which had filed for bankruptcy, confronted abuse claims of more than $500 million, and the Archdiocese of Los Angeles faced settlements with victims for an equivalent amount. In July 2005 Voice of the Faithful, a Catholic lay reform group, estimated that sexual abuse lawsuits ultimately could cost Catholic dioceses between $2 and $3 billion (Kusmer 2005).

Various reasons have been suggested for the lack of effective action to stem the tide of abuse. First, even though bishops have significant authority within the church hierarchy, church law prevents them from acting quickly to deal with priests accused of such misdeeds. Second, the Vatican likely chooses as bishops those priests who have developed a reputation for acting cautiously. Third, contemporary bishops came of age from the 1940s to the 1960s, when the church hierarchy was more rigid and before social attitudes had begun to change significantly. At the same time that the news media began to report revelations of child molestation by priests, additional stories came to light claiming the existence of a network of homosexuals in Catholic seminaries (Dreher 2002, 30). Although there is no necessary relationship between homosexuality and child molestation, the additional accounts lead more people to question the church leadership. In November 2005 the Vatican issued a decree, approved by Pope Benedict XVI, stating that men who practice homosexuality, have "deeply rooted" homosexual tendencies, or support the "gay culture" should not be admitted to seminary. Estimates place the proportion of priests who are gay anywhere from 10 percent to 50 percent (Ostling 2005, A6). To the extent that lay Catholics have challenged the authority of individual bishops and the United States Conference of Catholic Bishops, the ability of church leaders to influence public policy also may have been weakened.

The Episcopal Church also has faced internal controversy over sex-related issues. At the beginning of 2003 Episcopal clergy and laypeople, preparing for the triennial General Convention, faced the issue of blessing same-gender unions. Some more liberal bishops were already allowing the ordination of gay priests and ceremonies to bless same-gender unions. At the 2000 General Convention, the clergy and lay delegates had narrowly defeated a proposal to approve such blessings. In June 2003 clergy and lay delegates to a convention in the New Hampshire Diocese elected V. Gene Robinson, an openly gay priest, as bishop. Conservative Episcopalians in the United States and Anglicans around the world condemned the election as contrary to scripture as well as to denomination policy. The Lambeth Conference in 1998, a gathering of the primates of the Anglican Provinces occurring every ten years, had passed a resolution stating that homosexual practices were "incompatible with scripture" (Bates 2005, 6). Although conference resolutions are not considered binding on the member provinces, conservatives embraced the statement on homosexuality as mandatory policy. At the Episcopal Church General Convention in August 2003, both the House of Deputies and the House of Bishops approved Robinson's election. The convention also approved a measure stating that a diocese wishing to do so could conduct same-gender blessings without violating church doctrine.

In response to the strong criticism of the actions that the Episcopal Church had taken in electing a gay bishop, the Archbishop of Canterbury, Rowan Williams, called a meeting of the Anglican primates at Lambeth in October 2003. In the United States, approximately 2,700 Episcopalians who objected to the gay bishop met in Dallas in October and asked Williams to discipline the Episcopal Church, even though each Anglican province is self-governing and the Archbishop of Canterbury does not have the authority to sanction a member church (Kirkpatrick 2003, 3). At the Lambeth meeting, primates signed a statement warning that Robinson's final consecration as bishop could jeopardize the future of the Anglican Communion. Many in the United States speculated about the ultimate consequences, including the possible defection of conservative Episcopalians from the church and reductions in contributions, which could limit the ability of the Episcopal Church to fund social services and missions. The controversy raised anew conflicting interpretations of the Bible as well as the status of scripture in Christian belief. More liberal scholars noted that the Bible approved of slavery and polygamy and condemned divorce. The church has accepted contemporary attitudes on such issues, so should not the church accept changing perspectives on human sexuality? On the other hand, conservatives insisted on adhering to the Bible's condemnation of homosexual behavior, quoting from the Book of Romans (1:26–27): "For this reason God gave them up to degrading passions. Their women exchanged natural intercourse for unnatural, and in the same way also the men, giving up natural intercourse with women, were consumed with passion for one another. Men committed shameless acts with men and received in their own persons the due penalty for their error."

Thirteen conservative bishops agreed to explore the possibility of forming a new organization, the Network of Anglican Communion Dioceses and Parishes, and called for a constituting convention to be held in January 2004. The bishop of the Pittsburgh Diocese, Robert W. Duncan, agreed to serve as "moderator and convening authority" (*Houston Chronicle* 2003). In January 2004 the American Anglican Council sponsored the conference in Woodbridge, Virginia, where approximately 3,000 members examined possible actions that could be taken, including separation from the Episcopal Church. Sessions of the conference discussed the development of parishes for the newly created network (*Houston Chronicle* 2004a). Adding to the tension within the church, in March 2004 six parishes collaborated in holding confirmation services for 110 young members conducted by five retired bishops and a Brazilian bishop without seeking authorization from the Diocese of Ohio because the bishop had supported Robinson's election. When the House of Bishops met in Navasota, Texas, that same month, some conservative bishops decided to boycott the meeting (Vara 2004a). V. Gene Robinson attended the meeting. The bishops attempted to ameliorate the controversy by offering an objecting parish a visiting conservative bishop to provide "pastoral oversight" if the parish and the bishop of the diocese fail to reach reconciliation of differences (Vara 2004b). The American Anglican Council responded to the proposal by calling it "woefully inadequate" (*Houston Chronicle* 2004b). At the meeting, the bishops issued a statement criticizing the five retired bishops who took part in confirmation services in Ohio.

In an effort to avoid division in the church, moderate and liberal Episcopal clergy and laypeople from predominantly conservative dioceses in eight states met in late March 2004 in Atlanta to call for reconciliation (Weber 2004, 23A). As the debate continued, a panel in England attempting to heal the division in the Episcopal Church released a statement from U.S. Presiding Bishop Frank Griswold in which Griswold commented that Robinson's ordination as bishop occurred after thirty-five years of discussion within the church on homosexuality. He stated that cultural circumstances in the United States differ greatly from those that Anglicans face in other parts of the world. A representative of the

American Anglican Council responded that Griswold's letter represented a justification for sin and that the stated Episcopal policy contradicted scripture (*Houston Chronicle* 2004c).

In June 2004 the Anglican Church of Canada, at a national church meeting, weighed in on the issue, affirming the "integrity and sanctity" of same-gender relationships. However, gay supporters were dissatisfied that no decision was made on the authorization for local dioceses to decide for themselves whether to institute blessing ceremonies for same-gender couples (Ostling 2004). In July 2004 the Lambeth Commission, a group of seventeen Anglican Communion leaders working to draft an arrangement intended to preserve Anglican unity, continued to receive opinions from various national churches and other groups, including the Network of Anglican Communion Dioceses and Parishes, which requested that the Episcopal Church be disciplined in order to return it to the Anglican fold and that standards for Anglican membership be defined (*Houston Chronicle* 2004d). In February 2005 Anglican primates announced that, due to disagreements within the Episcopal Church and the Anglican Church of Canada, those churches were being asked to withdraw temporarily from the Anglican Consultative Council, a representative advisory group composed of bishops, clergy, and laypeople chosen by member churches of the Anglican Communion. The Consultative Council, with the Archbishop of Canterbury as president, provides guidance to the communion on mission and interchurch relations (Barr 2005, A19; Wall 2000, 8).

In January 2006, as the Episcopal Church prepared for the 2006 triennial General Convention in Columbus, Ohio, a church nominating committee announced the names of four candidates for the position of presiding bishop, succeeding Frank Griswold. Three of the four candidates had voted in favor of Robinson's selection as bishop of the Diocese of New Hampshire. Conservative Episcopal spokespersons expressed their dissatisfaction with all four candidates, viewing each of them as failing to abide by the orthodox principles of the church (Vara 2006, A12). The personal pressures of the controversy within the church apparently had affected Bishop V. Gene Robinson, who announced in February 2006 that he had begun treatment for alcohol abuse (Ostling 2006, F4).

At the Episcopal Church General Convention in June 2006, delegates reluctantly approved a resolution requesting that dioceses avoid selecting actively gay bishops. Both liberal and conservative participants found fault with the resolution, which also did not appear to placate Anglican bishops in Africa and Asia. The convention delegates selected as the denomination's new presiding bishop Katharine Jefferts Schori, who had voted in favor of Robinson's ordination and had previously expressed her support for the blessing of same-gender unions. Conservative parishes and dioceses continued to explore the possibilities of disassociating from the Episcopal Church and affiliating with another province within the Anglican Communion. In February 2007, Anglican primates from thirty-eight national churches in the Anglican Communion, meeting in Tanzania, called on the U.S. Episcopal Church to agree not to sanction the blessing of same-gender unions and not to approve any candidate for bishop who is involved in a same-gender relationship (Vara 2007). The primates set a September 30, 2007, deadline for meeting their demands.

The following month Episcopal bishops, meeting in Navasota, Texas, rejected the demands of the Anglican primates, including the proposal to form a pastoral council to supervise conservative congregations in the United States. Bishop Don Wimberly of Houston announced that, instead of accepting a pastoral council, the presiding bishop could appoint a "primatial vicar" to oversee conservative churches. The bishops emphasized continuing discussion, announcing that they would listen to the concerns of church members and meet again in September (Karkabi 2007). The ultimate fate of the church in the United States, once so prominent in the American political establishment, remains in doubt.

Other mainline denominations also face sexuality issues. In 2004 a court of thirteen United Methodist Church (UMC) pastors at the Pacific Northwest Annual Conference meeting in Bothell, Washington, held a trial for Karen Dammann, who was charged with violating church law by openly declaring that she was a lesbian living in a homosexual relationship with another woman. UMC law prohibits the ordination of "self-avowed practicing homosexuals" (Mitchell 2004, 9A). The trial court ultimately acquitted Dammann of the charges, announcing that the church failed to present convincing evidence to support the charge. The acquittal led to controversy at the subsequent UMC General Conference in April. The disagreement over sexuality was seen as symptomatic of the financial and membership difficulties the church faced, including a decline in membership from 10.7 million in 1965 to 8.3 million in 2004 (Vara 2004c, 1E). The General Council voted 551–345 to have the denomination's Judicial Council review the Dammann case. Although the court subsequently ruled that it did not have the authority to review the acquittal ruling, the delegates voted to maintain the church's position regarding the incompatibility of homosexuality and orthodox Christian teachings (Vara 2004d, 4A). The council overwhelmingly approved a unity resolution that appeared to overcome possible divisions in the denomination resulting from the sexuality controversy. However, the Reverend William Hinson, president of the Confessing Movement, a dissident conservative group, expressed his preference for biblical truth over denominational unity (*Houston Chronicle* 2004e).

The Presbyterian Church (U.S.A.), also facing declining membership, has confronted the issue of sexuality. In July 2004 the denomination's Legislative Assembly, by a narrow vote of 259–255, rejected a proposal to allow regional church organizations to ordain gay clergy and lay officers (*Houston Chronicle* 2004f). In May 2004 the permanent judicial commission for the Ohio and Michigan Synod ruled that a minister who conducted marriage ceremonies for same-gender couples did not violate church law, even though the highest court of the church ruled in 2000 that blessing same-gender unions was allowed, but not marrying same-gender couples. In 2005, a regional judicial commission in California acquitted another minister, Jane Spahr, who had conducted same-gender marriages, stating that the minister's actions accorded with the "normative standards of the region in which she served" (Leff 2006, F4).

The extent to which the controversies over sexuality issues threaten the unity of these mainline denominations remains uncertain. However, it appears that such conflicts have consumed the time, effort, and resources of those on both sides of the issue. To that extent, the denominations have been less able to focus on the policy issues that traditionally have informed their mission in the larger society. Although the denominations, especially the larger ones, have extensive bureaucracies to administer their programs, the possible reduction in resources due to members withholding contributions can restrict the effectiveness of their actions. An examination of the various areas of public policy in which mainline denominations engage will provide a perspective on their importance as well as further indication of the potential significance of internal divisions.

Capital Punishment

The leadership of all of the nine mainline denominations under discussion have taken public stands against the death penalty. However, although the clergy and lay leadership wish to persuade the membership regarding the nature of the death penalty, given the strong support for the death penalty in the general population, they ultimately may not express the views of parishioners. The Catholic Church affirms a doctrine of the sanctity of life that calls into question the use of the death penalty. The United States Conference of Catholic Bishops maintains a highly consistent policy, opposing any course of action that intentionally leads to the death of a human being, including abortion and euthanasia as well as the death penalty. The bishops have questioned the argument that the death penalty has a deterrent effect, preventing others from committing similar crimes. They also reject the death penalty as a form of retributive justice. The bishops advocate abolition as a means of ending what they consider a cycle of violence in American society, an expression of a belief in the worth of each individual from conception, a recognition that human life at every stage is sacred, and a course of action in accord with the example of Jesus (Overberg 2005).

In 2000 the General Assembly of the Presbyterian Church (U.S.A.) declared its continuing opposition to capital punishment and called for a moratorium on executions by the national government and all states that have instituted the death penalty. The General Assembly directed the stated clerk to present to the president of the United States, members of Congress, and the governors and legislators of the thirty-eight states that impose the death penalty the call for a moratorium. The assembly noted that states had imposed the death penalty disproportionately on minority defendants and that all states have failed to meet American Bar Association standards for providing counsel for indigent prisoners. The resolution declared that in a representative democracy, the death penalty makes citizens executioners (PCUSA General Assembly 2000).

In a resolution adopted in 2003, the General Assembly of the Christian Church (Disciples of Christ) (CCDC) declared that the death penalty is "contrary to God's passion for justice." As did other denominations, the CCDC noted the disproportionate numbers of poor and minority group members who are executed and claimed that such people receive inadequate legal defense. They asserted that the death penalty has not reduced the rate of crime. The resolution called for the elimination of the death penalty in the United States and encouraged church members and congregations to campaign for the abolition of the death penalty and to establish ministries to assist those who have lost loved ones to violent criminal acts as well as families of those sentenced to death (CCDC 2003).

The General Conference of the United Methodist Church has adopted several resolutions expressing the denomination's opposition to capital punishment. Church leaders have declared that they reject retribution and vengeance as reasons for taking human life, stating that capital punishment violates belief in God as the creator and redeemer of humankind. The General Conference called on church members to communicate with state governors and state and federal representatives to make known their opposition to capital punishment, and it has called for an immediate moratorium on executions (McAnally 2006).

The General Synod of the Reformed Church in America has expressed the denomination's opposition to capital punishment, stating that the death penalty has unsubstantiated deterrent value; is "an uneven and unfair instrument of justice," having been applied in a racially discriminatory way; and is subject to mistakes that cannot be undone. Foremost among the reasons for opposing the death penalty is the church's stated objection that the punishment fails to coincide with "the spirit of Christ and the ethic of love." The General Synod has declared the death penalty to contradict the Old Testament as well as the New Testament in that the punishment fails to address broader inequalities in society and has been applied more heavily on the poor and powerless. Unlike self-defense, which could justify killing, the General Synod rejected the application of the death penalty against people who are in custody, and therefore do not threaten others. (RCA 1999).

Embryonic Stem-Cell Research

In August 2001 President George W. Bush announced his decision to allow limited national government funding of embryonic stem-cell research. The funding would be restricted to sixty-four lines of human embryonic stem cells, which originated from in vitro fertilization clinics. Many Americans have a highly personal interest in stem-cell research, given the occurrence within the population of various diseases, such as Parkinson's, Alzheimer's, diabetes, and amyotrophic lateral sclerosis (ALS), as well as spinal cord injuries, stroke, cancer, and heart disease, for which stem-cell research might result in effective treatments. Although all denominations that responded to President Bush's decision as well as to the prospects of stem-cell research expressed concern for maintaining ethical guidelines, some were more willing to support such research. The policy-making bodies in the denominations made their policy recommendations based largely on the same biblical foundation, but came to differing conclusions.

Bishop Joseph A. Firoenza, the president of the United States Conference of Catholic Bishops, responded most negatively, referring to President Bush's decision as "morally unacceptable" (Shannon 2002). The pope and bishops have consistently held that the human embryo should be valued and treated as a person from the instant of fertilization and hence deserves absolute respect and protection. In other words, one human being (an embryo) cannot be killed in order to achieve benefits for other human beings. Assuming that many of the health problems for which stem-cell research would provide remedies are preventable, Catholics have suggested that, instead of concentrating limited public funds on highly expensive research that only the wealthier members of society can afford, resources should be devoted to policies that encourage behavior leading to the avoidance of diseases that many now face. Other mainline denominations, while expressing caution about the use of embryos in research, tended to express support for such research as holding promise for ameliorating human suffering and for saving lives that presently are being lost to incurable diseases.

The Presbyterian Church (U.S.A.) (PCUSA), in a resolution approved at the 2001 General Assembly noting that as Christians, church members are to assist in easing human suffering, affirmed that, with strict regulation, human embryonic stem cells should be used for research that could culminate in procedures to treat successfully those suffering from severe illness (Race 2005). The resolution distinguished between two sources of stem cells: aborted fetuses and early-stage embryos remaining from the process of in vitro fertilization. Although the use of tissue from fetuses is morally acceptable, assuming that the woman's decision to undergo an abortion is independent of the decision to donate fetal tissue for research, the resolution noted moral questions uniquely raised in the instance of stem cells. Unlike an aborted fetus, researchers must terminate the life of embryonic tissue for the conscious purpose of employing the tissue in research. As living tissue, human embryos have the potential of personhood. However, the respect for human embryos can be balanced against the potential for alleviating the suffering of many others. Therefore, research should be limited to embryos that will not be used in fertility treatments and will not be donated to other women. The General Assembly recommended strict regulation of any use of human embryos in the conduct of stem-cell research, including the prohibition of selling embryonic tissue. The PCUSA subsequently supported legislation proposed in Congress to extend national government financial support of stem-cell research.

The delegates to the 2001 General Synod of the United Church of Christ (UCC), noting the potential for developing treatments for serious diseases, called for national government funding of embryonic stem-cell research. The delegates noted that in 2001 there were approximately 25,000 frozen embryos at in vitro fertilization clinics that would likely be discarded and that the National Institutes of Health (NIH) had established guidelines for national government funding of stem-cell research, including the use of frozen human embryos resulting from in vitro fertilization that would be discarded following treatment. In the resolution, delegates noted that banning research would preclude the possibility of improving the lives of people now living. The resolution directed the general minister and president of the UCC to send a letter to President Bush, urging him to approve federal funding for embryonic stem-cell research within the guidelines that the NIH had established (Kershner 2001).

Deputies at the 2003 General Convention of the Episcopal Church approved a resolution urging the U.S. Congress to approve funding for research on embryonic stem cells that have resulted from in vitro fertilization. The resolution included four basic restrictions that should be placed on such research. First, the embryos to be used in research should no longer be required in the in vitro fertilization process and would otherwise be disposed of; second, those donating embryos consent to their use in research; third, the original purpose for creating the embryos was not to conduct research; and fourth, acquisition of the embryos did not result from a commercial agreement (Thompson 2003). During debate on the resolution in the House of Deputies, some expressed their opposition, demonstrating that basic questions of ethics and morality still remained. Some questioned the morality of creating embryos, knowing that they ultimately will be destroyed, and others recommended that unused embryos should be adopted for ultimate use by infertile women. Others claimed that the potential benefit of stem-cell research had been exaggerated and that, in any event, no human life (embryo) should be sacrificed to benefit others.

The United Methodist Church has gone on record calling for a ban on research that "generates waste embryos" (Bloom 2001). Following President Bush's announced policy regarding stem-cell research, James Winkler, general secretary of the General Board of Church and Society, stated that the members of the board were pleased with the limitation on national government funding of embryonic stem-cell research. Prior to Bush's announcement, Winkler had written to the president, urging him to establish a moratorium on funding research. Winkler opposed the destruction of human embryos in conducting research that he claimed showed little evidence of potential success in treating disease. Such destruction, he stated, raised serious moral and ethical questions. In 2004 delegates to the General Conference approved a resolution declaring that no more embryos than necessary should be created for reproductive purposes. However, delegates also expressed support for those who wish to donate early embryos remaining after the conclusion of in vitro fertilization, and called on the federal government to grant funding for research on such embryonic stem cells.

End-of-Life Decisions and the Right to Die

Terri Schiavo, the woman in a vegetative state for more than thirteen years who died in March 2005 after her husband Michael won a court battle against the woman's parents to have her feeding tube removed, raised anew difficult moral and ethical questions regarding end-of-life decisions and the right to die. The mass media followed the controversy closely, and people on both sides of the issue avidly stated their views. More conservative Christian leaders almost unanimously opposed the decision to allow Terri Schiavo to die. For instance, James Dobson, Focus on the Family founder, stated that "All human life is of value, regardless of the human's stage of development, level of health, or ability" (Gilgoff 2005, 16). Evangelicals and Catholics embraced the Schiavo case as an important instance of the battle between those who advocate the "quality of life" and those who champion the "sanctity of life." Undoubtedly, evangelical and Catholic spokespersons tended to identify the question of whether to allow Terri Schiavo to die with the issue of abortion. A strong stand on the abortion issue appeared to mandate an equally strong position on maintaining Terri's life.

Mainline denominations, which tend to perceive more complex questions in end-of-life decisions, remained on the edge of the conflict. Two fundamental empirical questions were debated: first, did Terri have any level of consciousness at all, and second, had Terri confided in her husband prior to her disability that she would not want to be kept alive in a vegetative state? Beyond these empirical questions, spokespersons stated varying positions regarding the preservation of life in circumstances of extreme disability. When Terri's feeding tube was removed for the last time, conservative Christians appeared to object on a number of grounds, including the possibility that Terri did have some level of consciousness, that her condition might not be irreversible, that she might experience severe pain through starvation, and that the decision represented the crass view of the value of life dominant in modern society. Reverend Larry Hollon, general secretary of United Methodist Communications, the official communications agency of the UMC, expressed his personal reaction to the intervention of the U.S. Congress in the Schiavo case. Hollon, who had faced a similarly difficult circumstance, described the death of his fifteen-year-old son and responded to comments that then–House majority leader Tom DeLay had made: "The kindest, most loving thing [family members] can do may be to allow their loved one to die naturally without intervening, but Rep. DeLay has framed this as a barbaric act" (Hollon 2005). This retort undoubtedly expressed the view of many laypeople in mainline as well as evangelical denominations. Eighty-two percent of those interviewed in a CBS News poll agreed that Congress and the president should not become involved in the Schiavo matter, and 75 percent of respondents in an ABC News poll indicated that they believed Congress had acted for political reasons in intervening in the case (ibid., 21).

Prior to the Schiavo case, many of the mainline denominations attempted to confront the often difficult end-of-life questions that many families must ultimately face, questions that involve the value of an individual human life, individual rights and freedom, perceptions of suffering, and religious beliefs about the person's duties to God.

The leadership in mainline denominations generally have taken a cautious position on end-of-life issues, calling for further investigations of the difficult topic. Delegates to the 2002 General Assembly of the Presbyterian Church (U.S.A.) requested that the assembly form a special committee to investigate the Christian and Reformed view of human life, including such practices as euthanasia and assisted suicide. Delegates hoped that such a study would provide a perspective different from current secular cultural standards.

In 1991 delegates at the General Convention of the Episcopal Church approved a resolution, "Establish Principles with Regard to the Prolongation of Life," that expressed basic values regarding end-of-life decisions. The resolution declared morally wrong the intentional taking of a human life for the purpose of ending suffering due to an incurable illness. However, the administration of drugs to relieve the pain of individuals suffering from incurable illnesses, even if those responsible for such administration know that it may bring death more quickly, does not violate the principle of the sanctity of life. In addition, extraordinary measures to prolong the life of someone who has no reasonable chance of recovery may be withheld. In such circumstances, the counsel of others in the church community should be sought in determining whether to withhold artificial life support, including water and nutrition. Any federal or state legislation should take into account the rights of individuals and should provide for the withholding of extraordinary life support technology. The resolution urged church members to make advance provision through a living will stating the individual's wishes regarding the use of life support systems (Episcopal Church 2005).

In 1977 the Task Force on Ethical Issues in Human Medicine of the American Lutheran Church, prior to the church's merger with other Lutheran denominations in 1988, issued a statement on facing death. The task force concluded that when death is "judged to be certain and imminent," it would be unjust to the person to employ "extraordinary technology." The continuation of artificial life support depends on the conscious choice of the individual. The task force distinguished between meaningful pain, called "redemptive suffering," and "the dehumanizing and mindless suffering of the artificially-maintained terminally ill." However, actions taken to cause death are wrong and impermissible. The task force affirmed a moral distinction between taking steps to end a person's life and allowing a person to die. Underlying these principles, the task force noted that the Christian faith includes a duty to preserve health, but that life is not an absolute value. Death, when it comes, should be accepted in "the hope of the resurrection" (*Journal of Lutheran Ethics* 2006).

In 1994 the Commission on Christian Action of the Reformed Church in America, in response to Oregon's Death with Dignity law as well as physician Jack Kevorkian's practice of assisting terminally ill patients to commit suicide, issued a report on physician-assisted suicide. The commission stated the belief that Christians do not belong to themselves, but are stewards of a gift from God. Therefore, a decision to take action to end one's life amounts to denying that the person belongs to God. The individual who suffers physical pain expresses "deep moral courage," and the Christian community has the obligation to provide support for the sufferer and for those providing care. The commission recognized a dilemma—called the principle of double effect—in providing medication to relieve pain. The medication can relieve suffering but also may lead to the death of the patient. The commission listed four criteria. First, the caregiver must intend the good effect of relieving pain, not the bad one of bringing about death. Second, the action must be good or, at minimum, "morally indifferent." Third, the good result must not come from an evil action. Finally, the good that results must exceed any evil. In addition to these standards, the physician must inform the patient of the possible bad consequences of the medication (RCA 1994).

Mainline denominations have wrestled with the various end-of-life issues that become more complex as medical technology continues to advance. Questions about which medical procedures amount to "extraordinary treatment," determining an unambiguous definition of when death occurs, and what ultimately constitute morally correct actions add to the intricacies of the subject. The mainline denominations have asked for input from lay members, an important element in a commitment to democratic decision making. Such a process may encourage differing perspectives but also may lead some, who have strong views about the uncompromising nature of God's commands, to object to what appears to be a relativistic stance of their denomination more characteristic of the secular culture than a group obedient to God.

Faith-Based Initiative

Mainline Protestant denominations traditionally have supported the separation of church and state. Any interaction between churches and government to achieve a public good should be buffered by intermediate organizations such as Lutheran Social Services, an arm of the Evangelical Lutheran Church in America and the Lutheran Church–Missouri Synod, and Catholic Charities. In 1996, as part of welfare reform legislation, the Personal Responsibility and Work Opportunity Reconciliation Act, Congress initiated charitable choice. This legislation mandated that national government officials provide religious organizations with the same opportunity to receive government funding as secular nonprofit organizations. Faith-based organizations that obtained government funding received protection of their religious character and mission. Government-funded religious groups were required to honor the religious liberty of clients, and funds could not be used to support such religious activities as worship or proselytization (Ryden and Polet 2005, 2). However, President Bill Clinton's administration did not push for the implementation of the new program, and few state officials received adequate information that would have allowed them to take advantage of charitable choice.

Soon after George W. Bush assumed the presidency in January 2001, he established the White House Office of Faith-Based and Community Initiatives in addition to faith-based centers in the departments of Justice, Education, Health and Human Services, Housing and Urban Development, and Labor (ibid., 3). The Bush administration then introduced legislation in Congress that would expand protections for faith-based organizations under charitable choice and provide tax incentives to encourage donations to religious groups engaged in charitable activities. However, when Congress failed to approve his proposals, President Bush announced in December 2002 executive orders that allowed the administration to implement policies geared to permit the national government to issue contracts that provide funding to faith-based organizations. The executive orders added two additional faith-based centers in the Department of Agriculture and the U.S. Agency for International Development and mandated that the seven faith-based offices in the various agencies inspect their departments' rules for any policies that might impede the issuance of contracts to faith-based groups; set aside funds for religious groups that applied for grants; and establish additional protections for the religious integrity of faith-based groups, including hiring rights. During fiscal year 2003 national government agencies dispensed more than $1 billion to religious nonprofit organizations, indicating that the Bush administration strategy of implementing faith-based funding via executive order had achieved some success (ibid., 4).

The United States Conference of Catholic Bishops (USCCB) strongly supported President Bush's faith-based initiative, but it expressed special concern over the hiring of staff for charitable activities funded by the federal government. The bishops wished to maintain control of employment decisions, taking into account the religious beliefs of potential employees. The bishops have opposed any provisions within proposed legislation that would limit the ability of religious organizations to hire those who share the religious values of the organization (USCCB 2005). This policy issue had become controversial in Congress. Those members of Congress more skeptical of the faith-based initiative expressed concern that religious groups receiving federal funding may use discriminatory hiring practices. Although Title VII of the Civil Rights Act of 1972 permitted religious groups to use religious beliefs as a criterion in making hiring decisions, legislation authorizing some social programs prohibits organizations that receive federal funding from discriminating against prospective employees on the basis of age, gender, race, or religion (Allen and Cooperman 2003, 14). Any religious group receiving government funding potentially faces a conflict between the group's wish to maintain basic moral values and the larger social value of avoiding discrimination. The USCCB strongly supported passage of the Charity Aid, Recovery and Empowerment Act (CARE), which would provide additional funding in the Social Services Block Grant for charities, both faith based and secular. The legislation also would allow non-itemizers who make charitable contributions to take a tax deduction and would create a Compassion Capital Fund to provide faith-based and community organizations with technical assistance (USCCB 2005).

In 2001 the Executive Council of the Episcopal Church, noting that the church traditionally had received public funding, supported the new faith-based initiative but urged the establishment of safeguards to ensure the separation of church and state. Unlike the USCCB, the Episcopal Church's Executive Council conditioned support for the program on eliminating any preference given to an employee or job applicant based on religious belief, national origin, sexual orientation, age, sex, or disability. The council also stated that recipients of assistance should not be required to engage in any religious activities as a condition for receiving services. With those conditions, the council resolved that governments be urged to increase assistance to faith-based and community service groups and that organizations within the Episcopal Church investigate the possibility of separate incorporation in order to distinguish more clearly between the delivery of social services and the religious mission of the church (Episcopal Church 2001).

After Congress initially passed legislation establishing a program of charitable choice in 1996, the Presbyterian Church (U.S.A.) conducted a sample survey of church members, elders, pastors, and specialized clergy. Majorities of these constituencies of the PCUSA stated that they did not believe that charitable choice threatened the principle of separation of church and state. Those questioned tended to believe that the provision of assistance to the poor offers an opportunity to the church to share the gospel message. The surveyed group also thought that charitable choice could benefit the financial circumstances of the church. However, respondents expressed concern that accepting government funding could lead to government regulation of faith-based organizations (Markum 2002).

Following passage of the 1996 legislation establishing charitable choice policy, members of the Board of Church and Society of the United Methodist Church issued a statement declaring that the program violated the establishment clause of the First Amendment to the U.S. Constitution. James Winkler, chief executive of the board, suggested that existing safeguards, including churches establishing separate corporations for the receipt and use of public funding, be enforced in order to prevent government regulation and inspection of church affairs. The 2000 UMC General Conference approved a resolution establishing criteria for the church groups receiving government funds. The resolution recommended that services provided should (1) contribute to meeting genuine need in the community; (2) avoid serving a religious purpose; (3) not discriminate on the basis of race, religious belief, or political preference; and (4) meet professional and administrative standards. Following President Bush's proposal to expand faith-based funding, three UMC agencies—the Board of Global Ministries, the General Council on Finance and Administration, and the Board of Church and Society—produced a guide to explain to local churches and other church organizations the purpose and requirements of faith-based funding.

In 2001 the presiding bishop of the Evangelical Lutheran Church in America, George Anderson, heading a denomination that traditionally has accepted government funding for the provision of social services, raised questions regarding the proposed faith-based initiative. His concerns were that such funding should not adversely affect the identity of religious groups; any funds received from governments should be used for a social benefit that serves the entire community; and the funding should not substitute for government programs aimed at the general welfare. Anderson raised concerns about possible limitations on a religious organization's freedom to hire employees and the potential need for additional staff that individual religious organizations may face in order to deal with regulations and paperwork (Anderson 2001).

Immigration

Mainline Christian denominations express an openness to immigration of people from other countries and a willingness to help them to succeed in the United States. In justifying a humane immigration policy, members note a fundamental Christian value that strangers be made welcome. They cite scripture in support of this position. In the Old Testament Book of Leviticus (19:33–34), God tells the Jewish people, "When an alien resides with you in your land, you shall not oppress the alien. The alien who resides with you shall be to you as the citizen among you; you shall love the alien as yourself, for you were aliens in the land of Egypt: I am the Lord your God." In the New Testament Book of Matthew (25:35–36), Jesus proclaims, "for I was hungry and you gave me food, I was thirsty and you gave me something to drink, I was a stranger and you welcomed me, I was naked and you gave me clothing, I was sick and you took care of me, I was in prison and you visited me." Therefore, welcoming and assisting immigrants is considered a biblical mandate.

After the U.S. House of Representatives approved the Border Protection, Antiterrorism, and Illegal Immigration Control Act of 2005 (House Resolution 4437), Cardinal Roger Mahony of the Catholic Archdiocese of Los Angeles declared the legislation an attack on immigrants and those who might offer them assistance. Mahony stated that the Catholic Church and other organizations would join together in an effort to protect "the rights of all" by ultimately defeating the legislation (Muñoz 2006). For several years mainline denominations have taken a similar position on immigration. In 2005 a large number of national and local religious groups, including Catholic Charities USA, the Episcopal Church, the Lutheran Immigration and Refugee Service, the stated clerk of the Presbyterian Church (U.S.A.), the United States Conference of Catholic Bishops, the General Board of Church and Society of the United Methodist Church, and the Wider Church Ministries of the United Church of Christ joined together in issuing a statement supporting comprehensive immigration reform. The religious groups noted the suffering that immigrant families endure when attempting to enter the United States and the exploitation they experience in the workplace, and advocated the establishment of a "safe and humane" immigration system that reflected Christian values (Institute on Religion and Public Policy 2005). The statement urged public officials to approve legislation that would regularize the status of immigrants who satisfy "reasonable criteria" and allow them to enter a process of attaining lawful permanent resident status and ultimately U.S. citizenship. Further, legislation should reduce the time that separated family members must wait before they are reunited. In addition, legislation should provide for procedures for workers and their families wishing to migrate to the United States to work in legal and safe circumstances and have their rights protected. Finally, policies established to maintain border security should be informed by humanitarian values. The statement emphasized that public policy should respect the human dignity of persons.

The Evangelical Lutheran Church in America (ELCA), in a statement on immigration policy, noted that U.S. history demonstrates an unfortunate tendency to exclude newcomers who differ from those who have already established themselves in the country. The ELCA calls on Americans to welcome immigrants, refugees, and those seeking asylum and to recognize the opportunities they can offer present citizens to become aware of new perspectives and the gifts such people bring with them. The statement claimed that the presence of new immigrants heightens understanding of the Christian belief that all people are God's creation and that all have a responsibility to respect their human dignity (ELCA 2006).

The 2004 General Assembly of the Presbyterian Church (U.S.A.) approved a resolution recommended by the Advisory Committee on Social Witness Policy advocating the establishment of a program for the legalization of undocumented persons in the United States. Immigration policy should provide for a more expeditious and humane process for family reunification. Exploitation of workers was declared a violation of just treatment that "all children of God" deserved. The resolution also called for the PCUSA to join with other faith-based and secular groups that are working to achieve the legalization of immigrants (PCUSA General Assembly 2004). When the immigration legislation came before the U.S. Congress in December 2005, Clifton Kirkpatrick, stated clerk of the PCUSA's General Assembly, commented that the proposed legislation in Congress contradicted the intentions of the resolutions that the General Assembly had passed in 2004. Kirkpatrick interpreted the legislation as potentially making religious organizations and private citizens subject to criminal prosecution for assisting undocumented immigrants. He commented that the legislation also would classify undocumented immigrants as "aggravated felons" subject to imprisonment and deportation without a hearing. In the context of the broader implications of the legislation, Kirkpatrick claimed that the new law could disrupt the U.S. economy by failing to establish procedures by which needed laborers could enter the country legally (Silverstein 2005).

The Reformed Church in America (RCA) also has taken stands over the years regarding the treatment of immigrants. In 1983 delegates to the General Synod approved resolutions calling on the U.S. Congress to enact legislation that includes "economically and racially just" policies regarding undocumented immigrants and amnesty for undocumented aliens presently in the United States. The delegates called for strict enforcement of existing fair labor standards in order to eliminate the motivation to hire and exploit illegal aliens. The 1984 General Synod delegates noted that, given the denomination's objective of developing congregations composed of newly arrived Americans and biblical mandates such as Exodus 23:9 ("You shall not oppress a resident alien; you know the heart of an alien, for you were aliens in the land of Egypt"), they supported just immigration reform. In 1993 a report from the RCA's Christian Action Commission, "Welcoming the Strangers in Our Midst," emphasized "God's special love for resident aliens" and the church's mission of "welcoming strangers" through the formation of immigrant churches. In 1993 delegates to the General Synod passed resolutions to encourage citizenship classes in local congregations and to make available worship materials in various languages. In 1995 the Christian Action Commission objected to the inclusion of provisions in the Republican Party's Contract with America that would deny legal immigrants certain rights of U.S. citizenship (RCA 1995).

The Executive Council of the Episcopal Church, meeting in March 2006, called on church members to "follow the call of the Baptismal Covenant" in their ministry to illegal immigrants even though a proposed federal law might make such assistance a criminal act. The council strongly objected to legislation that could make illegal the actions of faith-based organizations following the biblical mandate to alleviate the suffering of illegal immigrants. The council interpreted the proposed legislation to mean that taking part in such activities as working in a soup kitchen could fit the definition of "alien smuggling." Bishop Jon Bruno of Los Angeles submitted a letter to the Los Angeles City Council decrying what he considered an "irrational fear" within the nation that is leading to policies "reminiscent of the rounding-up of Japanese immigrants" during the Second World War. Bruno declared that the scriptures call on Christians to "embrace the strangers in our midst, for in them we see the face of Christ" (Schjonberg 2006).

In March 2007 Alexia Salvatierra, executive director of Clergy and Laity United for Economic Justice and an ELCA pastor, announced that religious leaders from various denominations, including the Catholic, Lutheran, Methodist, and Presbyterian churches, were planning to revive the sanctuary movement to provide illegal immigrants with shelter and help them avoid deportation (Prengaman 2007).

Iraq War

By early 2006 support among the American public for the U.S. military intervention in Iraq had declined significantly as that country appeared to move ever closer to civil war between the Sunni and Shia populations. The initial rationale for the military action, that Iraqi leader Saddam Hussein had been actively developing chemical, biological, and nuclear weapons—weapons of mass destruction—and that Iraq was a center for worldwide terrorist activity, had long ago lost credibility. As the insurgency developed momentum, the United States focused on restoring civil order, training Iraqis to take control of security operations, and molding democratic institutions and practices that would bridge the ethnic, cultural, and religious divisions within the country. The leadership of the mainline Christian denominations remained cautiously hopeful that the United States could attain such noble goals, but many expressed doubts about the practicality of such objectives and the justice and morality of the military action and its consequences.

Prior to the U.S. invasion, spokespersons for these denominations advised the Bush administration against conducting a preemptive attack on another country. In September 2002 various religious leaders, including the moderator and the stated clerk of the General Assembly of the Presbyterian Church (U.S.A.), the general secretary of the Reformed Church in America, the presiding bishop of the Episcopal Church, the presiding bishop of the Evangelical Lutheran Church in America, the general minister and president of the United Church of Christ, the president of the Council on Christian Unity of the Christian Church (Disciples of Christ), and the general secretary of the General Board of Church and Society of the United Methodist Church signed a letter to President George W. Bush stating that, although Saddam Hussein remained a threat to his own people and Iraq's neighbors, engaging in preemptive military action was wrong on moral grounds and ultimately harmful to U.S. interests. The religious leaders declared that military action could result in many civilian deaths and injuries and suffering for huge numbers of innocent people. U.S. military action could destabilize the region and lead to increased militant activities in Arab and Islamic-majority countries. Instead of military action against Iraq, the religious leaders urged the president to focus attention on gaining a peace settlement between Israel and the Palestinians (Churches for Middle East Peace 2002).

The concept of a just war informed the views of many religious leaders and laypeople. According to the principles of just war doctrine, in order to be considered just, a war can be fought only after all nonviolent avenues have been tried and the cause must be judged just; it must be fought by a legitimate authority, to right a wrong, and with a reasonable probability of success; the establishment of a peaceful condition preferable to the situation prior to the war must be the likely outcome; the violence used should be proportional to the objective of rectifying a wrong; and the weapons and tactics used must allow for the ability to distinguish between combatants and noncombatants. Bishop Wilton D. Gregory of the United States Conference of Catholic Bishops addressed a letter to President Bush in which the bishop, although noting that "people of good will" may come to differing judgments, raised serious questions regarding whether the proposed U.S. military action against Iraq would meet the requirements of the just war doctrine. Gregory asked whether there existed "clear and adequate" evidence of a connection between the Iraqi regime and the suicide attacks of September 11, 2001, or of an impending attack. The bishop questioned whether the objective of limiting the proliferation of weapons of mass destruction justified a preemptive military attack. With regard to a just war being fought by a legitimate authority, Gregory suggested the need for an international sanction, which would most clearly mean action by the United Nations Security Council. As for probability of success and proportionality, he feared that a war against Iraq could have unpredictable consequences for that nation and its civilian population as well as for the stability of the Middle East. Gregory urged the president to pursue alternatives to military action, including the resumption of weapons inspections, enforcement of a military embargo, and "carefully-focused" economic sanctions (Gregory 2002).

Richard L. Hamm, general minister and president of the Christian Church (Disciples of Christ), informed members of his denomination that he believed the United States had "squandered the good will that the world community felt toward the United States immediately after 9-11" because of the Bush administration's policy of taking unilateral military action. Hamm claimed that many in other countries had come to view the United States as "arrogant and ignorant." He viewed the issue to be primarily moral and ethical rather than political and urged fellow church members to pray for peace and to express their views to their representatives in Congress and to the president (Hamm 2002).

The pleas of mainline religious leaders notwithstanding, the Bush administration initiated military action against Iraq in March 2003. Religious groups then turned their attention to concern for the safety of U.S. military personnel and Iraqi civilians. Mark S. Hanson, presiding bishop of the Evangelical Lutheran Church in America, commented in April 2003 that the reconstruction of Iraq should include reestablishing "relationships between nations and the United Nations" and that U.S. objectives should focus on resolving the broader conflicts in the Middle East (Hanson 2003). More than a year later, in June 2004, Hanson reported that he had discussed Iraq with U.N. Secretary General Kofi Annan. The bishop emphasized that the United Nations should play a significant role in moving from U.S. occupation to Iraqi self-governance and that the United States must surrender leadership in the reconstruction of Iraq to the international community and the Iraqi people. Hanson expressed concern that the United States did not understand how its unilateral actions had adversely affected the way the nation was being perceived around the world (Hanson 2004).

In May 2004 the Council of Bishops of the United Methodist Church, noting the failure to determine the presence of weapons of mass destruction in Iraq as well as any connection between the Al Qaeda terrorist organization and the Saddam regime, approved a resolution deploring the continued military action by the United States and coalition forces, called on the U.S. government to ask the United Nations to take part in the transition to a new Iraqi government, recommended the creation of a multinational development plan for rebuilding Iraq, and asked United Methodists to pray for peace and "advocate for public policies that promote justice, life, and reconciliation among adversaries" (UMC Council of Bishops 2004). In July 2004 the General Assembly of the PCUSA approved measures condemning U.S. preemptive military actions as ethically indefensible and contrary to just war doctrine. The assembly registered the concern of Presbyterians regarding the alleged abuse of prisoners in Iraq and at the Guantanamo prison facility (Smith 2004).

In 2006 Bishop Thomas Wenski, chairman of the Committee on International Policy, presented the United States Conference of Catholic Bishops' position on the conflict in Iraq, noting that bishops had often communicated "grave moral concerns" about the U.S. military action in Iraq and the "unpredictable and uncontrollable negative consequences" of the operation. The bishops concluded that, based on available information, it was difficult to justify the use of military force in Iraq. Wenski advised that U.S. forces should stay in Iraq only until a "responsible transition" had occurred. In achieving the transition, the bishop stated that the United States must resist "excessive military responses" that can result in civilian casualties or the abuse of prisoners, religious freedom must be protected, the United States must cooperate with other nations in assisting refugees leaving Iraq, and public officials should not use the cost of the war to justify a failure to meet the needs of the poor in the United States and in other nations. The conference urged Congress to face these challenges of transition in Iraq and to deal with terrorism without depending only on military methods (USCCB 2006).

The efforts of mainline religious groups to influence U.S. policy toward Iraq, both before and after the military invasion, proved unsuccessful. Moral and ethical considerations usually do not play a prominent role in foreign policy making, which tends to be controlled by some variation of the realist perspective of power politics. Foreign policy, unless it should gain the public's attention or is widely recognized as unsuccessful, tends to be driven by a relatively small number of policy makers in the executive branch of the federal government. These policy makers welcome the input of religious leaders most often when that input supports decisions already made.

Abortion

For more than thirty years the issue of legalized abortion has divided the nation. The U.S. Supreme Court decision *Roe v. Wade* in 1973 declared that state laws making abortion illegal invaded women's right to privacy and therefore violated the due process clause of the Fourteenth Amendment. During the first trimester of pregnancy, state governments could not interfere with the decision a woman made in consultation with her physician regarding the medical procedure of abortion. The court decision allowed state governments to regulate abortion in subsequent months of pregnancy, restricting the procedure to circumstances where the health of the woman was in danger. Following the point of fetal viability, states could prohibit late-term abortion procedures with the highly restricted exceptions involving the protection of the life or the health of the woman. Already in 1966 the Family Life Bureau of the United States Conference of Catholic Bishops, headed by Reverend James McHugh, had established the National Right to Life Committee to monitor state policies regarding abortion in order to maintain restrictions. Following the *Roe* decision, mainline denominations began to develop positions on the issue.

The Catholic Church has taken the most adamant position on the issue of abortion as well as other issues regarding the sanctity of human life. In 1968 Pope Paul VI issued the encyclical *Humanae Vitae*, banning Catholics from using artificial means of birth control. Although many U.S. Catholic clergy, scholars, and laypeople objected to the encyclical, it has remained the official Catholic statement regarding the point at which life begins, thus supporting the position that abortion at whatever stage of pregnancy involves the ending of a sacred human life. In 1994 Pope John Paul II issued *Evangelium Vitae*, an encyclical pronouncing the church's position on the evil of abortion. Although large proportions of lay Catholics in the United States do not support these encyclicals (Varacalli 2006, 65), they provide devout Catholics the inspiration for opposing any policy that allows for legalized abortion.

Mainline Protestant denominations generally did not take as absolute a stance on the issue of abortion as did the Catholic Church. There arose disagreement within the denominations and hence the decision-making bodies had to arrive at statements that recognized what were considered the complexities of the issue. In the same year as the *Roe* decision, the General Synod of the Reformed Church in America adopted a statement expressing the view that "abortion ought not to be practiced at all" but at the same time recognizing that in actual complex circumstances where often "one form of evil is pitted against another form of evil"—hence acknowledging the possibility of moral dilemmas—exceptions to general guiding principles may arise. The synod members supported restrictions on any abortion that might be performed "to insure individual convenience" and called on those who counsel women with problem pregnancies to "uphold the Christian alternatives to abortion." The General Synod called on church members to support a constitutional amendment to establish legal protections for the unborn (RCA 2006).

In 1991 the delegates at the Churchwide Assembly of the Evangelical Lutheran Church in America adopted a lengthy "social teaching statement" on abortion. In the statement, the delegates recognized that claims of rights in absolute language should be avoided. "A developing life in the womb does not have an absolute right to be born, nor does a pregnant woman have an absolute right to terminate a pregnancy." The statement, citing biblical references, recognized the basic Christian belief that God has granted life as a gift. For instance, the Old Testament Book of Jeremiah (1:5) states, "Before I formed you in the womb I knew you, and before you were born I consecrated you." The statement concluded that if an abortion is an option, it should be one of last resort; the church and the larger society must take responsibility for providing circumstances conducive to giving birth to new life; sex education should emphasize responsibility and the need for abstinence prior to marriage; and the church should encourage women in most circumstances of unintended pregnancy to give birth. It also promoted adoption as an important option to abortion. However, there may be acceptable reasons for ending a pregnancy with an abortion, including pregnancy resulting from circumstances in which women are oppressed to such an extent that they have no choice regarding sexual intercourse.

With regard to public policy, the Lutheran statement called for sex education in the schools, community pregnancy prevention programs, parenting classes, and the development of new methods of contraception. The government has a legitimate role to play in regulating abortion, and public policy should protect prenatal life as well as acknowledge women's dignity and their right "to make responsible decisions in difficult situations." The church opposes legislation that would either fail to regulate abortion at all or outlaw abortion in all circumstances. The statement declared that "in cases where the life of the mother is threatened, where pregnancy results from rape or incest, or where the embryo or fetus has lethal abnormalities incompatible with life, abortion prior to viability should not be prohibited by law or by lack of public funding of abortions for low income women." However, the church recognizes a conflict of values regarding public funding of abortions: "equity of access to legal medical services" can conflict with the use of people's tax revenues for what some may consider morally objectionable purposes (ELCA 1991).

In 1994 the Episcopal Church, in a resolution passed at the seventy-first General Convention, reaffirmed previous resolutions regarding abortion. The resolution declared the belief that all life is sacred from conception to death and that abortion has a "tragic dimension." While recognizing that every woman has the legal right to undergo an abortion, that right should be exercised "only in extreme situations." The resolution opposed abortion for purposes of birth control, family planning, selecting the gender of a child, or "mere convenience," but also opposed any government action at the local, state, or national level that restricts the right of women to "reach an informed decision about the termination of a pregnancy" or that limits women's access to safe methods of taking action according to their decision (Episcopal Church 1994).

In 1992 the Presbyterian Church (U.S.A.) General Assembly approved a position statement noting that while no scriptural references speak directly about abortion, "taken in their totality," scripture contains many references stating that a woman and child before and after birth deserve respect. The statement declared that women, "guided by the Scriptures and the Holy Spirit, in the context of their communities of faith," are able to make "good moral choices" regarding pregnancy and that the decision to terminate a pregnancy can be "a morally acceptable, though certainly not the only or required, decision." Circumstances that could justify the decision to undergo an abortion include the medical determination of "severe physical or mental deformity" of the fetus, pregnancy resulting from rape or incest, or situations in which "the physical or mental health of either woman or child would be gravely threatened." The General Assembly asserted that laws and administrative decisions should not limit access to abortion nor limit information regarding the abortion option or public funding for the disadvantaged requiring "necessary abortions." No law should restrict access to, or use of, means of contraception (PCUSA 2006).

The United Methodist Church has initiated a policy regarding abortion that affirms a belief in the sanctity of the unborn human life. Although reluctant to approve abortion, the church recognizes the obligation to the well-being of the mother, and thus the "tragic conflicts of life with life" could justify the decision to undergo an abortion. Therefore, the church supports the abortion option when such circumstances arise. However, abortion must not be used as a means of birth control or of gender selection. The church has declared its opposition to the late-term abortion procedure dilation and extraction, also know as "partial-birth abortion," except when the life of the woman is endangered or in cases of "severe fetal anomalies incompatible with life." The church also encourages members, social service agencies, and the government to assist in adoptions as an alternative to abortion (UMC 2005).

Values and Public Policy

As the so-called culture war indicates, values can and do conflict. Although mainline Christian denominations have provided value positions on the issues discussed in this chapter, the messages conveyed are subject to at least three restrictions. First, other groups, both secular and religious, hold conflicting value positions and, as in traditional interest group competition, the differing arguments that various groups present can result in less clear alternatives for the public as well as for decision makers. Second, the message from a particular denomination may be muted because of internal disagreements over value questions. As James A. Reichley has observed (2002, 240), such disagreements have occurred between the clergy and lay members. For instance, during the Vietnam conflict, the rank-and-file members of mainline churches remained far more supportive of the war effort than did the clergy. This disagreement may lead to a more weakly stated position or to "minority reports" that essentially side with an interest outside the denomination. When clergy and laity agree on an issue, such as happened during the civil rights movement of the 1950s and early 1960s, a denomination can take a much stronger stand and potentially increase its influence on public policy. Third, the extreme complexity of policy questions—such as making end-of-life decisions—may militate against any categorical value positions; those holding similar values can honestly disagree about what policy they should recommend. Perhaps with the exception of the Catholic Church, the mainline denominations appear to experience significantly less success in establishing strongly worded recommendations than do more fundamentalist and evangelical groups.

References

Allen, Mike, and Alan Cooperman. 2003. "Praying for a Hiring Exemption: Bush Supports Religious Groups' Employment Rules." *Washington Post National Weekly Edition* (June 30–July 13):14.

Anderson, George. 2001. "Faith-based Initiatives and the Church." http://www.elca.org/bishop/text/010315.html.

Barr, Robert. 2005. "Anglicans Face Split over Gay Issues." *Houston Chronicle* (February 25): A19.

Bates, Stephen. 2005. *A Church at War: Anglicans and Homosexuality.* London: Hodder and Stoughton.

Bloom, Linda. 2001. "Church Official Lauds Bush's Stem Cell Research Decision" (August 10). http://www2.umc.org/umns/news_archives2001.asp?ptid=2&mid=3365.

Christian Church (Disciples of Christ) (CCDC). 2003. "Resolution on the Death Penalty." http://www.disciples.org/ga/pdf/pastassemblies/03/resolutions/0324.pdf.

Churches for Middle East Peace. 2002. "Letter to President Bush on Iraq" (September 12). http://www.cmep.org/letters/2002Sep12_BushReIraq.htm.

Dreher, Rod. 2002. "Sins of the Fathers: Pedophile Priests and the Challenge to the American Church," *National Review* (February 11): 27–30.

Episcopal Church. 1994. "Reaffirm General Convention Statement on Childbirth and Abortion." http://www.episcopalarchives.org/cgi-bin/acts/acts_resolution-complete.pl?resolution=1994-A054.

Episcopal Church. 2001. "Executive Council Resolution: Regarding Public Funding for Faith-Based Social Service Programs." http://www.episcopalchurch.org/1866_70075_ENG_HTM.htm.

Episcopal Church. 2005. "Establish Principles with Regard to the Prolongation of Life." http://www.episcopalchurch.org/3577_60370_ENG_HTM.htm.

Evangelical Lutheran Church in America (ELCA). 1991. "What We Say about Public Life: Abortion." http://elca.org/socialstatements/abortion/.

Evangelical Lutheran Church in America (ELCA). 2006. "What We Say about Public Life: Immigration." http://www.elca.org/socialstatements/immigration/.

Gilgoff, Dan. 2005. "Life and Death Politics: The Schiavo Case Is Just the Latest Front in a Much Nastier War." *U.S. News and World Report* 138 (April 4): 14–18, 21.

Gregory, Wilton D. 2002. "Letter to President Bush on Iraq" (September 13). http://www.mtholyoke.edu/acad/intrel/bush/bishops.htm.

Hamm, Richard L. 2002. "We Still Look for Peace." http://www.homelandministries.org/PEACE/HAMMstatement.htm.

Hanson, Mark S. 2003. "End of Overt Hostilities in Iraq War" (April 16). http://www.elca.org/bishop/m_iraq_041603.html.

Hanson, Mark S. 2004. "Public Church Reflections" (June). http://www.elca.org/bishop/m_0604letter.html.

Hollon, Larry. 2005. "Commentary: Schiavo Case Underscores Need for End-of-Life Discussion." http://www.interpretermagazine.org/interior.asp?ptid=2&mid=7066.

Houston Chronicle. 2003. "Episcopal Bishops' Network Counters Gay's Consecration" (December 18): 8A.

Houston Chronicle. 2004a. "Episcopalians Meet to Discuss Split" (January 10): A17.

Houston Chronicle. 2004b. "Unauthorized Service Angers Church Leaders" (March 25): 5A.

Houston Chronicle. 2004c. "Episcopal Memo Released" (April 10): 2E.

Houston Chronicle. 2004d. "Anglican Conservatives Want Action against Gay Bishop" (July 1): 7A.

Houston Chronicle. 2004e. "Methodists Choose Unity over Schism" (May 8): 12A.

Houston Chronicle. 2004f. "Presbyterian Vote Rejects Gay Ordination" (July 3): 10A.

Houston Chronicle. 2005a. "Archdiocese OKs Deal in Abuse Cases" (March 10): A8.

Houston Chronicle. 2005b. "Settlement OK'd in Church Abuse" (July 6): A4.

Institute on Religion and Public Policy. 2005. "Interfaith Statement in Support of Comprehensive Immigration Reform" (October 14). http://www.religionandpolicy.org/show.php?p=1.1.1686.

Journal of Lutheran Ethics. 2006. "Death and Dying: An Analysis Offered by Task Force on Ethical Issues in Human Medicine, ALC (1977)." http://elca.org/jle/article.asp?k=199.

Karkabi, Barbara. 2007. "Episcopal Bishops Spurn Demands from Anglicans." *Houston Chronicle* (March 22): A8.

Kershner, Tim. 2001. "Synod OKs Federally-Funded Embryonic Stem Cell Research." http://www.ucc.org/ucnews/gsa01/stem.htm.

Kirkpatrick, Frank. 2003. "The Anglican Crackup." *Religion in the News* 6 (Fall): 2–4, 20.

Kusmer, Ken. 2005. "Lay Catholics Question Cost of Abuse." *Houston Chronicle* (July 10): A8.

Leff, Lisa. 2006. "'Her Right of Conscience:' Panel Exonerates Minister Who Presided over Same-Sex Unions." *Houston Chronicle* (March 11): F4.

Markum, Jack. 2002. "Charitable Choice." *Presbyterians Today* (March): 7.

McAnally, Tom. 2006. "Official Church Statements on Capital Punishment." http://archives.umc.org/umns/news_synd.asp?ptid=2&story=%7B6C69E3F8-5173-4737-A8D2-AC0EF8564777%7D&mid=883.

Mitchell, Melanthia. 2004. "Supporters Arrested at Gay Pastor's Church Trial." *Houston Chronicle* (March 18): 9A.

Muñoz, Rosalio. 2006. "Cardinal Mahony Initiates Immigrant Rights Campaign." *People's Weekly World* (February 7). http://www.pww.org/article/view/8536/.

Ostling, Richard N. 2004. "Canada's Anglicans Affirm Gay Relationships." *Buffalo News* (June 4): A4.

Ostling, Richard N. 2005. "In U.S., Vatican's Anti-Gay Edict Draws Mixed Responses." *Houston Chronicle* (November 24): A6.

Ostling, Richard N. 2006. "Too Great an Expectation? Pressure to Live Up to Ideals Can Make Some Clergy More Susceptible to Alcohol Abuse." *Houston Chronicle* (February 18), F4.

Overberg, Kenneth R. 2005. "The Death Penalty: Why the Church Speaks a Countercultural Message." *Catholic Update*. http://www.americancatholic.org/Newsletters/CU/ac0195.asp.

Prengaman, Peter. 2007. "Churches Set To Help Immigrants." *Houston Chronicle* (March 17): A8.

Presbyterian Church (U.S.A.) (PCUSA). 2006. "Abortion Issues." *Presbyterian 101*. http://www.pcusa.org/101/101-abortion.htm.

Presbyterian Church (U.S.A.) (PCUSA) General Assembly. 2000. "Moratorium on Capital Punishment." http://ccmn2.tripod.com/sitebuildercontent/sitebuilderfiles/Presbyterian_Teachings_on_the_Death_Penalty.pdf..

Presbyterian Church (U.S.A.) (PCUSA) General Assembly. 2004. "Resolution Calling for a Comprehensive Legalizing Program for

Immigrants Living and Working in the United States." http://www
.pcusa.org/acswp/pdf/immigration-resolution.pdf.

Race, Carolynn. 2005. "Next Steps: Federal Funding for Stem Cell
Research." http://www.pcusa.org/washington/issuenet/hc-050802
.htm.

Reformed Church in America (RCA). 1994. "A Christian Response to
Physician-Assisted Suicide." http://www.rca.org/NETCOMMUNITY/
Page.aspx?&pid=505&srcid=491.

Reformed Church in America (RCA). 1995. "Position on Immigrants
and Immigration." http://www.rca.org/NETCOMMUNITY/Page
.aspx?&pid=504&srcid=491.

Reformed Church in America (RCA). 1999. "Position on Capital
Punishment." http://www.rca.org/NETCOMMUNITY/Page
.aspx?&pid=496&srcid=491.

Reformed Church in America (RCA). 2006. "Summary of General Synod
Statements on Abortion." http://www.rca.org/NETCOMMUNITY/
Page.aspx?&pid=4928&srcid=491.

Reichley, A. James. 2002. *Faith in Politics*. Washington DC: Brookings
Institution.

Ryden, David K., and Jeffrey Polet. 2005. "Introduction: Faith-Based
Initiatives in the Limelight." In David K. Ryden and Jeffrey Polet, eds.
Sanctioning Religion? Politics, Law, and Faith-Based Public Services, 1–8.
Boulder, CO: Lynne Rienner.

Schjonberg, Mary Frances. 2006. "Executive Council Opposes 'Unjust'
Immigration Laws." *Episcopal News Service* (March 9). http://www
.episcopalchurch.org/3577_72778_ENG_HTM.htm.

Shannon, Thomas A. 2002. "Stem-Cell Research: How Catholic Ethics
Guide Us." http://www.americancatholic.org/Newsletters/CU/
ac0102.asp.

Silverstein, Evan. 2005. "Stated Clerk Calls on Congress to Rethink
Proposed Immigration Bill." *Presbyterian News Service* (December 8).
http://www.pcusa.org/pcnews/2005/05680.htm.

Smith, Alexa. 2004. "Measures Condemn Iraq War, Prisoner Abuse."
http://www.pcusa.org/ga216/news/ga04122.htm.

Steinfels, Peter. 2004. *A People Adrift: The Crisis of the Roman Catholic
Church in America*. New York: Simon and Schuster.

Thompson, Richelle. 2003. "Committee Passes Guidelines for Stem Cell
Research." http://www.episcopalchurch.org/3577_17341_ENG_HTM.
htm.

United Methodist Church (UMC). 2005. "Abortion." http://archives
.umc.org/interior.asp?mid=1732.

United Methodist Church (UMC) Council of Bishops. 2004. "Resolution
on the War in Iraq" (May 11). http://archives.umc.org/interior.asp?
ptid=1&mid=5143.

United States Conference of Catholic Bishops (USCCB). 2005. "Faith-
Based Initiative." http://www.usccb.org/sdwp/national/200510fbi
.htm.

United States Conference of Catholic Bishops (USCCB). 2006. "Iraq"
(February). http://www.usccb.org/sdwp/international/200602iraq
.htm.

Vara, Richard. 2004a. "Bishops to Discuss Gay Ordination." *Houston
Chronicle* (March 19): 8A.

Vara, Richard. 2004b. "Clergy Devises Plan to Deal with Gay Bishop
Split." *Houston Chronicle* (March 24): 4A.

Vara, Richard. 2004c. "Sexuality Issues, Weak Budgets on the
Methodists' Front Burner." *Houston Chronicle* (April 24): 1E.

Vara, Richard. 2004d. "Methodist Delegates Uphold Homosexuality
Condemnation." *Houston Chronicle* (May 5): 4A.

Vara, Richard. 2006. "Leadership Slate Upsets Episcopal Conservatives."
Houston Chronicle (January 16): A12.

Vara, Richard. 2007. "What Will the Church Decide?" *Houston Chronicle*
(March 10): F1.

Varacalli, Joseph A. 2006. *The Catholic Experience in America*. Westport,
CT: Greenwood.

Wall, John N. 2000. *A Dictionary for Episcopalians*. Cambridge, MA:
Cowley.

Weber, Harry R. 2004. "Episcopalian Meeting Ends with Call for Unity."
Houston Chronicle (March 28): 23A.

3

Worldwide Perspective

Most of the mainline churches in the United States can trace their origins to Europe: the Episcopal Church and the United Methodist Church to Great Britain, the Evangelical Lutheran Church in America to Germany and the Scandinavian countries, and the Presbyterian Church (U.S.A.) to England and France. While the United States has maintained a tradition of formal separation of religious institutions and the state, many of these European countries have a tradition of state-supported religious organizations. Some, such as England, continue to maintain a state-supported church; others, such as Sweden, have severed such relationships; and yet others, like France, have a history of anticlericalism and secularism while at the same time maintaining past religious traditions. The continent of origin for U.S. denominations today has become far more secularized than the United States. Danièle Hervieu-Léger (2006, 46) notes the claim among students of religion that Europe, not the United States, represents the exception because it is the only region in the world where religion plays a significantly diminished role in public life. Whereas more than 90 percent of U.S. respondents to attitude surveys over several decades consistently have expressed a belief in God, William Murchison (2005, 36) reports that just 41 percent of Europeans report believing in a personal God. Recent surveys indicate that less than 25 percent of Europeans consider religion "very important" in their lives, and only 15 percent attend a worship service once a week. In Great Britain it is estimated that more Muslims attend Friday prayers than Anglicans attend Sunday worship services (ibid.).

Many in the United States have reacted negatively to the general lack of Christian belief and observance in Europe. For instance, George Weigel, an American Catholic theologian, has speculated about the possible consequences Europe faces as a result of increasing secularization—what international legal scholar Joseph Weiler terms "Christophobia" among European intellectuals (Weigel 2005, 19–20). Many Europeans regard their societies to be "post-Christian." Weigel notes that Weiler identifies several elements of Christophobia, including the belief that the genocidal attack against Jews during the Second World War resulted from a long history of Christian anti-Judaism; the youth rebellion of the late 1960s that included a reaction against traditional European Christian identity; reaction against the once-dominant role that Christian Democratic parties played in post–Second World War Europe; the tendency to trace the roots of democracy in Europe only to the Enlightenment, ignoring the pre-Enlightenment Christian roots of democracy; and the mocking of Christianity in popular culture (Simpson 2006).

Of particular concern to Weigel is the refusal of officials to mention the contribution of Christian heritage to European civilization in the preamble to the new constitution for the European Union. Despite the urging of Pope John Paul II and other Christians, the draft European constitution on which 2004 negotiations were based referred to classical Greek and Roman heritage as well as the Enlightenment, but, as Weigel (2005, 57–58) comments, "fifteen hundred years of Christian influence on the formation of what is now Europe went unremarked." Those opposing such a reference argued that no religious language should appear in the constitution in order not to offend those of different faiths or who have no religious beliefs. Weigel quotes Pope John Paul II as saying in response that "One does not cut off the roots from which one is born" (ibid., 143). This quote brings to mind American novelist and Catholic Walker Percy's comment that those who attempt to maintain the values that Christianity established while dispensing with Christianity itself are like the cartoon characters who run off a cliff and remain suspended in midair, not realizing they no longer have any support under them. Similarly, David Martin (2006, 64–65), reflecting on religion in Europe, asks whether "the specifically religious gold standard" is still required to support the values of European civilization, and responds that the "hidden gold standard" does provide a "permanent backing for secular enlightened usage."

Reflecting on the present status of religious belief in Europe, Weigel (2005) presents four possible futures. First, Europe could succeed in maintaining economic prosperity and integrating increased immigrant populations and new states into the European Union. However, Weigel identifies serious difficulties that Europe faces, including the ability to discover the "moral resources" he deems necessary to withstand social and political divisions associated with an increased Islamic population in Europe, estimated at 25 million. In a similar vein, David Martin (2006, 78) observes that the Muslim populations of Europe maintain characteristics distinct from and in opposition to the weakened religious commitment of most Europeans. Martin claims that Muslim communities, while using the language of freedom, rights, and multiculturalism, remain "integral, organic, monocultural and patriarchal." Muslims and native Europeans have very different perceptions of religion, with the latter increasingly viewing religious belief as an individual choice and the former understanding belief as a communal inheritance (Martin 2006, 82). Second, Weigel suggests that European nations could "muddle through," with the native population failing to reproduce itself and an increased Islamicization of the population. Third, with the assistance of immigrants from Christian parts of the non-Western world, Europeans could return to old traditions, finding in Christianity "the spiritual, intellectual, and moral resources to sustain and defend its commitments to toleration, civility, and human rights" (Weigel 2005, 148). Weigel finds some hope for this possible future in various remaining Christian communities in Europe. Finally, Europe could fail to reverse the low birthrates that threaten demographic decline; the population, without Christian roots, would become more demoralized, and an increasingly aggressive Islamic population would prevail, resulting in "a thoroughly nonhumanistic theism" (ibid., 156). Italian journalist Oriana Fallaci expressed this fear, criticizing European officials and intellectuals for accommodating Muslim immigrants who refuse to adopt Western values and customs (Wilkinson 2006b, A20). Although Weigel correlates the decline in the birthrate throughout Europe to the weakening of religious belief, interestingly some have associated the recent and pronounced decline in Eastern Europe to the elimination of Communist-era incentives to have children, such as free housing and subsidized child care. In addition, women in Europe have entered the workplace and thus have delayed motherhood or dispensed with that option completely (Rosenthal 2006, A20). It remains an open question whether a renewal of religious belief would alter these social conditions that militate against child bearing. Nonetheless, some suggest that young Europeans' estrangement from religious institutions is a partial explanation for a pronounced decline in the marriage rate. For instance, in 2004 the rate was 4.3 per 1,000 people in France and 5.1 in England, compared to 7.8 in the United States (Moore 2006, 18).

Although from Weigel's perspective a comparison of the status of religious belief in the United States with that of Europe has consequences beyond a simple contrast of understandings of separation of church and state and the relationship of churches with government, the levels of participation in the traditional denominations, and church participation in social and economic reform movements. This chapter deals primarily with these sorts of questions, attempting to compare and contrast the status of religion in the United States with that of various European nations. I examine the place of Christian churches in six European countries—England, France, Germany, Italy, Poland, and Sweden—highlighting the similarities as well as the differences among European countries regarding the role played by religious organizations in these societies. Poland, a former member of the Communist bloc of Eastern European nations allied with the Soviet Union, represents a major exception to the other five countries in that religious belief and church attendance there are much higher, comparing favorably with that of the United States. The status of religious institutions and religious belief in these six countries will provide a context in which to understand better the position of the mainline Christian denominations in the United States as well as the more general role that religion plays in U.S. politics and society. I will provide brief accounts of the historical evolution of religious belief and institutions in these countries and highlight the religious conflicts that arose in Europe but that were largely absent in the United States.

England

The Church of England began over a highly complex dispute between major political and Catholic religious leaders of the sixteenth century. King Henry VIII and Pope Clement VIII engaged in a confrontation over Henry's request that the pope consent to the annulment of the king's marriage to Catherine of Aragon, the daughter of Ferdinand and Isabella of Spain. Catherine had given birth to several children, but only one—Mary—had survived, thus failing to provide the king with a male heir. Henry's marriage to Catherine itself was of questionable legitimacy. In 1504 Henry's older brother, Arthur, at the age of fourteen, had married Catherine. Shortly thereafter Arthur died, thus denying his father, Henry VII, a generous dowry. In order to retain the dowry, Henry VII intended to have his second oldest son, the future Henry VIII, wedded to Catherine. Church law, which prohibited a man from marrying his brother's wife, stood in the way. Although there were doubts regarding the pope's authority to set aside church law, he acceded to Henry VII's request, and in 1509 Henry the younger married Catherine. The doubtful legality of the marriage provided the justification for Henry's request that the marriage be annulled. When the pope repeatedly refused to agree to an annulment, the king separated from Rome and in 1529 had the question referred to the universities, which, under pressure, agreed to the king's wishes. In 1531 a convocation of the English church declared that Henry was "the singular protector, the only and supreme lord, and as far as permitted by the law of Christ, even the supreme head" of the church (Latourette 1975, 801).

The pope excommunicated Henry, declaring once more the validity of Henry's marriage to Catherine. In 1534 Henry succeeded in having Parliament pass the Act of Succession and the Act of Supremacy, which declared the king to be the only head of the Church of England. Earlier, Henry had published under his name a book claiming to refute Martin Luther's theology, for which the pope had named him the "Defender of the Faith," a title the king continued to use. In addition to the formal break with Rome, Henry had the monasteries repressed, thus altering the basic structure of religious life in England. Various religious organizations were dissolved and the assets transferred to the royal treasury. Parliament repealed prohibitions on the printing and distribution of the scriptures and legalized the marriage of priests, actions that very possibly contributed to the ultimate emergence of a variety of religious groups other than the Church of England.

When Henry's daughter Elizabeth succeeded to the throne in 1558, the ingredients of religious conflict that engulfed France appeared to be present in England. However, Elizabeth concerned herself more with the actions than the beliefs and opinions of her subjects; she focused mainly on political stability and the maintenance of a strong nation rather than religious convictions. As long as Catholics did not engage in treasonous acts and Puritans did not overstep their bounds, they could enjoy freedom of thought and conscience (Harbison 1955, 121).

The early eighteenth century saw the beginning of Methodism in England, largely through the efforts of two brothers, John and Charles Wesley. While at Oxford in 1729, Charles established a club with two others in order to improve their studies. When John, a priest like his father in the Church of England, returned to Oxford after helping in his father's parish, he became the leader of the study group. Called the Holy Club, the group came to be known as the Methodists in reference to the systematic methods that characterized the members of the group. The members retained the name, which subsequently became the official title of the new religious movement.

In 1735 the Wesley brothers, missionaries in the Society for the Propagation of the Gospel in Foreign Parts, left England for Georgia, a newly founded colony in the New World that gave refuge to debtors and Protestants escaping persecution in Germany (Latourette 1975, 1024). Charles, suffering from illness, returned to England in 1736, and John, involved in disputes with colonists, soon followed. In 1738 John had a religious experience that confirmed for him the fundamental Protestant belief in salvation by faith alone. As John carried his emotional message to the general population, he experienced strong critical reaction. Nonetheless, by 1790, shortly before his death, the Methodist movement had attracted more than 71,000 members in Great Britain, making it the largest independent Protestant group in England. Although John considered Methodism to be an appendage of the Church of England, at his death in 1791, followers formally established the Wesleyan Methodist Church. Various differences over such issues as the nature of the group's relationship with the Church of England and disagreement over Arminianism—the doctrine, supported by John Wesley, that human free will played a role along with God's sovereignty in salvation—and the Calvinist belief in predestination and election—the preferred doctrine of fellow Methodist George Whitefield—led to divisions in the movement.

In the nineteenth century the Church of England faced serious challenges from a rapidly changing social and intellectual climate.

The vast population of the nation, which suffered from the dislocation brought about by industrialization, looked upon the church as an institution of privilege concerned only with the interests of the upper classes. Changes occurred within the Church of England itself. For instance, those in the Anglo-Catholic movement called for the adoption of Catholic practices, such as introducing greater ritual within the Church of England. As a result of the use of such Catholic traditions, those in independent groups drifted further from the Church of England, forming in 1846 the Evangelical Alliance in order to bring together Evangelicals from various splinter groups (Latourette 1975, 1171). As scientific knowledge increased and social awareness developed, some reacted negatively to such changes, refusing to make any compromises with such innovation, while many others left the church completely. Some attempted to find common ground with those critical of a fundamentalist interpretation of the Bible, accepting the historical study of scripture, and with scientists such as Charles Darwin who appeared to threaten traditional Christian beliefs. Various forms of socialism developed in an attempt to address the social evils of the day. In accordance with that trend, various Christian social movements were established to ameliorate economic and social problems. The Church of England, which spread throughout the world as the British Empire expanded, moved to unify the various Anglican churches that had followed the flag. The church began holding the Lambeth Conferences, meetings of bishops in the Anglican Communion, which first gathered in London in 1867 and subsequently met at ten-year intervals.

The First World War devastated the younger population of England and other countries on the European continent, and the social, political, and economic disruption resulting from the conflict decreased the influence of religion in the country. Churches nonetheless attempted to reestablish their standing among the population. For example, in 1924 various churches joined in the Conference on Christian Politics, Economics, and Citizenship to plan a strategy for reaching out to those who had fallen away from the church. Others worked to heal divisions through the union of dissenting groups. For instance, in 1929 the Church of Scotland and the United Free Church of Scotland combined after more than eighty years of separation, and in 1932 the larger Methodist groups agreed to unite (ibid., 1387). The Church of England, demonstrating a level of tolerance, permitted a variety of theological approaches and organizational understandings, from conservative Evangelicals to Anglo-Catholics who hoped for a reunion with the Catholic Church and advocated the Church of England's recognition of the pope as the leader of Christians but without the strict hierarchy of the Catholic Church or the doctrine of infallibility.

In the early twentieth century, Parliament and church officials agreed to certain policies to allow for greater independence of the Church of England from the government. The Enabling Act of 1919 introduced such policies as permitting the residents of a parish to participate in the choice of a pastor. In 1921 the Church Assembly was established, a body composed of lay as well as clerical members (ibid., 1391). Despite such reforms, the intellectual movements hostile to traditional Christian belief that arose in the nineteenth century continued to influence general attitudes as the country entered the twentieth. Such noted authors as George Bernard Shaw and D. H. Lawrence rejected the authority of the Christian establishment, and the continued influence of industrialization and the creation of large numbers of factory jobs, with workers drawn away from traditional rural society, also contributed to the weakening of established religious institutions. The Great Depression, beginning in 1929, added to the adverse influences on the churches. With economic hardship, donations declined, and the creation of government programs took from churches one of their traditional social functions. People in the upper classes, who had been major financial supporters of church organizations, contributed more heavily to such government programs in the form of taxes, and the poor came to depend not on religious charity but on government programs (ibid., 1392). The Second World War, like the First World War, caused major social disruptions, further diminishing the status of religious organizations, and German bombing raids early in the war destroyed many churches' physical structures. Following the war the number of people interested in becoming pastors increased briefly, but by the 1950s the Church of England experienced a further decline in the number of clergy.

In contrast to the difficulties the Church of England faced, the Catholic Church experienced significant growth during the first half of the twentieth century. While the total number of Catholics in England and Wales was estimated at approximately 1.8 million in 1914, their numbers had risen to more than 2.6 million by 1950. The growth was attributed to conversion by marriage and the high birthrate in Catholic families (Latourette 1975, 1395). The great majority of the population of the Republic of Ireland, which became independent of Great Britain in 1949, was Catholic. The majority of the population of Northern Ireland, which remained part of Great Britain, was Protestant, but the presence of a significant Catholic minority led to major civil conflict. The ill will between Catholics and Protestants in Northern Ireland has continued into the twenty-first century. In 2006 Ian Paisley, noted Protestant leader of the Democratic Unionist Party, rejected the call to take part in a power-sharing executive group to recommence the peace process with Sinn Fein, the Irish Republican Army's political wing (*Houston Chronicle* 2006). However, in March 2007 Paisley and Sinn Fein leader Gerry Adams, under pressure from British Northern Ireland Secretary Peter Hain, agreed to cooperate in forming a coalition government, thus raising hopes that the long hostility between Protestants and Catholics would soon end (Katz 2007).

The English monarch today retains the title of Defender of the Faith, promising in the coronation oath to support and maintain the Christian church. She is the "supreme governor" of the Church of England. On the recommendation of the prime minister, the monarch approves the appointment of archbishops and deans and formally opens sessions of the General Synod, the governing body of the church. The church plays important symbolic roles during public occasions. Bishops and priests perform state weddings and funerals, conduct memorial services, and officiate at major events such as coronations.

The Church of England and the British government are intertwined. Twenty-six bishops, including the archbishops of Canterbury in the south and of York in the north, along with the bishops of London, Durham, and Winchester, serve in the House of Lords and have the title of Lords Spiritual. Given greater religious pluralism within English society, questions have been raised regarding the possible extension of membership to other Christian denominations. Although the English constitution contains no principle of religious freedom, in practice various religious groups freely associate, engage in worship activities, and present their religious views publicly. The Church of England is within the worldwide Anglican Communion, and the archbishop of Canterbury serves as that group's formal spiritual leader, although he has little authority to command compliance from member churches in other countries.

A bishop and at least one assistant bishop preside over each of forty-three dioceses in the two provinces of Canterbury and York. The clergy and lay members of each synod elect members of the General Synod, which meets in London or York at least twice a year. Synod members serve five-year terms and are divided into three houses: the House of Bishops, the House of Clergy, and the House of Laity. Any church law that the General Synod may pass must receive the agreement of the monarch, and some church laws require parliamentary approval. The Church of England includes more than 16,000 churches and forty-two cathedrals. The parish, the basic unit of the Church of England, is governed by a priest, called a vicar or rector, who is sometimes assisted by a deacon or a parish lay worker. The priest collaborates with a parochial church council composed of the members of the congregation. The council, in collaboration with the bishop, appoints the priest and is responsible for maintaining church buildings (BBC 2006).

Church attendance in England has continued to decline in recent years. Approximately a million people attend services in the Church of England each Sunday. They tend to be older people, with far fewer of those between the ages of fifteen and thirty attending regularly. Declining participation in church services notwithstanding, contributions actually have increased each year. Although the Church of England is the country's official religious institution, each parish assumes the financial responsibility for maintaining the local church. Despite declining regular church attendance, participation in religious holiday events has remained relatively high. For instance, in 2002 approximately 40 percent of church members reportedly attended church services on Christmas (BBC 2006).

Members and clergy of the Church of England have faced some of the same controversies as mainline denominations in the United States. For instance, in 1992 the General Synod approved the ordination of women. However, responding to objections, the next year it provided a mechanism by which a parish could refuse to accept a woman priest. The first woman priest was ordained in 1994, and presently approximately 20 percent of priests are female. The next step would be to approve women as bishops. Officially, the Church of England permits the ordination of gay priests if they are celibate. Along with the rest of the Anglican Communion, the Church of England has struggled with the question of whether the church should bless same-gender unions. In February 2007 the

General Synod of the Church of England affirmed the position that homosexuality does not disqualify a person from full participation in the church, but rejected a proposed statement committing the church to "respect the patterns of holy living to which lesbian and gay Christians aspire" (*Houston Chronicle* 2007b). Since 2003, when the Episcopal Church elected an actively gay bishop, Archbishop of Canterbury Rowan Williams has struggled to maintain unity within the worldwide Anglican Communion.

France

Like other European countries in recent years, France has become increasingly secularized. Unlike England, France has a 100-year tradition of separation of church and state. Although approximately two-thirds of the population identify with the Catholic Church, the proportion of the population taking part in various religious observances such as baptisms and weddings has declined significantly over the last fifteen years. In recent surveys, less than half of younger French residents claim they believe in God, and 40 percent state they have no religious affiliation (French Embassy in Australia 2000). The French Catholic Church faces a crisis of personnel similar to that of the U.S. Catholic Church. In 1960 the church had 45,000 priests, but today that number has dropped to 22,000. Ordinations of new priests have declined to approximately 100 per year, down from about 1,000, and the number of nuns has declined from 100,000 to 52,000. The Catholic Church has attempted to counter these troubling trends by trying to attract younger people to the church, organizing religious activities such as the annual World Youth Day, at which the pontiff is invited to speak.

Although the storm of the sixteenth-century Reformation was centered in Germany, from 1562 to 1593 France also experienced significant social and political disruption, called the Wars of Religion, resulting from the rise of the Calvinist movement. By 1560 the French Calvinists, called Huguenots, had gained strength in the nation's larger towns; attracted significant support among artisans, tradesmen, and farmers; and succeeded in gaining converts among the nobility (Harbison 1955, 106). In 1561, although legally prohibited, the Huguenots had established approximately 2,500 churches. The vast majority of the population as well as the major social structures, including the monarchy and the theologians of the University of Paris, remained firmly in the Catholic fold throughout the period of civil strife. For both sides in the conflict, loyalty to the religious cause overshadowed commitment to the monarchy or the nation, and both sides were guilty of committing atrocities. For instance, in 1572, in an event called the Massacre of St. Bartholomew, major Calvinist leaders were murdered in Paris and subsequently more than 10,000 Huguenots around the country were killed.

In 1594 Henry of Navarre, a Protestant, agreed to convert to Catholicism in return for becoming Henry IV, King of France. He famously commented that "Paris was well worth a mass" (Latourette 1975, 767). The new king pledged to protect the Huguenots, and this promise ultimately led to peace. In 1598 Henry issued a compromise statement, the Edict of Nantes, that granted to the Huguenots liberty of conscience, freedom of worship in several designated towns, and civic and legal rights on an equal basis with Catholics, including the right to hold public offices, to attend universities and schools, and to be admitted to hospitals. The edict notwithstanding, Henry's son, Louis XIII, conducted three campaigns against the Huguenots. In 1629 the Peace of Alais reaffirmed many of the assurances granted to the Protestants in the Edict of Nantes. Although the Huguenots never made up more than 11 or 12 percent of the population, as long as religious guarantees were honored, they prospered, gaining influence in national and local affairs. However, during the reign of Louis XIV, increased restrictions were placed on the Huguenots, including the destruction of churches and the removal of Protestant children from their families to be raised by Catholics. Finally, in 1685 the edict was revoked completely. Many Huguenots fled, settling in other countries, and Protestantism significantly declined in France (ibid., 769). Not only Protestants but also Catholics suffered reverses under Louis XIV, for the notion of the divine right of kings superseded the claims to authority of both Catholics and Calvinists (Harbison 1955, 112).

In the late eighteenth century, as economic and political conditions in France worsened, the country moved toward the revolution of 1789. The Catholic Church, identified with the old aristocracy and considered an enemy of the revolution, suffered confiscation of property and restrictions on its role in French society. With the fall of Napoleon in 1814 and the restoration of the Bourbons to the monarchy, conservative Catholics tended to regard the revolution as a great crime, and the most extreme among them claimed that God had granted absolute authority to the king and the pope. Following the revolution of 1848, the hostility between the church and supporters of the revolution subsided. The view developed that democracy and the Catholic faith were compatible, and several of the clergy participated in the first National Assembly of the Second Republic (Latourette 1975, 1106). Nonetheless, in 1870, with the fall of Louis Napoleon and the Second Empire and the establishment of the Third Republic, many Catholic clergy and leading lay members, such as Joseph Marie de Maistre, renewed their support for the restoration of the monarchy. The new government thus resumed the animosity toward the Catholic Church and imposed restrictions on the church. The parliament took various measures contrary to church doctrine, including legalizing divorce and permitting labor on Sunday. However, Pope Leo XIII took steps to ease the hostility between Catholics and the new republic. Finally, in 1892 the pope issued an encyclical exhorting Catholics to accept the existing governing system.

Relations between the Catholic Church and the government once again worsened in the 1890s with the controversial case of Alfred Dreyfus, the Jewish army officer unfairly convicted of treason. Catholics tended to oppose Dreyfus's cause, which resulted in popular opinion unfavorable to the church. In 1901 the French parliament approved the Association Act, which required formal government approval of the existence of any religious organization in France. The difficult process of gaining such approval led to the closing of various religious orders and several thousand Catholic schools (ibid., 1107). In 1905 the French government ended the Concordat of 1801 that had established the relationship between church and state, thus disestablishing the Catholic Church and relegating it to a status comparable to any other denomination. Pope Pius X criticized the actions of the French government, and in 1907 the French parliament eased the restrictions on the church but did not undo the disestablishment decision. State policies undoubtedly advanced the secularization of French society. By the 1940s just over three-fourths of the population had been baptized in the Catholic Church, including children living in France's capital, Paris. However, observers questioned whether baptism was anything more than a lingering social convention. The proportion of Catholics who regularly practiced their faith was estimated to vary between 2 percent in the munici-palities and 38 percent in rural areas (ibid., 1367). Following the Second World War, secularization continued, with the non-Christian movements of existentialism and Marxism coming increasingly into vogue. In the twentieth century France followed a policy called *laïcité*, which involves the separation of church and state and the guarantee of religious freedom. Government officials traditionally have avoided making public statements referring to religious considerations when debating public policy questions. Although the United States and France both adhere to the doctrine of separation of church and state, the French government actively promotes secularism to a much greater extent than the United States. For instance, in 2001 the French parliament (composed of the National Assembly and the Senate) approved a law banning religious groups from engaging in activities to establish psychological dependence among followers (Creswell 2002).

The French government owns and cares for all church buildings built before 1905. In addition, the state pays the salaries of some church workers, such as prison, military, and hospital chaplains. Approximately 15 percent of students attend Catholic schools, and the church has negotiated agreements with the government whereby the state provides funds for teacher salaries (Minkenberg 2003, 204). One exception to the separation principle in France is the region of Alsace, which was part of Germany at the time the nation established that principle.

Today, Protestants constitute between 2 and 3 percent of the French population. Restricted prior to the official separation of church and state in 1905, Protestants finally gained a status equal to that of Catholics. The Protestant Federation of France comprises fifteen churches. Participation among Protestants in religious observances is very low, with more than 50 percent participating little or not at all. While more than half of Catholic priests are older than sixty, Protestant clergy are significantly younger, and 15 percent of them are women. The Reformed Church, France's largest Protestant denomination with 300,000 adherents, in recent times has lost nearly half of its membership and nearly a third of its ministers (Ecumenical News International 2005).

With the decline in Christian religious participation, Islam has grown in significance. Muslims make up between 5 and 10 percent of the French population. Muslim youth rioted in the poorer suburbs of Paris and in other parts of France in fall 2005; although the riots were motivated largely by the dim economic future of these youth and alleged racism rather than religion per se, Fouad Ajami (2005, 50), director of Middle East Studies at Johns Hopkins University, claimed that radicalized Islam contributed to the intensity of the turmoil. The riots raised deeper concerns among Christians about the future of the country as a secular state when a large minority population holds significantly different cultural and religious norms (Tolson 2005, 35).

Germany

Germany was the original site of the Protestant Reformation of the early sixteenth century. Ever since, the nation essentially has been divided between Protestant and Catholic populations. Today, Protestants and Catholics each make up approximately one-third of the population, with about 30 percent of Germans having no religious affiliation. The German Basic Law, ratified in 1949, contains five articles on religion taken from the liberal Weimar Constitution of 1919. Among the provisions are a no-establishment clause, protection of freedom of religion and belief, and a prohibition on discrimination based on religious affiliation or beliefs. Germany does not have a state church, and legally churches are public corporations. Both Protestants and Catholics engage in discussions of significant social and political issues, such as disarmament, labor policy, abortion, and the environment (Germany Info 2006). Although the German constitution establishes separation of church and state, interactions between the government and religious institutions reach a level that would be looked upon with concern, if not completely rejected, in the United States. The relationship between church and state has been called one of "positive neutrality." Because religious organizations contribute to the public life of the nation, the government grants them certain benefits (Monsma and Soper 1997, 172). For instance, churches may provide religious instruction in the public schools to children of adherents. Also, the German government cooperates with religious institutions in having taxes collected from church members. The major religious groups that take part in these activities are the Catholic Church, the Evangelical Church in Germany, and Jewish organizations. In 1995 the Constitutional Court ruled that the display of the crucifix in public school classrooms violated the principle of separation of church and state and that a crucifix must be removed if any student or teacher protests (Minkenberg 2003, 203).

Following Martin Luther's break with the Catholic Church beginning in 1517, violent social and political disruptions occurred in Germany. The Peasants' War of 1524 and 1525, a rebellion involving religious differences but primarily concerning economic issues such as taxation and deflation, brought attacks on the nobles, including church officials, whom the peasants blamed for their plight. Although Luther expressed sympathy for the peasants' cause, he strongly objected to violence against the nobility and urged the princes to use stern force against the rebels, which the princes were most willing to do. Although Luther issued a pamphlet asking for mercy on the captives taken by the princes, the peasants came to view him as a traitor (Latourette 1975, 725). Such events led Luther to distrust the peasants, to have greater concern for establishing civil order, and to be willing to rely on the princes for maintaining peace. Approximately a century later, Germany was the major focus of the Thirty Years' War, another religiously based conflict that attracted the participation of other European countries and led to the destruction of German cities and a breakdown of social stability (ibid., 894).

In the early nineteenth century a new European intellectual movement began, arising from Deism and the Enlightenment, that was centered in German universities. Students from Scandinavia, Great Britain, the United States, and other predominantly Protestant countries studying in Germany carried the views of German theologians and philosophers back to their own countries. Participants in the movement would have a major influence on mainline Protestant theologians and denominations in the United States. This movement engaged in a scientific and rationalistic examination of the Bible and Christian history, an approach that came to be known as "higher criticism." Johann Salomo Semler, an eighteenth-century theologian and progenitor of the movement, argued that although the Bible contained revelation and timeless truths, not all portions of scripture carried the same value. According to Semler, the contents of books were influenced by the time periods in which they were written. Similarly, Johann Gottfried von Herder, an eighteenth-century preacher, claimed that the books of the Bible could be understood only within the context of the time periods in which they were written. The great eighteenth-century German philosopher Immanuel Kant also contributed greatly to a revised understanding of the nature of Christianity (ibid., 1051).

In the mid-nineteenth century, the German territories moved toward unification, largely through the efforts of conservatives, of whom Otto von Bismarck, the German Empire's first chancellor, was most prominent. The consolidation did not include Austria, where the population was predominantly Catholic, so the result was a Protestant majority in the new country. However, various religious currents flourished, including more orthodox beliefs; pietism; religious influences from other countries such as Great Britain and the United States; and the official church of Germany, the *Landeskirchen* (ibid., 1120). Following the First World War the religious denominations, including Catholics, prospered under the Weimar Republic. However, with the rise of Hitler in the early 1930s, churches came under increasing restriction. In 1933 the National Socialist regime disbanded the Center Party, the political organization many Catholics had supported. That same year the Vatican, attempting to guarantee the religious freedom that had prevailed prior to the Nazi takeover, negotiated a concordat with the German government. However, the following year the government repressed Catholic labor organizations and severely restricted Catholic publications. In 1935 the Nazi regime began a program of indoctrination in Catholic schools and subsequently restricted Catholic education in order to win the loyalty of children away from the church. To weaken them further, Nazi officials brought various criminal charges against religious organizations (ibid., 1368).

The Lutheran church perhaps found it more difficult to resist the Nazi regime, given that Lutherans traditionally were more willing to accept secular authority. Many religious leaders bowed to the wishes of the Nazi regime, organizing the Faith Movement of German Christians, a group that opposed communism, advocated German traditions and what it considered the legacy of Martin Luther, and attempted to create a unified church organization parallel to the Nazi movement (ibid., 1375). However, other religious leaders, including Lutheran pastors such as Dietrich Bonhoeffer, opposed the Nazi regime. Bonhoeffer, who became involved with anti-Nazi conspirators, was imprisoned in the Buchenwald concentration camp in 1943 and executed in 1945 (Chadwick 1990, 366).

Following the Second World War the Allies divided Germany into separate zones, which became East and West Germany, with East Germany controlled by the Soviet Union. Predominantly Protestant areas were included in East Germany, and the church came under severe pressure from the new Communist regime. During forty-five years under Communist rule, the regime in East Germany strongly discouraged the population from participating in religious observance. Therefore, participation rates were much lower than in West Germany, and when Germany reunited, the rates of participation for the nation as a whole dropped.

A controversial court case in early 2007 demonstrated that Germany, like other European countries, was finding it difficult to accommodate increasing religious pluralism. A Muslim woman, born in Germany but with a Moroccan cultural background, requested that a judge grant an accelerated divorce, claiming that her husband beat her. The judge, herself a woman, denied the request, citing a verse from the Quran that appears to sanction husbands beating their wives for disobedience (Landler 2007). Although the judge ultimately was replaced, and public officials, legal experts, and German Muslim leaders strongly objected to the ruling, arguing that all people living in the country should be governed by the German legal code, the case suggested that Germans may need to develop a clearer understanding of their contemporary secular culture in the context of a Christian tradition and new religious influences.

Italy

For most of two millennia Italy has been the spiritual center of the Christian faith, with the Catholic pope, with few exceptions, located in the city of Rome. Not surprisingly, more than 85 percent of the Italian population claim Catholicism as their religious affiliation, at least nominally. Like residents in other European countries, few Italians participate in worship services; estimates indicate that just 20 percent of Italian Catholics participate regularly in church life. According to recent polls, 14 percent of Italians identify themselves either as atheists or agnostics.

As Italy developed into a unified nation in the late nineteenth century, the papal states were dissolved. In the early nineteenth century, nationalist leaders such as Giuseppe Garibaldi supported unification of the country with the pope playing a significant political role. Although Pope Pius IX initially supported unification, he ultimately opposed the nationalist goals. Count Camillo Benso di Cavour, who succeeded in establishing the Kingdom of Italy, designed the country's constitution and served as the first prime minister. He was a strong anticleric and took action against certain parts of the church. Until 1870 the pope, with French military support, maintained control of Rome and the immediate environs. However, with the withdrawal of French forces, the Italian army occupied the city and the pope remained essentially a prisoner in the Vatican. In 1871 Cavour attempted to appease the papacy, offering the pope sovereignty over the church's properties, including the Vatican and the Lateran in Rome, and an annual pension in compensation for the loss of the papal states. However, Pope Pius IX refused to agree, requesting that Catholic princes reinstate his political position. In 1868 he prohibited Catholics from participating in the new government, which nonetheless continued to provide clergy salaries, to prohibit divorce, and to allow the church to offer religious instruction in the schools. However, the government also expropriated a large proportion of church property, reduced the number of monasteries, and assumed responsibility for charitable activities. Although many Catholics refused to abide by the pope's prohibition on political participation, many did, which resulted in the government being controlled by those indifferent, or hostile, to the church, thus increasing the distance between church and state (Latourette 1975, 1112–1113).

Protestants in Italy have always represented a small minority of the population. In the nineteenth century the Waldenses, a Christian group that traced its history back to the twelfth century, rejected the papacy and such Catholic elements as the mass, purgatory, and indulgences, stressing instead the simple gospel message. By the mid-nineteenth century, King Charles Albert of Savoy had granted the Waldenses religious and civil rights. Protestants in Great Britain and the United States provided financial aid to the group, and the Kingdom of Italy instituted measures recognizing religious liberty (ibid., 1154).

The Catholic Church's status in the newly created nation remained in flux until after the Fascist government under Benito Mussolini came to power in 1922. In 1929 the Vatican entered into an understanding regarding church-state relations, called the Lateran Treaty, which established an uneasy truce between Pope

Pius XI and Mussolini. The treaty reestablished the pope's secular authority by creating Vatican City as a separate state, recognized the pope as a sovereign prince, and compensated the pope for the loss of income from confiscated lands. A concordat, also agreed to in 1929, normalized relations between the Vatican and the government of Italy. The agreement made instruction in the Catholic religion mandatory in the secondary schools, exempted seminary students from military service, and authorized government stipends for priests and bishops (Donovan 2003, 97–98). In return, the government received the right to participate in the appointment of clergy. The agreements notwithstanding, the relationship between the church and the Fascist government remained uneasy. For instance, Mussolini required Catholic youth organizations to be included within the Fascist structure, and the Fascist government disbanded young Catholic men's groups and attempted to exercise government control over church schools (Latourette 1975, 1365). Although Pope Pius XI challenged the Fascist regime by declaring, in response to the Italian invasion of Ethiopia, that such wars of aggression were unjust, the Catholic Church failed to mount an unqualified protest, instead using the circumstance to increase papal authority over the Catholic Church in Ethiopia (ibid., 1365). When Italy entered the Second World War, the pope appealed successfully to both sides to treat Rome as an open city off limits to bombing and destruction.

After the Fascist regime of Benito Mussolini disintegrated during the Second World War, the Catholic Church stood as a major force in opposition to the Communist party, which was competing for the opportunity to govern Italy. The provisions of the Lateran Treaty were incorporated into the new constitution of 1948, and the Catholic Church allied itself with the Christian Democratic Party (DC), mobilizing Catholic voters, including parish priests and members of youth organizations and women's groups, to support its candidates. Pope Pius XII worked to reaffirm the traditional status of Christianity in Italy and Europe (Donovan 2003, 100). The DC became the dominant party in Italy, winning 48.5 percent of the vote in the 1948 elections and more than half of the seats in the Chamber of Deputies. However, although the DC depended on the pope to encourage political unity among the nation's Catholics and the capacity of the church to mobilize voters, party leaders wished to establish their independence within the political realm. The church's authority in society remained limited during the 1950s. Given the difficulties the DC faced in governing and the church's association with the party, the Catholic Church's reputation declined (ibid., 102). A national referendum in 1974 resulted in legalizing divorce, a major defeat for the Catholic Church, and in 1978 the Italian parliament approved an abortion measure, which voters ratified by referendum in 1981.

A revision of the Lateran agreement in 1984 established the principle of the secular state while maintaining government support of religious institutions (U.S. Department of State 2005). Christian denominations other than the Catholic Church—including Adventists, Assemblies of God, Baptists, and Lutherans—have negotiated agreements with the Italian government to receive certain privileges such as ministerial access to hospitals, prisons, and military facilities; registration of religious marriages; and exemptions of students from school attendance on religious holidays. The agreement provided for regulation of the Vatican bank—which had suffered from scandal—and subjected church property to taxation, but it also established tax deductions for religious donations and the use of the tax structure to make voluntary contributions to the church. An estimated 40 to 45 percent of taxpayers make such contributions (Donovan 2003, 103).

In contrast to the United States, where public displays of religious symbols such as the Ten Commandments have created significant political and legal controversy, in Italy Christian images such as the crucifix regularly appear in schools and other public buildings. In 2004 the Constitutional Court ruled constitutional a 1928 statute mandating the display of crucifixes in classrooms, and in 2005 a court determined that crucifixes could remain at polling stations. Although the Italian constitution prohibits government support for private schools, the Catholic Church has sought government assistance to support its large number of private schools, which have suffered from declining enrollment. Although the revised concordat ended the religious teaching requirement in the schools, the government allows the church to choose Catholic teachers who are paid by the government to teach religion courses in the public schools. Students are not required to attend these courses and may register for alternative classes. Government agencies provide land for places of worship and can subsidize their construction. The Italian government also plays a role in maintaining historic places of worship, where many artistic and cultural artifacts are housed.

By 1995 the DC had ceased to exist and its heir apparent, the Italian Popular Party, failed to provide a satisfactory alternative for the Catholic Church. Anticommunism had been a major rallying point for the DC, but with the fall of communism in the late 1980s as well as revelations of corruption within the party, no sufficiently cohesive force remained to maintain a single political organization for Catholics. Several political parties along the political spectrum declared affiliation with the Christian cause, and the Vatican initiated a policy of partisan nonalignment. Church advocacy then shifted toward interest group action, the efforts of influential individuals, and the operation of formal church-state interaction. The church hierarchy backed candidates who supported its value positions, including the defense of human life, advocacy of the family within the institution of marriage, liberty in education, support for local government, and a preference for assisting the less advantaged in society (ibid., 109). However, Mark Donovan has noted that measures of Italian public opinion indicate that the population tends to object to the church intervening in the public arena to make policy recommendations (ibid., 113).

Nonetheless, the Catholic Church continues to maintain a presence in public policy. For instance, in 2004 the church successfully backed legislation that declared an embryo to be equivalent to human life, banned the use of sperm for artificial insemination, and restricted the use of embryos in scientific research. Commenting on the draft constitution for the European Union, Pope John Paul II and Cardinal Joseph Ratzinger (the future Pope Benedict XVI) declared that the document should recognize Europe's Christian heritage. In such ways, the Catholic Church in Italy appears to have taken on a role comparable to that of mainline denominations in the United States, which periodically issue statements on public policy in an essentially secularized society.

In 2006 Pope Benedict XVI became involved in a worldwide controversy over a speech that he delivered at the University of Regensburg in his native Germany. The pope angered Muslims by quoting the fourteenth-century Byzantine Emperor Manuel II Paleologus who, in a dialogue with an "educated Persian," stated, "Show me just what Muhammad brought that was new, and there you will find things evil and inhuman, such as his command to spread by the sword the faith he preached" (Wilkinson 2006a, A15). Following sometimes violent reaction, including the murder of a Catholic nun in Somalia that some associated with the pope's comments, Benedict issued a statement of regret, commenting that the quote did not express his personal view. Those reporting on Benedict's speech emphasized that the pope also focused his presentation on increased secularism and a decline in European Christian vitality. The incident suggested that the pope, although no longer a major authoritative participant in Italian politics, still plays a significant symbolic role in world politics. The pope's comments appeared to echo the attitudes of others in Italy and other European countries. For instance, Italian journalist Oriana Fallaci, who died in September 2006, had begun a public campaign against Islam following the September 11, 2001, terrorist attacks, referring to Islamists as "SS and Black Shirts who wave the Quran" (Wilkinson 2006b). In November 2006 Pope Benedict traveled to Turkey, a trip that had been planned prior to his controversial comments. Turkey, an overwhelmingly Muslim nation, does not legally recognize the Catholic Church. Before becoming the pontiff, Benedict had expressed reservations about Turkey entering the European Union. However, on this trip, he altered his view, expressing support for Turkey's inclusion. Nonetheless, Benedict emphasized that Muslim countries would be expected to respect the religious beliefs of Christians just as Western European countries should recognize the rights of those from other cultures. The pontiff has stated that peace can be ensured only through "respect for the religious convictions and practices of others, in a reciprocal way in all societies" (Carosa 2006).

Poland

Although the Catholic Church traditionally had been suspicious of the development of democratic government, following the Second World War the church in Poland came to support the formation of democratic institutions. John Anderson (2003, 144) attributes this shift to Catholic opposition to Communist rule and to the liberalizing results of the Second Vatican Council held from 1962 to 1965. In Poland, a predominantly Catholic country, the Catholic Church followed such a policy of advocating democratic reforms during the period of Communist rule.

In 1925 the Vatican established relations with Poland through a concordat, and the church at that time acceded to the establishment of a nondemocratic government. Poland had a significant Orthodox Ukrainian population, which the government and the Catholic Church attempted to convert to Catholicism. Many Orthodox clergy were imprisoned and executed (Latourette 1975, 1371). When Germany and the Soviet Union invaded Poland at the beginning of the Second World War, the Catholic Church became the target of repression. The pope maintained contact with the Polish government-in-exile and allowed its ambassador to stay in the Vatican. In 1947 the Communist faction within the country gained complete control of the Polish government and attempted to sever ties between the Polish church and the Vatican. In 1950 the government and the Polish bishops signed an agreement guaranteeing freedom of worship and religious education, but doubts quickly arose regarding the effectiveness of this agreement (ibid., 1372).

Although the Catholic Church in Poland followed a defensive strategy during the first decades following the Second World War, by the 1970s the church began aggressively to oppose the Communist regime, forming an alliance with intellectual and working groups (Anderson 2003, 144). The election in 1978 of Polish priest Karol Wojtyla as Pope John Paul II strengthened this alliance. The workers, forming Solidarity (*Solidarność*), an independent labor union backed by the Catholic Church, objected primarily to the economic conditions in Poland, but the church provided a religious and moral justification for the struggle. In 1980 union leader Lech Walesa led a strike to gain recognition for Solidarity and a forty-hour work week (McElroy 2006, 30). As the Communist regime began to weaken in the late 1980s, the Catholic Church became increasingly critical of those in power, and when the regime crumbled, church leaders played significant roles in the shift to a new structure of government. However, the transition to a democratic system posed the significant question regarding what role the church, which had acted as an opponent to the previous Communist government, would play in a democracy. Having struggled against an authoritarian regime for so long, church leaders insisted that the church should receive special status within the new constitution and laws. After several drafts, the constitution backed by the Solidarity party recognized the centuries-long

Christian heritage. In addition, the document identified a right to life that began at conception and required the government to support the teaching of religious beliefs in the public schools. As the Constitutional Commission debated the proposed constitution, representatives of the Catholic Church emphasized three points: avoiding an explicit statement of separation between church and state, including a reference to God and Christian values, and protecting the fetus (Anderson 2003, 145). Ultimately, Article 53 of the constitution guaranteed the religious rights of all citizens.

Politically, the Catholic Church offered to support those involved in creating political parties that were friendly to the interests of the church. Immediately following the fall of the Communist regime, the church supported the Solidarity coalition in the elections in 1989. In several instances, church officials allowed Solidarity electoral committees to meet on church property. In 1990 Polish bishops suggested that religious education should be mandatory. During the following school year, several school officials did introduce the subjects of religion and ethics, apparently on a voluntary basis. The bishops expressed concern about the moral character of media broadcasting, although the church received permission to broadcast masses and to establish Catholic radio stations. In the 1995 presidential campaign, church officials, while taking an officially neutral stance, recommended to voters that they withhold support from those candidates who participated in the former Communist regime. Instances of bishops attempting to persuade voters did not succeed, leading John Anderson (2003, 148) to conclude that the political influence of the church should not be overstated. On the issue of abortion, in 1992 the church succeeded in having a bill passed in the National Assembly that restricted the practice. However, when the Socialists returned to power in 1995, the National Assembly, over the objections of the church leadership, eased the restriction somewhat. The church attempted to have a provision introduced into the constitution, but achieved limited results. Therefore, the efforts of church leaders notwithstanding, Poland permitted a limited right to abortion as well as divorce. Solidarity, the initial spark that brought greater freedom in the 1980s, lost its most prominent member, Lech Walesa, who resigned his membership, claiming that the organization no longer stood for its founding principles. The leaders of the Law and Justice faction, identical twins Lech and Jaroslaw Kaczynski, won the 2005 election for president and prime minister, respectively, and promised to eliminate corruption and establish a new Poland based on Christian values (Reiter and Rakoweic 2006, A21).

The difficulties of the Communist era continued to influence the attitudes and actions of Polish citizens and to affect Catholic Church officials. In December 2006 the news media reported rumors that the newly appointed archbishop of Warsaw, Stanislaw Wielgus, had collaborated with Sluzba Bezpieczenstwa, Poland's security service, in the 1970s. With continued media reports, Wielgus abandoned his initial denials and admitted that the collaboration accounts were true, although he still claimed never to have informed on anyone. After consulting with Vatican officials, Wielgus bowed to pressure and announced his resignation just hours before the scheduled mass to celebrate his elevation to archbishop (Fleishman and Kasprzycka 2007). These events illustrated the continuing significance of the Communist era and the Catholic Church to the Polish nation. Researchers estimate that as many as 10 percent of Poland's priests, monks, and nuns collaborated in some way with the secret police. Some in the church claim that knowledge of collaboration was available for years but was not publicized, perhaps out of respect for Pope John Paul II, or even at his direction (*Houston Chronicle* 2007a).

Sweden

Sweden traditionally has been called the nation of empty churches. Today a smaller percentage of Swedes profess a faith in God than the residents of any other country in Europe. Less than 10 percent of the Swedish population regularly attends church. However, 70 percent still receive baptism. The number of youths taking part in confirmation has declined significantly in recent years, and today approximately 40 percent of fifteen-year-olds attend religious classes in preparation for confirmation (Olofsson 2004, 35). Approximately 50 percent of couples marry in the church. Until recently the Lutheran Church was the official state religion, receiving government assistance to maintain church buildings and to pay pastors' salaries. Unless they expressed an alternative preference, all Swedish citizens were considered members of the church. Before 1950 Swedes could not leave the Evangelical Lutheran National Church (the Church of Sweden) unless they joined another church approved by the king. Unlike churches in the United States that are called "evangelical," referring to fundamentalist beliefs and a personal conversion experience, the term as used in the Swedish church's name refers to its origins in the Protestant Reformation in the sixteenth century. Although the church-state relationship was severed in 2000, more than 80 percent of Swedes still remained members of the Lutheran Church, and most continued to pay an annual church tax of approximately 1.25 percent of annual income (ibid., 32).

Each of the church's 2,225 parishes is governed by a parish council, which, along with the pastor, makes policy regarding educational, social, and evangelistic activities (Church of Sweden 2005). A bishop leads each of the thirteen dioceses of the Church of Sweden. The priests of the dioceses, along with an equal number of lay delegates, elect the bishop. The archbishop of Uppsala heads the national church organization. Karl Gustav Hammar served as archbishop from 1997 to 2006. Conservative members of the church criticized Hammar for some of his theological statements regarding the virgin birth of Jesus and Jesus's bodily resurrection, as well as his public stands on political questions. For instance, Hammar criticized the U.S. invasion of Iraq, recommended a boycott of items produced in Israel, and supported the rights of homosexuals.

Christianity first came to Sweden in the ninth century when the Frankish Benedictine monk Ansgarious, devoted to extending the Roman church to new territories, preached the Christian message in the trading town of Birka (Pleijel 1960, 13). Around the year 1000 the first Swedish king converted to Christianity. Christian influences from Britain as well as Germany shaped early Christian practices in Sweden. The church established its organizational structure, forming bishoprics throughout the country and requiring tithes and tax exemption for church property. With the Reformation, Lutheran doctrine spread quickly to Sweden, due in part to the education of many Swedish clergy in Germany and to King Gustav Vasa's desire to establish independence from the influence of Rome and hence gain greater sovereignty for Sweden.

With the Reformation, the king became head of the church, assuming the role in religion formerly played by the pope. The Uppsala Council in 1593, headed by Duke Charles, who would later become King Charles IX, accepted the Augsburg Confession as the fundamental Lutheran statement of faith and declared that the national church of Sweden would be Evangelical-Lutheran (Gustafsson 2003, 51). The Canon Law of 1686 authorized the king to supervise and defend the church. The government of Sweden established severe church regulations, including restrictions on freedom of religion, largely to protect the Lutheran denomination from the intrusion of Catholics and Calvinists. Church and state became closely associated, with priests not only serving the church but also serving the state, performing various nonreligious duties as civil servants. The local parish clergyman served as the leader in spiritual as well as temporal matters. As Hilding Pleijel (1960, 20) has noted, church and state "entered into a relationship so close that religious orthodoxy and civic loyalty had become practically synonymous." The government did not allow citizens to leave the church and considered straying from church teaching or repudiating doctrines of the Lutheran Church crimes punishable by exile. For instance, Baptists faced imprisonment because they held worship services independently of the Lutheran clergy, and the children of Baptists were required to be baptized (Gustafsson 2003, 51). Subsequently, the official Lutheran Church became the only permitted religion in Sweden, although exceptions were allowed beginning in the seventeenth century. In the early seventeenth century, under the rule of Gustavus II Adolphus, Sweden expanded territorially and, in accord with Lutheran doctrine, the Bible was translated into the various languages of the new provinces.

By the eighteenth century various so-called free churches were established, including Methodists, Baptists, Quakers, and the Salvation Army. By the early decades of the twentieth century Seventh Day Adventists had established approximately a hundred churches. Followers of such movements as pietism and Moravianism spread their influence in various Swedish provinces, thus influencing the character of religious tradition among the population. During the first half of the nineteenth century Sweden underwent a series of economic, social, political, and religious changes associated with the transformation from an agrarian to an industrialized society. By 1860 the presence of other churches, including the Catholic and Methodist-Episcopal, was officially recognized (Ahrén 1960, 32). In 1878 Peter Waldenström gathered many within the free-church movement into the Swedish Mission Covenant. Without permission from government authorities to celebrate the Lord's Supper and to preach, the Mission Covenant group built many chapels throughout Sweden while remaining officially within the Church of Sweden (Latourette 1975, 1147). The Church of Sweden itself gained from the government greater control of its own activities.

Clergy and lay members attempted to reach workers in the factories, especially the younger people, with their message regarding the evils of strong drink. Some pastors became politically active, especially in the Social Democratic movement, and a few even gained seats in the Riksdag, the Swedish parliament (ibid., 1148). In the late twentieth century the Social Democratic–controlled government had continued the campaign against alcohol consumption, scrupulously regulating the sale of alcoholic beverages and strictly enforcing drunk driving laws (Heclo and Madsen 1987, 27).

In the nineteenth century two separate theological paths developed within the Church of Sweden, each associated with one of the major Swedish universities. At Uppsala, there evolved a more philosophical and subjective view of Christianity that deemphasized the formal church structure, while the faculty at Lund tended to promote the formalism of the church. Protestants in Sweden became active in social policy in an attempt to confront various problems arising from industrialization and the resulting social change. In 1863 the government permitted the formation of a national ecclesiastical council, which was composed of clergy and laypeople representing the dioceses and the two major universities. The council took part in making decisions affecting the church. In addition to alternative religious denominations, others, primarily those in academics and the labor movement, challenged the structure and beliefs of the state church. The critical and historical study of the Bible, which originated in Germany, reached Sweden via the Swedish students who attended German universities. The faculty at Uppsala University tended to welcome the new approach to religion and biblical study, but others reacted negatively to the new approaches. In addition to these academic influences, Marxism attracted many workers in Swedish industry, thus alienating them from the church. The more educated Swedes, although often maintaining official adherence to the church, in fact became critical of traditional religious beliefs. Faculty at the University of Lund in the twentieth century—particularly Gustaf Emanuel Hildebrand Aulén and Anders Nygren—expressed strong criticism of the liberal influences of the nineteenth century and supported the major theologians of the earlier centuries in an attempt to preserve what they considered to be the true Christian faith. They emphasized God's love as a fundamental ingredient in Christianity (Latourette 1975, 1385).

The state church softened its traditional policy of exclusiveness as the official church, initiating interaction with various Christian groups. In 1863 a rule requiring all church members to receive communion at least once each year was repealed. Each citizen was subject to the authority of a secular borough as well as a parish, and the parish had the right to assess taxes on anyone living in the parish in order to finance the activities of the religious organization. The Church Assembly, established in the 1860s, consisted of bishops, clergy, and lay representatives and was elected by the parishes. This body had veto power over any policy related to religion. Prior to 1908 the Swedish government required that every marriage must be conducted within the Church of Sweden, but in that year a new law provided the option of marriage through a civil ceremony. In the late 1920s education, which had been the responsibility of the parishes, began to be transferred to secular authorities. In 1930 the Riksdag determined that in the larger parishes, church councils would be elected by a system of proportional representation. This move introduced the political parties into the representative structure of the Church of Sweden.

In 1952 the Riksdag approved legislation that finally established the formal principle of religious liberty. Under this legislation, no persons could be required to be a member of the Church of Sweden against their wishes, and people could withdraw their church membership at their own choosing. However, few people took advantage of this option; members of the Lutheran Church continued to make up nearly 99 percent of the Swedish population (Gustafsson 2003, 55). In the 1950s many Swedes voiced their concern about the continuation of the Lutheran Church as the official state church, arguing that such an arrangement violated the principle of religious freedom. Nonetheless, at that time more than 85 percent of children were baptized in the church and a similar percentage were confirmed (Ahrén 1960, 32). In 1958 a commission was established to examine the official status of the state church. After ten years, the commission issued a final report that presented four possible models for an altered relationship between church and state, extending from no significant change to establishing a church that was completely independent of the state. Thus began several years of political negotiations to determine the precise details of the altered status of the church in Swedish society. The church continued to lose its civil functions, which included the keeping of the vital statistics of citizens, such as birth and death records, in the local rector's office, and maintaining cemeteries.

In 1991 civil registration of citizens was transferred from the priests of the church to the secular tax authority. In 1994 the Preparatory Committee on Church Matters presented a proposal that the church should be separated from the state but that the Riksdag should approve a new law affirming that the Church of Sweden would remain an Evangelical-Lutheran denomination, that all regions of the country would be included in a parish, and that the church would have a democratic organization. Although the church would no longer have the authority to levy taxes, the state would assist in collecting fees from members. The government also would provide financial assistance in maintaining historic churches (Gustafsson 2003, 66). With the changes in church status taking effect on January 1, 2000, many expected that membership would decrease significantly. However, the loss of members was minimal. Elections to the various levels of church organization occurred in September 2001, with a turnout rate of 14 percent (ibid., 69). Various political parties gained representation, which exceeded that of representatives unaligned with any party. This outcome led some to conclude that although the church has gained greater independence from government, it still is closely tied to the political system, with political parties able to exercise influence within the church.

Other Scandinavian countries are contemplating greater independence of the church from the state. In Norway, a government-appointed committee in January 2006 recommended that the Storting (Norwegian parliament) and the king no longer take part in church affairs, including the selection of bishops. A modification of church-state relations would require amending the nation's constitution before going into effect (Stoichevski 2006, 36). Denmark also is considering the separation of church and state. In 2003 Finland's parliament approved the Freedom of Religion Act, which established a less complicated procedure for Evangelical-Lutheran Church members to leave the church.

Although there are other denominations in Sweden, the Lutheran Church continues to dominate, with approximately 7.6 million members, even though many are associated with the church in name only. The Lutheran Church has joined with other denominations to form the Christian Council of Sweden, which includes twenty-five member churches and three "observers" categorized into four groups: the Lutheran Church; the Catholic Church, with approximately 165,000 members; the free churches, which include various Protestant denominations (including Baptist, Methodist, Reformed, Mission Covenant, and Pentecostal churches) consisting of 250,000 members; and the Eastern Orthodox and Oriental Orthodox churches, with a total membership of 100,000. These churches participate in ecumenical discussions as well as evangelism activities (Christian Council of Sweden 2005).

The Church of Sweden participates in activities outside the nation's boundaries. Through Church of Sweden Aid, the church offers emergency relief as well as more extended development assistance to other nations. The organization works with local churches to provide economic assistance and to protect the environment, and also advocates debt cancellation for poor countries and fair-trade policies. The Church of Sweden Mission, founded in 1874, conducts foreign missionary work at the invitation of other countries and in cooperation with local congregations. The organization assists local congregations, provides medical assistance, and advocates respect for human rights.

Just as with mainline denominations in the United States, conservative members and clergy in the Swedish Lutheran Church have objected to liberal trends, including the decision to allow the ordination of women beginning in 1960 and, more recently, more accepting attitudes toward homosexuals and gay marriage (Olafsson 2004). However, due to the tradition of having an official state church, Swedish clergy are much more closely tied to government policy than are clergy in the United States, where a very different tradition of separation of church and state prevails.

Conclusion

European countries have a long history of interaction between church and state, which frequently led to violent conflict. In the United States, although the original thirteen states practiced the establishment of religion, the last state-established church came to an end in Massachusetts in 1833. The countries discussed here have to various degrees accepted the principle of separation of church and state, although church-state relations beyond those usually considered constitutionally acceptable in the United States continue. The level of religious observance in Europe pales in comparison to that of the United States. The long history of official church recognition and the resulting controversy and conflict may contribute to explaining the increased levels of apparent indifference to formal religious institutions and the lack of organizational structures geared toward religious influence in politics that tend to pervade the U.S. political process.

Does the present state of religious organization and belief in Europe portend the status of religion in the United States in the future? Observing that the mainline churches can trace their roots back to Europe, and noting membership declines in recent decades, we might answer in the affirmative. However, other factors suggest a negative response. The shift from the mainline churches to more evangelical denominations and nondenominational churches points to a continuing relevance of religious affiliation to a large segment of the U.S. population. In addition, if Europeans' attitudes toward religion are taken as the exception in a world where the norm is significant religious belief and commitment, there may be little reason to expect the United States to follow in the footsteps of Europe. The religious beliefs of U.S. citizens and elected officials may be expected to continue to influence public policy making. However, the extent to which that influence comes from the mainline denominations remains an open question.

References

Ahrén, Per-Olov. 1960. "Organization and Legal Status." In Robert Murray, ed., *The Church of Sweden: Past and Present*, 31–44. Malmö, Sweden: Allhem.

Ajami, Fouad. 2005. "The Boys of Nowhere." *U.S. News and World Report* (November 21): 50.

Anderson, John. 2003. "Catholicism and Democratic Consolidation in Spain and Poland." In John T. S. Madeley and Zsolt Enyedi, eds., *Church and State in Contemporary Europe: The Chimera of Neutrality*. London: Frank Cass: 137–156.

British Broadcasting Company (BBC). 2006. "The Church of England." http://www.bbc.co.uk/religion/religions/christianity/cofe/cofe_1.shtml.

Carosa, Alberto. 2006. "Holding a New Line: Pope Benedict, Islam, and the Media." *Chronicles* (December): 20.

Chadwìck, Owen. 1990. "Great Britain and Europe." In John McManners, ed., *The Oxford Illustrated History of Christianity*. New York: Oxford University Press.

Christian Council of Sweden. 2005. "Four Church Families." http://www.skr.org/english/fourchurchfamilies.4.ec944110677af1e83800015088.html.

Church of Sweden. 2005. "Facts about the Church of Sweden." http://svenskakyrkan.se/ArticlePages/200508/16/20050816074719_svkhjs928/20050816074719_svkhjs928.dbp.asp.

Creswell, Mike. 2002. "Leaders Assess Impact of New French Religion Law." Baptist News Service. http://www.rickross.com/reference/general/general426.html.

Donovan, Mark. 2003. "The Italian State: No Longer Catholic, No Longer Christian." In John T. S. Madeley and Zsolt Enyedi, eds., *Church and State in Contemporary Europe: The Chimera of Neutrality*, 95–116. London: Frank Cass.

Ecumenical News International. 2005. "French Religion Faces New Future 100 Years after Church-State-Law." http://www.eni.ch/articles/display.shtml?05-0791.

Fleishman, Jeffrey, and Ela Kasprzycka. 2007. "New Archbishop Resigns Hours Before Inauguration." *Houston Chronicle* (January 8): A8.

French Embassy in Australia. 2000. "Religion in France." http://www.ambafrance-au.org/article-imprim.php3?id_article=462.

Germany Info. 2006. "Religion." http://www.germany.info/relaunch/culture/life/religion.html.

Gustafsson, Göran. 2003. "Church-State Separation Swedish-Style." In John T. S. Madeley and Zsolt Enyedi, eds., *Church and State in Contemporary Europe: The Chimera of Neutrality*, 51–72. London: Frank Cass.

Harbison, E. Harris. 1955. *The Age of Reformation*. Ithaca, NY: Cornell University Press.

Heclo, Hugh, and Henrik Madsen. 1987. *Policy and Politics in Sweden: Principled Pragamatism*. Philadelphia: Temple University Press.

Hervieu-Léger, Danièle. 2006. "The Role of Religion in Establishing Social Cohesion." In Krzysztof Michalski, ed., *Religion in the New Europe*. New York: Central European University Press.

Houston Chronicle. 2006. "Leader Rejects Power Sharing." (May 23): A9.

Houston Chronicle. 2007a. "Church in Poland Reels Over Cold War Scandal" (January 10): A10.

Houston Chronicle. 2007b. "Anglicans Affirm Policies on Gay Communicants" (March 1): A16.

Katz, Gregory. 2007. "N. Ireland Leaders Strike Pivotal Accord." *Houston Chronicle* (March 27): A10.

Landler, Mark. 2007. "German Judge Stirs Protest by Citing Quran." *Houston Chronicle* (March 23): A19.

Latourette, Kenneth Scott. 1975. *A History of Christianity, Volume II: Reformation to the Present.* New York: Harper and Row.

Martin, David. 2006. "Integration and Fragmentation: Patterns of Religion in Europe." In Krzysztof Michalski, ed., *Religion in the New Europe.* New York: Central European University Press.

McElroy, John Harmon. 2006. "Workers of Another World United: A Personal Commemoration of Poland's Solidarity 25 Years Later." *Touchstone* (December): 28–33.

Minkenberg, Michael. 2003. "The Policy Impact of Church-State Relations: Family Policy and Abortion in Britain, France, and Germany." In John T. S. Madeley and Zsolt Enyedi, eds., *Church and State in Contemporary Europe: The Chimera of Neutrality.* London: Frank Cass.

Monsma, Steven V., and J. Christopher Soper. 1997. *The Challenge of Pluralism: Church and State in Five Democracies.* Lanham, MD: Rowman and Littlefield.

Moore, Molly. 2006. "Romance, But Not Marriage." *Washington Post National Weekly Edition* (November 27–December 3): 18.

Murchison, William. 2005. "Vanishing Sea of Faith: European Islam and the Doubtful Future of Christian Europe." *Touchstone* (October): 36–40.

Olofsson, Folke T. 2004. "A Grief Observed: On Being a Living Priest in a Dying Church in Sweden." *Touchstone* (November): 32–39.

Pleijel, Hilding. 1960. "The Church of Sweden: An Historical Retrospect." In Robert Murray, ed., *The Church of Sweden: Past and Present,* 13–28. Malmö, Sweden: Allhem.

Reiter, Natalia, and Malgorzata Rakoweic. 2006. "Former President of Poland Leaves Solidarity Behind." *Houston Chronicle* (September 1): A21.

Rosenthal, Elisabeth. 2006. "European Birthrates Are Still Declining: Numbers at an All-Time Low as Many Find Having Children Too Costly." *Houston Chronicle* (September 4): A20.

Simpson, Victor L. 2006. "Bishops Balking at Satirical Stabs Aimed at Vatican." *Houston Chronicle* (November 26): A25.

Stoichevski, William. 2006. "No More State Church in Norway?" *The Lutheran* (August 2006): 36–37.

Tolson, Jay. 2005. "An Education in Muslim Integration: Could Islamic Schools Be Part of the Solution?" *U. S. News and World Report* (November 21): 37–38, 40.

United States Department of State Bureau of Democracy, Human Rights, and Labor. 2005. "Italy: International Religious Freedom Report 2005." http://www.state.gov/g/drl/rls/irf/2005/51560.htm.

Weigel, George. 2005. *The Cube and the Cathedral: Europe, America, and Politics without God*. New York: Basic Books.

Wilkinson, Tracy. 2006a. "Benedict Drops Bombshell with Quote on Islam." *Houston Chronicle* (September 13): A15.

Wilkinson, Tracy. 2006b. "Italian Author Was Country's Most Provocative Journalist." *Houston Chronicle* (September 16): A20.

4

Chronology

This chronology highlights the current activities of the mainline denominations as well as their historical roots, pinpointing their first appearance on the North American continent and their various organizational transformations; the issues that led to internal divisions and the current expression of these divisions in the context of the larger social and political conflicts within American society known as the culture war; moves toward unity among denominations; and the larger issues in the public realm with which the denominations have become involved.

1628   Dutch settlers in New Amsterdam (subsequently New York City) establish a Reformed congregation when an ordained minister arrives from the Netherlands.

1631   Roger Williams arrives in Massachusetts and quickly clashes with the Puritan leadership when he asserts that the civil authority should not enforce adherence to those parts of the Ten Commandments dealing solely with the relationship between individual human beings and God.

1634   Catholics, led by Cecil Calvert, establish a colony in Maryland.

1644   Roger Williams issues *The Bloudy Tenet of Persecution for the Cause of Conscience Discussed*, in which he defends religious liberty. Having left Massachusetts in 1636 because of disagreements with the authorities over religious questions, Williams allows Baptists who

1644 (*cont.*)	have been expelled from Massachusetts to live in the new settlement of Providence.
1647	A Massachusetts law declares that any person in the colony who derives authority from the Catholic pope in Rome will be considered a disturber of the public peace and safety and an enemy of the true Christian religion.
1706	Presbyterians in Philadelphia establish the first presbytery in North America.
1707	Baptist adherents establish the Philadelphia Baptist Association, composed of five congregations in Pennsylvania and New Jersey.
1734	Jonathan Edwards, a Calvinist minister, theologian, and effective speaker, begins a religious revival in Northampton, Massachusetts. The revival contributes significantly to the religious movement called the Great Awakening that is sweeping through the colonies.
1773	Ten preachers from three colonies hold the first annual conference of American Methodism at St. George's Church in Philadelphia on July 14.
1784	Methodist ministers meet in Baltimore and establish the Methodist Episcopal Church in America.
1785	The Episcopal Church holds its first General Convention in Philadelphia. The delegates begin work on a constitution and revisions to the *Book of Common Prayer*.
1787	John Leland, a Virginia Baptist pastor, withdraws his opposition to the proposed Constitution when James Madison assures him that, once ratified, the document will be amended to guarantee religious freedom.
1789	John Carroll, a member of the Society of Jesus, is selected as the first Catholic bishop in the United States. Georgetown College is established as the country's first Catholic institution of higher education.
1800	Followers of Philip William Otterbein and Martin Boehm establish the Church of the United Brethren, a predominantly German-speaking denomination.
1801	Presbyterians and Connecticut Congregationalists agree to the Plan of Union, which encourages cooperation among missionaries of the two denominations.

The plan leads to increased expansion of the churches in the western territories. Although Presbyterians benefit most from the agreement, conservative (Old School) Presbyterians object to the lack of exclusive control over missionary activities.

1804   Separating themselves from the Presbyterian Church, Barton W. Stone and five colleagues establish a religious organization that will ultimately become the Christian Church (Disciples of Christ).

In a eulogy for Alexander Hamilton, who has been killed in a duel with Aaron Burr, Presbyterian minister Eliphalet Nott condemns the practice of dueling, calling it an absurd practice originating in a barbarous age.

1809   Thomas Campbell, organizer of the Christian Association of Washington, Pennsylvania, issues the *Declaration and Address,* in which he expresses the basic principles of the New Testament and the objective of Christian unity.

1812   Congregational ministers in New England vote to denounce the War of 1812 and present antiwar sermons to their congregations.

1816   Experiencing discrimination within the church, disaffected African Americans leave the Methodist Episcopal Church to establish the African Methodist Episcopal Church.

1819   Dutch Reformed congregations incorporate as the Reformed Protestant Dutch Church.

1821   As happened in 1816, another group of disaffected African Americans leaves the Methodist Episcopal Church and establishes the African Methodist Episcopal Zion Church.

1828   Lyman Beecher, a Presbyterian minister, joins with other Christians to found the General Union for Promoting the Observance of the Christian Sabbath. The group attempts to use boycotts and persuasion to get people to observe the Sabbath.

1830   Thomas Campbell and his son Alexander, who emigrated from Ireland, leave the Baptist organizations with which they originally joined, forming the

1830 (*cont.*)	Disciples, a precursor of the Christian Church (Disciples of Christ).
	Approximately 5,000 ministers and laypeople, dissatisfied with insufficient lay representation in the Methodist Episcopal Church, leave the denomination to form the Methodist Protestant Church.
1837	At the General Assembly meeting of the Presbyterian Church, Old School proponents, having gained a majority of representatives, end the 1801 Plan of Union with the Congregationalists, whom they consider to have aided the New School partisans. This move eliminates four synods that were formed under the plan, thus decreasing the strength of the New School. The issue of revivalism—which the Old School opposes and the New School encourages—as well as controversy over abolition result in the division of the Old and New School Presbyterians.
1844	When the New England Convention of Christians ratifies a resolution condemning slavery, Southern Christian congregations form the Southern Christian Association.
	Delegates to the General Convention of the Methodist Episcopal Church (MEC) vote to suspend a Southern bishop who has refused to free slaves that he owns. Southern delegates quickly devise a plan to separate from the MEC, forming the Methodist Episcopal Church, South.
1845	The American Baptist Foreign Mission Society decides that no candidate who owns slaves will be appointed for service, and the American Baptist Home Mission Society concludes that separate northern and southern conventions should be established. As a result, members in the Southern states establish the Southern Baptist Convention separate from a group of northern Baptist societies.
1853	The Congregational Church in Butler, New York, ordains a woman, Antoinette Brown, and calls her to the ministry.
1854	More than 3,000 clergymen in New England sign a petition opposing the Kansas-Nebraska bill, which will allow the extension of slavery beyond the limits

set in the Missouri Compromise of 1821 by providing for the creation of two new territories—Kansas
and Nebraska—with the expectation that Kansas will
permit slavery and Nebraska will not. With the backing of Senator Stephen A. Douglas, President Franklin
Pierce, and Southern representatives, the bill becomes
law.

1855   Congregational minister Henry Ward Beecher proclaims from the pulpit of Plymouth Church in Brooklyn, New York, his support for John Brown and those
fighting to maintain Kansas as a free state. He raises
money to purchase rifles, called "Beecher's Bibles,"
for those opposing slavery.

1857   As the Civil War approaches, New School Presbyterians divide into northern and southern groups.

1859   Charles Darwin publishes *The Origin of Species*, in
which he presents a theory of evolution based on
natural selection. Disagreements arise in Christian
denominations between those who attempt to accommodate their religious beliefs to Darwin's theory and
those who argue that the new science contradicts the
Genesis account of creation, replacing purpose and
spirituality with a random and materialistic understanding of human existence.

1860   Unlike the Presbyterians who are divided over the
slavery issue, the Campbell-Stone movement, which
will become the Christian Church (Disciples of Christ),
avoids division by stating that the issue is not a matter
of faith but of opinion.

1861   With Southern state secession, northern and southern
Old School Presbyterians divide into two separate
groups. The southern group becomes the Presbyterian
Church in the Confederate States of America.

1866   Following the Southern defeat in the Civil War, the Old
School Presbyterians in the South rename themselves
the Presbyterian Church in the United States (PCUS).

      The German Reformed Church joins with the
Dutch Reformed Church to establish the Reformed
Church in the United States.

1867   The Congregational Church becomes the first denomination officially to allow the ordination of women.

1867 (*cont.*)	The Reformed Protestant Dutch Church, incorporated in 1819, changes its name to the Reformed Church in America.
1870	Northern Old School and New School Presbyterians, divided since the Civil War, merge to form the Presbyterian Church in the U.S.A. (PCUSA).
1874	Francis Landey Patton, professor of theology at the Presbyterian Theological Seminary of the Northwest in Chicago, accuses David Swing, popular minister at Fourth Presbyterian Church in Chicago, of heresy. Patton charges that Swing's sermons and book, *Truths for Today*, deny the teachings of the Westminster Confession of Faith. Swing responds that human creeds are imperfect and must be revised to correspond with current cultural circumstances. Although the Presbytery of Chicago acquits Swing of all charges, Swing leaves the denomination when Patton announces his intention to appeal the case to the Northern Illinois Synod. Swing continues as an independent minister, and his views encourage the ascendance of theological liberalism in the late nineteenth century.
1878	The General Conference of the Southern Methodist Church censures Vanderbilt University professor Alexander Winchell for abandoning a literal interpretation of the Genesis account of creation in favor of a more allegorical reading. When Winchell refuses to resign, the Methodist university eliminates his teaching position.
1882	Catholics found the Knights of Columbus in New Haven, Connecticut. This association of men encourages fraternity, benevolence, and tolerance.
1884	James Woodrow, a theologian in the Southern Presbyterian denomination, a scientist, and uncle of future President Woodrow Wilson, states in an address that the church should not take a position on the issue of evolution, declaring the subject outside the sphere of religious belief. The pronouncement raises a great deal of controversy within the denomination.
1886	The Southern Presbyterian General Assembly permanently removes James Woodrow from the faculty of the Presbyterian seminary in Columbia, South Carolina,

because Woodrow has declared that the church should not take a stand either in support of or in opposition to evolution theory because the topic exceeds that institution's jurisdiction. The assembly votes 137–13 in favor of a statement proclaiming that Adam had no natural animal forebears.

1889   U.S. Catholic bishops found Catholic University of America in Washington DC.

1891   Pope Leo XIII issues the first modern social encyclical, *Rerum Novarum* (On the Condition of the Working Class), which proclaims the basic right of workers to attain an adequate material and spiritual life. Thus, the Catholic Church avoids taking a stand of unqualified support for the capitalist system that is developing in the United States.

1892   Delegates to the 1892 General Assembly of the Presbyterian Church in the U.S.A., meeting in Portland, Oregon, approve a declaration, called the Portland Deliverance, that affirms the inerrancy of the Bible and requires all ministers in the denomination to accept this doctrine.

The Presbytery of Cincinnati tries and convicts Henry Preserved Smith, professor of the Old Testament at Lane Theological Seminary, on charges that he has denied the verbal inspiration and inerrancy of the Bible, a position he expressed at the 1891 Presbyterian General Assembly in defense of Augustus Briggs, a major advocate of higher criticism of the Bible. The presbytery suspends Smith from the ministry. Smith subsequently publishes his views in *Inspiration and Inerrancy*.

1893   The Presbyterian assembly convicts of heresy Charles Augustus Briggs, a prominent Old Testament scholar, chair of biblical studies at Union Theological Seminary, and advocate of the higher critical approach to biblical scholarship, even though his presbytery has acquitted him of the charges. Although the assembly suspends Briggs from the ministry, the board of directors of the seminary refuses to accept the ruling, retaining Briggs on the faculty.

1899   Pope Leo XIII issues the encyclical *Testem benevolentiae* (On the Heresy of Americanism), in which he warns

1899 (*cont.*)	Catholics about heretical attitudes contrary to the faith, including tailoring beliefs to the larger culture. Although both liberal and conservative groups within the U.S. Catholic Church interpret the statement as supporting their position, the conservative camp ultimately claims the victory.
1907	Established in the mid-nineteenth century as the northern group of Baptists, the American Baptist Missionary Union reorganizes as the Northern Baptist Convention.
1908	The northern Methodists establish the Federation for Social Service to adopt progressive social principles and guide the denomination's social welfare projects.
	Mainline Protestant denominations join in establishing the Federal Council of Churches, an ecumenical organization intended to increase the churches' influence on social and economic matters.
1910	The General Assembly of the Northern Presbyterian Church approves a social statement that will become an important ingredient in the Federal Council of Churches. Among the proposed social reforms are improving working conditions for women, ending child labor, establishing workmen's compensation, limiting the length of the workweek, and providing higher wages for industrial employees.
	Francis James Grimké, an African American Presbyterian minister who has spoken against racism and segregation in the Presbyterian Church and the wider American society, plays a significant role in the creation of the National Association for the Advancement of Colored People (NAACP), a civil rights organization.
1914	Norman M. Thomas, a Presbyterian minister (better known later as the leader of the Socialist Party), forms the Association of Pacifist Ministers to oppose Christian involvement in warfare.
	The Presbyterian Church in the United States (PCUS), the United Presbyterian Church of North America (UPCNA), the Presbyterian Church in the U.S.A. (PCUSA), and the Associate Reformed Presbyterian Synod issue the "United Declaration of Christian Faith and Social Service," which calls on religious

groups to oppose social injustice and asks individuals to engage in social, political, and economic interactions that adhere to the principles of love and justice. However, the declaration recommends that congregations refrain from taking positions and acting on particular political and social issues.

1917 Beginning the merger process of Lutheran denominations, three Norwegian synods combine to form the Norwegian Lutheran Church in America (NLCA). Various Lutheran groups cooperate to establish the National Lutheran Commission to assist U.S. military personnel.

With the cooperation of President Woodrow Wilson, the Catholic Church establishes the National Catholic War Council to coordinate Catholic assistance in the war effort. The formation of the council represents a significant first step in creating a national organization dedicated to larger social activities and is the precursor to the United States Conference of Catholic Bishops.

1918 Continuing the unification process among Lutheran groups, three German synods combine to form the United Lutheran Church in America (ULCA).

1919 Monsignor John A. Ryan, who is beginning his twenty-six-year tenure as director of the National Catholic Welfare Council's social action department, issues the pamphlet "Social Reconstruction: A General Review of the Problems and Survey of Remedies." Ryan advocates such reforms as child labor bans, government-supported unemployment and retirement insurance, the right of workers to organize, and equal pay for men and women for equivalent labor.

1922 Harry Emerson Fosdick, a Baptist minister and pastor of the First Presbyterian Church in New York City, preaches the sermon "Shall the Fundamentalists Win?" in which he questions the virgin birth of Jesus, the inerrancy of the Bible, and the literal second coming of Jesus. Ivy Lee widely distributes copies of the sermon, retitled "The New Knowledge and the Christian Faith." Because of the views expressed in the sermon, Fosdick becomes the focus of controversy in the Presbyterian Church in the U.S.A.

1924   A group of Presbyterian Church in the U.S.A. ministers meets in Auburn, New York, to prepare a response to the Five Point Deliverance statement adopted by the 1910 General Assembly and reaffirmed in 1916 and 1923. The Five Point Deliverance specifies that clergy must adhere to such beliefs as the inerrancy of the Bible, the virgin birth, the substitutionary atonement and bodily resurrection of Jesus, and the factual accuracy of miracles recounted in the Bible. One hundred and fifty ministers attending the meeting publish the Auburn Affirmation, which does not deny any of these beliefs but considers them theories about facts for which other explanations could be offered. Therefore, the ministers oppose making adherence to the Five Points a requirement for ordination or orthodoxy. The affirmation is reissued in May with 1,274 signatures.

1927   Following several years of controversy between fundamentalists and more progressive members, the Presbyterian Church in the U.S.A. General Assembly approves a resolution stating that the assembly cannot pronounce any belief essential without employing the precise wording of the Westminster Confession.

1928   Alfred E. Smith, governor of New York and a Catholic, wins the Democratic nomination for president but loses decisively to Herbert Hoover in the general election. Political analysts attribute Smith's defeat in part to his religious affiliation.

1930   Three German Lutheran groups merge to establish the American Lutheran Church (ALC).

The National Lutheran Commission, originally created at the start of the First World War to offer assistance to U.S. military personnel, begins a program of assistance within the United States.

1931   The Congregational Churches and the Christian Church merge to form the Congregational Christian Churches.

Pope Pius XI issues the encyclical *Quadragesimo Anno* (Forty Years After), establishing the Catholic Church's understanding of its relationship with the larger society. The statement calls for "subsidiarity," or the presence of organizational structures to mediate between individuals and the state as a protection against the domination of social and economic institutions.

Charles Cofflin, a Catholic priest, begins radio broadcasts in which he presents his views on current social and political issues. Originally a supporter of President Franklin Roosevelt's New Deal programs, Cofflin becomes a major critic of the New Deal.

1933　Dorothy Day, a left-leaning journalist turned Catholic, and Peter Maurin, a French Catholic populist, found the Catholic Worker movement and begin establishing hospitality houses around the United States to feed and house the poor. Day and Maurin emphasize spiritual as well as material needs, pacifism, and the importance of love.

1934　The Evangelical Synod and the Reformed Church combine to form the Evangelical and Reformed Church.

1936　J. Gresham Machen founds the Presbyterian Church of America (later called the Orthodox Presbyterian Church) after the Presbyterian Church in the U.S.A. suspends him from the ministry for establishing the Independent Board for Presbyterian Foreign Missions.

1939　The Methodist Episcopal Church; the Methodist Episcopal Church, South; and the Methodist Protestant Church join to form the Methodist Church.

1944　Notwithstanding past statements supporting social change to benefit the less advantaged, delegates to the General Assembly of the Presbyterian Church in the U.S.A. proclaim that the church has failed to act effectively to improve economic and industrial relations.

1946　The Evangelical Church and the United Brethren Church unite to form the Evangelical United Brethren Church.

1950　Members of the Northern Baptist Convention reorganize, changing the group's name to the American Baptist Convention.

Various Protestant, Anglican, Orthodox, Evangelical, and African American churches join in establishing the National Council of Churches of Christ in the U.S.A. The organization replaces the old Federal Council of Churches and other ecumenical organizations.

1951 Catholic Bishop Fulton J. Sheen begins a television program, "Life Is Worth Living," which attracts a large audience. The program acquaints many Americans with the Catholic faith.

1953 New Orleans Archbishop Joseph Francis Rummel issues a letter titled "Blessed Are the Peacemakers," in which he denounces racism and the practice of racial segregation.

1955 New Orleans Archbishop Joseph Francis Rummel orders the desegregation of Catholic schools in the archdiocese.

1957 The Congregational Christian Churches—formed by the merger of the Congregational Churches and the Christian Church in 1931—and the Evangelical and Reformed Church—established in 1934 through the merger of the Evangelical Synod and the Reformed Church—meeting at the General Synod in Cleveland, Ohio, join to establish the United Church of Christ (UCC). Cleveland becomes the location for the new denomination's national headquarters.

 In August a group of religious activists, primarily Quakers and Catholic Workers, hold a protest at the gates of a Nevada nuclear test site. Eleven of the protesters trespass onto the test-site grounds and are arrested.

1958 After discussions during the early 1950s, the Presbyterian Church in the U.S.A. and the United Presbyterian Church of North America (UPCNA), a denomination originally formed in 1858, join to create the United Presbyterian Church in the United States of America (UPCUSA). The Presbyterian Church in the United States (PCUS) rejects union with the predominantly northern denomination.

 Methodists agree to eliminate, over a ten-year period, the Central Jurisdiction, which includes exclusively black Methodist churches.

1959 The General Synod of the United Church of Christ calls for effort and prayer to end racial segregation and discrimination in the United States.

1960 Danish and Norwegian Lutheran groups merge with the American Lutheran Church, originally a predominantly German denomination.

John Kennedy, a Catholic, wins the Democratic presidential nomination, challenging the common view that a Catholic cannot be elected president. He is the first Catholic to be nominated since Al Smith in 1928. In a speech to the Houston Ministerial Association, Kennedy assures the American public that he believes in absolute separation of church and state, stating that he does not speak for his church on public matters, and the church does not speak for him. He declares that if elected president, he will make decisions independent of the Catholic hierarchy.

Northern Presbyterians declare that laws and customs mandating racial discrimination are violations of the law of God, and therefore Christians can justifiably disregard such laws if they do so in a peaceable and orderly way.

1962   The United Lutheran Church in America joins with German, Slovak, Icelandic, Swedish, Finnish, and Danish groups to form the Lutheran Church in America (LCA).

Pope John XXIII convenes the Second Vatican Council, which will meet three months each year from 1962 to 1965. The council examines the Catholic Church's position in the modern world. Deliberations lead to significant reforms in the Catholic Church, including changes in the national church organization that allow priests, nuns, and laypeople greater opportunity to express their views within the church hierarchy.

1965   The Methodist General Board of Christian Social Concerns recommends that President Lyndon Johnson's administration surrender responsibility for resolving the Vietnam conflict to the United Nations.

1966   With a mandate from the Vatican Council, the Catholic bishops in the United States establish the National Conference of Catholic Bishops (NCCB) and the United States Catholic Conference (USCC). The NCCB, composed entirely of bishops, exercises control over the church's affairs in the country, and the NCCB's committees, composed of laypeople and clergy as well as bishops, deal with issues in the larger society.

The Family Life Bureau of the National Conference of Catholic Bishops establishes the National Right

1966 to Life Committee, which is dedicated to maintaining
(*cont.*) existing restrictions on abortion.

Henry I. Louttit, Episcopal bishop of the Central Archdeanery of South Florida, leads a group that demands that Reverend James Pike be tried for heresy. Pike, the dean of the Cathedral of St. John the Divine in New York, has publicly rejected such orthodox Christian beliefs as the virgin birth of Jesus and the doctrine of the Trinity. The House of Bishops ultimately approves a mild censure of Bishop Pike.

1967 Referring to the results of the Second Vatican Council, which concluded in 1965, progressive Jesuit educators along with Father Theodore Hesburg, president of the University of Notre Dame, issue the Land O'Lakes declaration that calls for greater academic freedom in Catholic institutions of higher learning. The declaration recommends increased openness to ecumenical initiatives and secular scholarship in order to advance the educational quality of Catholic institutions.

After nine years of development, the General Assembly of the Presbyterian Church in the U.S.A. adopts a new confession of faith. Christian reconciliation emerges as the main theme of the confession, which focuses on four major areas for reform: discrimination in society, international conflict, the continuation of poverty amid affluence, and the relative status of males and females in society. Conservatives object to the confession, referring to the weakening of the orthodox view of scriptural authority and the deity of Christ, the failure to mention the virgin birth of Christ, and the omission of the doctrine of predestination.

1968 A representative assembly meeting in Kansas City, Missouri, approves the Provisional Design for the Christian Church (Disciples of Christ).

The Methodist Church and the Evangelical United Brethren unite, establishing the United Methodist Church.

Pope Paul VI issues the encyclical *Humanae Vitae* (Of Human Life), which prohibits Catholics from using artificial means of birth control and states that sexual intercourse naturally should result in the procreation of children. Many U.S. Catholic clergy and a large majority of laypeople object to, or simply ignore, the encyclical. The encyclical initiates subsequent dissent among American Catholics on a number of issues.

Conservative lay Catholics establish Catholics United for the Faith, an organization that defends the traditional Catholic faith against progressive influences.

Good News Magazine, published by Good News, a dissenting organization within the United Methodist Church, includes an article strongly criticizing the denomination's adult Sunday school curriculum, claiming that the material lacks grounding in biblical theology.

1972   Members of the American Baptist Convention reorganize the group, changing the name to American Baptist Churches in the U.S.A. (ABC).

The Reformed Church in America approves the ordination of women as elders and deacons.

1973   Following disagreements within the Southern-based Presbyterian Church in the United States (PCUS) over adherence to strict Calvinist theology, the denomination's involvement in the civil rights movement, and the ordination of women, conservative members of the denomination establish the Presbyterian Church in America (PCA).

The U.S. Supreme Court rules in *Roe v. Wade* that state laws restricting abortion violate the Fourteenth Amendment to the U.S. Constitution and women's right to privacy, thus beginning a long conflict between "pro-life" and "pro-choice" groups as well as efforts by mainline denominations to formulate moral positions on the issue. The Catholic Church first takes the initiative in attempting to reduce or eliminate abortions in the United States.

Delegates to the General Synod of the Reformed Church in America adopt a resolution expressing opposition to the practice of abortion, but recognizing that the procedure might be the lesser of two evils in some situations. The resolution supports limitations

1973 (*cont.*)	on abortions performed for "individual convenience" and urges women with "problem pregnancies" to choose an alternative to abortion.
	The Reformed Church in America ordains the denomination's first woman minister.
1974	The majority of students and faculty at the Lutheran Church–Missouri Synod (LCMS) Concordia Seminary in St. Louis leave the seminary in protest against LCMS policies and establish Seminex ("seminary-in-exile"), which will become the Evangelical Lutheran Church in America's Lutheran School of Theology in Chicago.
1976	More moderate members and clergy of the Lutheran Church–Missouri Synod leave to form the Association of Evangelical Lutheran Churches (AELC).
	The Fellowship of Catholic Scholars is established to oppose secularization in the Catholic Church and Catholic institutions of higher learning.
1977	The Task Force on Ethical Issues in Human Medicine of the American Lutheran Church concludes that when the death of a person is certain, the decision to withhold extraordinary medical technology is morally acceptable; however, any action intended to cause the death of such a person is wrong.
	Paul Moore, an Episcopal bishop in New York, ordains a practicing lesbian. Following objections from others in the denomination, Moore issues a statement of regret.
1979	Representatives from the American Lutheran Church, the Lutheran Church in America, and the Association of Evangelical Lutheran Churches form a committee to develop a plan for a merger among the three groups.
1981	A group dissatisfied with the claimed leftist causes advocated by mainline denominations, such as feminism, pacifism, multiculturalism, and sexual liberation, establishes the Institute on Religion and Democracy. The organization advocates the return to traditional Christian values within the mainline denominations.
1982	Catholics, Quakers, and other religious activists hold the first Lenten Desert Experience at a Nevada nuclear

test site, combining observance of the 800th birthday of St. Francis of Assisi and a protest of nuclear testing.

The American Lutheran Church, the Lutheran Church in America, and the Association of Evangelical Lutheran Churches, each holding simultaneous conventions, agree to a proposal to form the Commission for a New Lutheran Church, which will prepare for a merger among the three Lutheran groups.

1983   With the more fundamentalist members having left the church to form the Presbyterian Church in America, the Presbyterian Church in the United States joins with the northern Presbyterian Church (UPCUSA). The merged denomination takes on the name Presbyterian Church (U.S.A.) (PCUSA).

Delegates to the General Synod of the Reformed Church in America, advocating "economically and racially just" immigration policies, approve resolutions that ask the U.S. Congress to pass legislation providing for amnesty for undocumented aliens presently residing in the United States.

The National Conference of Catholic Bishops issues a pastoral letter on nuclear war, "The Challenge of Peace: God's Promise and Our Response." Joseph Cardinal Bernardin takes a leading role in developing the letter. In a lecture series, Bernardin calls on Americans to protect human life from nuclear war as well as abortion.

1984   Catholics, Quakers, and other religious activists hold the annual forty-day vigil at a Nevada nuclear test site, to protest nuclear weapons and to commemorate the destruction of the Japanese cities of Hiroshima and Nagasaki at the end of the Second World War.

1985   A Louisiana priest is convicted of sexually molesting several boys in the Diocese of Lafayette, beginning a series of lawsuits against the church.

1986   The American Lutheran Church, the Lutheran Church in America, and the Association of Evangelical Lutheran Churches, holding simultaneous conventions, approve a new constitution that unites the three groups as the Evangelical Lutheran Church in America (ELCA),

1986 (*cont.*)	becoming the fourth largest Protestant denomination in the United States.

American Catholic bishops issue a pastoral letter, "Economic Justice for All," which states that poverty and unemployment levels in a nation as rich as the United States represent "a social and moral scandal" that Americans cannot ignore. Government should strive to ensure justice and economic rights for all Americans, including such measures as instituting job creation programs and increasing the minimum wage. The letter appears to have little effect nationally on the discussion of economic policy. Archbishop Rembert Weakland of Milwaukee, Wisconsin, a Benedictine monk identified with the liberal faction within the Catholic Church, plays a major role in developing the letter.

1988 The merger of the American Lutheran Church, the Lutheran Church in America, and the Association of Evangelical Lutheran Churches, agreed to in 1987, takes effect.

Conservative members of the Presbyterian Church (U.S.A.) organize Presbyterians for Renewal to work for maintaining the biblical standards of the denomination.

1989 Members of the Presbyterian Church (U.S.A.) who are concerned about the direction of the denomination meet to establish formally Presbyterians for Renewal.

1990 With the publication of *Ex corde Ecclesiae* (Out of the Heart of the Church), the Apostolic Constitution on Catholic Colleges and Universities, Pope John Paul II attempts to restore traditional Catholic education in the United States and elsewhere. Although Catholic bishops are expected to establish norms of scholarship in keeping with the Apostolic Constitution, many progressive bishops and educational personnel in the United States begin an effort to delay implementation.

1991 Delegates to the Episcopal Church General Assembly approve a resolution, "Establish Principles with Regard to the Prolongation of Life," declaring that the intentional taking of human life in order to end suffering resulting from incurable illnesses is morally wrong.

However, the resolution states that the administration of drugs to relieve suffering is permissible even if such drugs might bring death more quickly. The resolution also states that extraordinary measures to prolong the life of someone with no hope of recovery can be withheld.

Delegates to the Churchwide Assembly of the Evangelical Lutheran Church in America adopt a "social teaching statement" on the issue of abortion. Rather than calling for a legal ban on the practice of abortion, the statement declares that abortion should be a last-resort option and that the church and society should assist in ensuring that pregnant women face conditions conducive to giving birth, including providing sex education in the schools, pregnancy prevention programs, parenting classes, and the development of new contraception methods.

1992 The General Assembly of the Presbyterian Church (U.S.A.) approves a statement recognizing that under certain conditions—such as severe physical or mental abnormality of the fetus, rape, or incest—the abortion option can be justified. In addition, the statement declares that no legal restrictions should be placed on methods of contraception.

The Society of Catholic Social Scientists is created to combine Catholic teaching with social science and public policy research.

1994 The Commission on Christian Action of the Reformed Church in America, responding to passage of the Death with Dignity law in Oregon, issues a report stating the belief that Christians do not belong to themselves, that life is a gift from God, and that human beings are stewards of that gift. Pain-relieving drugs that can hasten death may be administered, but under strict control.

Pope John Paul II issues the encyclical *Evangelium Vitae* (The Gospel of Life), which condemns the practice of abortion, thus providing devout Catholics in the United States with added inspiration for opposing legalized abortion.

The General Synod of the Episcopal Church approves a resolution declaring that life is sacred

1994
(*cont.*)

from conception to death and recognizing that while women have the legal right to undergo an abortion, that right should be exercised only in extreme circumstances and should not be used as a means of birth control, gender selection, or simply for convenience.

1995

A group of Episcopal bishops, scholars, and laypeople who believe that the Episcopal Church must return to the basic truths of the Christian faith initiates steps toward creating the American Anglican Council.

Members of the Christian Action Commission of the Reformed Church in America oppose items in the Republican Party's Contract with America that call for denying legal immigrants rights that American citizens enjoy.

1996

A small group of Evangelical Lutheran Church in America clergy and laypersons who are dissatisfied with a proposal to establish full communion with the Episcopal Church begin the Word Alone Network as an electronic discussion group to facilitate communication among those opposed to the union.

Congress passes the Personal Responsibility and Work Opportunity Reconciliation Act, legislation that introduces charitable choice to allow faith-based organizations to obtain federal government funding for such social welfare activities as job training and drug rehabilitation. The legislation does not require religious organizations to separate social programs from religious activities or to adhere to national laws mandating equal treatment regardless of race, gender, or sexual preference.

Members of the Board of Church and Society of the United Methodist Church issue a statement declaring that the new legislation creating a program of charitable choice violates the establishment clause of the First Amendment. James Winkler, chief executive of the board, recommends that safeguards be maintained to prevent government intervention in church operations.

George Anderson, presiding bishop of the Evangelical Lutheran Church in America, raises concerns regarding the charitable choice legislation and recommends that government funding of religious organizations not affect religious group identity.

A larger group of disaffected Episcopal Church members meets to develop an organizational structure and incorporate as the American Anglican Council.

1997 New York Bishop Paul Moore, Jr., ordains a lesbian woman, Ellen Marie Barrett, as a priest in the Episcopal Church. This action causes a great deal of controversy within the denomination.

1998 Pope John Paul II defrocks Father John Geoghan, who has been accused of multiple instances of child molestation.

Reversing, at least in part, five centuries of disagreement, representatives of the Catholic Church and the Evangelical Lutheran Church in America sign the "Joint Statement on the Doctrine of Justification." Although the agreement opens the door to further discussion between Lutherans and Catholics, the agreement appears to have few practical implications for lay members of the two churches.

1999 The Churchwide Assembly of the Evangelical Lutheran Church in America adopts Called to Common Mission, an agreement of full communion with the Episcopal Church. The agreement includes the sharing of ordained clergy and adoption of the Episcopal ideal of apostolic succession through bishops, who retain the sole authority to ordain ministers. Many Lutherans strongly oppose the agreement, particularly those involved in the Word Alone Network, claiming that the notion of apostolic succession violates fundamental Lutheran beliefs.

2000 In March members of the Evangelical Lutheran Church in America who object to the ELCA's agreement, Called to Common Mission, with the Episcopal Church hold a constituting convention in Mahtomedi, Minnesota, formally establishing the Word Alone Network, a dissenting organization within the ELCA.

Delegates to the Presbyterian Church (U.S.A.) General Assembly declare the denomination's continuing opposition to capital punishment and call on

2000
(*cont.*)

the federal government and all state governments that have death penalty laws to institute a moratorium on executions.

Sister Helen Prejean, a resident of a New Orleans housing project and a member of a group opposed to the death penalty, takes part in presenting 2.5 million signatures collected from around the world to U.N. Secretary General Kofi Annan.

2001

Soon after taking office, President George W. Bush establishes the White House Office of Faith-Based and Community Initiatives and faith-based offices in the departments of Justice, Education, Health and Human Services, Housing and Urban Development, and Labor in order to facilitate the eligibility of religious organizations to receive federal government funding for charitable activities. The Bush administration introduces legislation in Congress to encourage faith-based funding.

In March several disaffected congregations in the Evangelical Lutheran Church in America join together to form an alternative denominational organization, Lutheran Congregations in Mission for Christ (LCMC).

The Catholic Church combines the National Conference of Catholic Bishops and the United States Catholic Conference to form the United States Conference of Catholic Bishops.

Bishop Joseph A. Firoenza, president of the United States Conference of Catholic Bishops, objects to President George W. Bush's decision to allow for limited government funding of embryonic stem-cell research using sixty-four lines of embryonic stem cells originating from human embryos received from in vitro fertilization clinics. The bishop calls President Bush's decision morally unacceptable.

Delegates to the Presbyterian Church (U.S.A.) General Assembly approve a resolution calling for the careful regulation of human embryonic stem-cell research and affirming the use of stem cells for research that may result in returning to health those suffering from serious illnesses.

Delegates to the General Synod of the United Church of Christ call for federal government funding of embryonic stem-cell research as a possible means of developing treatments for serious illnesses.

James Winkler, general secretary of the General Board of Church and Society of the United Methodist Church, states that board members support President Bush's announcement of a limitation on government funding of stem-cell research.

The Executive Council of the Episcopal Church announces the denomination's support for President Bush's proposed faith-based initiative, but recommends that any program include appropriate safeguards to ensure the separation of church and state.

2002   In January the *Boston Globe* begins an exposé of Catholic priests in Boston who are accused of sexually abusing minors. The news accounts claim that the church hierarchy ignored complaints and reassigned priests accused of abuse. The news stories spur legal action against the Catholic Church in Boston and other parts of the country.

Catholic Church members concerned about the revelations of sexual abuse of children by priests establish Voice of the Faithful, an organization dedicated to holding the church leadership responsible for any sexual abuse committed by priests and to increasing the influence of lay members in the denomination.

Gallup poll data indicate that during 2002, Catholic Church attendance has declined by 7 percent, which many interpret as one consequence of new revelations about sexual abuse in the church.

Bishop Wilton D. Gregory of the United States Conference of Catholic Bishops writes to President George W. Bush, questioning whether the imminent U.S. military operation in Iraq meets the conditions for a just war. Gregory raises doubts about any solid evidence of a relationship between Iraq and the September 11, 2001, terrorist attacks and questions the use of a preemptive military attack to limit the spread of weapons of mass destruction.

2002
(*cont.*)

In September religious leaders, including representatives from the Presbyterian Church (U.S.A.), the Reformed Church in America, the Episcopal Church, the Evangelical Lutheran Church in America, the United Church of Christ, the Christian Church (Disciples of Christ), and the United Methodist Church, sign a letter addressed to President Bush stating that preemptive war is morally wrong and harmful to the nation's interests. Such action, they argue, could lead to many civilian injuries and deaths, destabilize the Middle East, and encourage further militant actions.

Richard L. Hamm, general minister and president of the Christian Church (Disciples of Christ), informs denomination members that he believes the Bush administration, by taking unilateral military action, is losing the support of the world community. He asks church members to contact representatives and senators in Congress and the president to express their views on the impending conflict.

The Vatican, concerned about impending U.S. military action against Iraq, sends a senior cardinal and personal friend of former President George H. W. Bush to the United States to present in private to President George W. Bush the views of Pope John Paul II.

In December Cardinal Bernard Law, Catholic archbishop of Boston, shortly before his forced resignation over the sexual abuse scandal, warns against U.S. military involvement in Iraq.

In December, given congressional failure to pass legislation to establish faith-based funding, President Bush announces executive orders allowing the administration to issue federal government contracts to faith-based institutions. Additional faith-based centers are instituted in the Department of Agriculture and the U.S. Agency for International Development. Faith-based offices in the various agencies are ordered to determine if regulations unduly restrict the issuance of contracts to faith-based groups and to set aside funds for grants to religious group applicants.

The United Church of Christ congregation in Jaffrey, New Hampshire, protesting the Boy Scouts of America policy of excluding gay scout masters, announces that the local troop may no longer hold meetings in the church's facilities.

2003   Following the U.S. invasion of Iraq in March, Presiding Bishop Mark S. Hanson of the Evangelical Lutheran Church in America states that the reconstruction of Iraq should include cooperation with the United Nations and that U.S. policy should strive to resolve the larger conflict in the Middle East.

The Permanent Judicial Commission of the Presbyterian Church (U.S.A.) upholds the decision of church moderator Fahed Abu-Akel to refuse to call a special assembly requested by conservative church members to deal with the issue of enforcing the ban on gay clergy. However, the commission admonishes Abu-Akel for appealing to those asking for the meeting to withdraw their petition.

The Episcopal Diocese of New Hampshire elects an openly gay priest, V. Gene Robinson, as bishop. Conservatives in the denomination, particularly members of the American Anglican Council, quickly denounce the election as contrary to biblical mandate.

In August both the House of Deputies and the House of Bishops of the Episcopal Church General Convention approve Robinson's elevation to the position of bishop of the New Hampshire Diocese.

Delegates to the Episcopal Church General Convention approve a resolution supporting federal government funding of strictly regulated research on embryonic stem cells derived from in vitro fertilization.

Approximately 2,700 Episcopalians opposed to the election of an actively gay bishop meet in Dallas and ask the Archbishop of Canterbury to discipline the Episcopal Church for violating the resolution passed by the 1998 Lambeth Conference of Anglican primates that declared homosexual practices to be incompatible with scripture.

In October, at the invitation of Archbishop of Canterbury Rowan Williams, thirty-eight national primates of the Anglican Communion meet in London to discuss the consecration of V. Gene Robinson as

2003
(*cont.*)
bishop of New Hampshire. Bishops prepare a statement claiming that the actions of the Episcopal Church in the United States threaten the unity of the Anglican Communion.

Thomas Reilly, attorney general of Massachusetts and a practicing Catholic, issues a strong criticism of the Catholic Archdiocese of Boston, outlining a history of sexual abuse by church officials.

The Catholic Archdiocese of Boston reaches a legal settlement with those claiming to have been sexually abused by priests, agreeing to pay $85 million.

The Catholic Diocese of Orange, California, agrees to pay $100 million to those claiming to be victims of child abuse by priests.

Delegates to the Christian Church (Disciples of Christ) General Assembly adopt a resolution declaring the death penalty "contrary to God's passion for justice," noting the disproportionate number of poor and minorities who are executed.

2004
In January approximately 3,000 Episcopal Church members who oppose V. Gene Robinson's election as bishop of the New Hampshire Diocese attend a conference in Woodbridge, Virginia, sponsored by the American Anglican Council, to discuss options for dissenting church members, including the establishment of a new parish network called the Network of Anglican Communion Dioceses and Parishes.

In January Catholic Archbishop Raymond Burke of St. Louis declares that he would refuse to allow presidential candidate John Kerry, a Catholic, to participate in the sacrament of holy communion because of Kerry's pro-choice stand on the issue of abortion. Although antiabortion Catholics urge other bishops to take a similar position, others recommend a broader consideration of moral issues during the campaign, such as poverty and the war in Iraq.

On January 20 dissenting Episcopalians representing twelve dioceses, meeting in Plano, Texas, launch the Network of Anglican Communion Dioceses and Parishes. The delegates adopt its Structural Charter; affirm its Theological Charter; and elect Robert Duncan, bishop of Pittsburgh, the new organization's moderator.

In March V. Gene Robinson is invested as bishop of New Hampshire at a ceremony held at St. Paul's Church in Concord, New Hampshire.

Participants at the Word Alone Network's annual convention adopt a resolution opposing any change in the Evangelical Lutheran Church in America's interpretation of biblical teaching on sexual relations and marriage.

A court of thirteen United Methodist Church pastors at the Pacific Northwest Annual Conference hold a trial for Karen Dammann, a pastor charged with living in a lesbian relationship with another woman. Although UMC law forbids the ordination of "self-avowed practicing homosexuals," the court acquits Dammann of the charges.

In April the Reformed Church in America (RCA) merges its publication division with that of the Christian Reformed Church (CRC). Publication operations for both denominations will be handled by the CRC's Faith Alive Christian Resources division located in Grand Rapids, Michigan. The RCA's director of operations and support comments that the denomination can no longer financially support its own publications division.

In May the permanent judicial commission of the Ohio and Michigan Synod of the Presbyterian Church (U.S.A.) rules in favor of a minister who conducted same-gender marriage ceremonies. The ruling reverses the decision of a lower church court.

The Council of Bishops of the United Methodist Church recommends that the U.S. government allow the United Nations to participate in the development of a new Iraqi government and asks denomination members to support policies that will promote justice and reconciliation among the warring parties.

In June Presiding Bishop Mark S. Hanson of the Evangelical Lutheran Church in America, following a meeting with U.N. Secretary General Kofi Annan, reiterates his position stated more than a year earlier

2004
(*cont.*)

that the United Nations should play a major role in the reconstruction of Iraq and the return of that country to self-rule. The bishop expresses concern for the way people in other nations view the United States.

In July the Presbyterian Church (U.S.A.) General Assembly passes a resolution supporting the creation of a legalization program for undocumented persons in the United States. The resolution denounces the exploitation of workers who are in the United States illegally.

In a separate decision, the PCUSA General Assembly narrowly rejects (259–255) a proposal to allow regional denominational organizations to ordain gay clergy and lay officers.

The Evangelical Lutheran Church in America Conference of Bishops, meeting in Chicago from September 30 to October 4, hold a closed session with sexuality task force members to discuss various possible recommendations regarding the blessing of same-gender unions and the status of pastors involved in same-gender sexual relationships.

In October the Lambeth Commission on Communion issues a statement asking the Episcopal Church to apologize for electing V. Gene Robinson, an openly gay priest, as the bishop of New Hampshire and to refrain from consecrating openly gay bishops and blessing same-gender unions until the Anglican Communion develops a policy on these issues.

In November the United States Conference of Catholic Bishops elects William Skylstad, bishop of Spokane, Washington, as the organization's new president. Skylstad is elected just days after he announces that the Spokane diocese will enter Chapter 11 bankruptcy, claiming that the amount of damages being sought in lawsuits charging the diocese with failure to address cases of sexual molestation of children exceeds the diocese's financial resources.

2005

In February Anglican primates announce that the Episcopal Church in the United States and the Anglican Church of Canada are being asked to withdraw temporarily from the Anglican Consultative Council due to disagreements within these provinces on issues of sexuality.

Following the death of Pope John Paul II in April, the College of Cardinals elects Cardinal Joseph Ratzinger as the next pontiff. Ratzinger takes the title of Pope Benedict XVI. Pope Benedict is expected to follow the conservative policies of his predecessor.

MeLinda Morton, an Evangelical Lutheran Church in America chaplain at the Air Force Academy in Colorado Springs, Colorado, resigns, citing an atmosphere of religious intolerance at the academy. Academy officials release interim guidelines that encourage sensitivity to religious beliefs and distinguish between official communications and personal expressions of religious belief.

In July the General Synod of the United Church of Christ approves by a large margin a resolution accepting same-gender marriage. Although not binding on individual congregations, the resolution requests that member churches consider instituting marriage policies that do not discriminate on the basis of gender. The resolution also asks local congregations to consider advocating legislation that allows gay and lesbian couples to marry. Delegates also approve a resolution declaring that the denomination "celebrates and reaffirms our church's faith in Jesus Christ," but reject language that would require the question "Do you profess Jesus Christ as Lord and Savior?" to be asked of clergy in ordination vows.

In July the General Assembly of the Christian Church (Disciples of Christ) elects Sharon Watkins to a six-year term as general minister and president of the denomination beginning in that month.

In other actions, delegates approve a resolution to be communicated to President George W. Bush, Alaska Governor Frank H. Murkowski, and members of Congress disapproving of any oil and gas exploration in the Arctic National Wildlife Refuge.

In a separate resolution, delegates support passage of legislation to guarantee workers and their families a living wage.

2005
(*cont.*)

The Catholic Diocese of Covington, Kentucky, pays $120 million to settle lawsuits brought by those claiming to be victims of sexual abuse by priests.

The Catholic reform group Voice of the Faithful estimates that sexual abuse lawsuits could cost dioceses between $2 and $3 billion.

In August the American Baptist Churches in the U.S.A. Minister's Council defeats a proposal that would call for its members to adhere to the belief that sexual intimacy is appropriate only in heterosexual marriage.

In September the board of directors of the Pacific Southwest region of the American Baptist Churches in the U.S.A. votes to recommend leaving the denomination. The ABC's decision to allow "gay-affirming" congregations to remain in the denomination motivates the Pacific Southwest region's decision.

The United States Conference of Catholic Bishops strongly backs passage of the Charity Aid, Recovery and Empowerment Act, which will offer additional funding to charities, both religious and secular, through the Social Services Block Grant.

A Presbyterian Church (U.S.A.) regional judicial commission in California acquits a minister who conducted same-gender marriages, stating that her actions were in agreement with the normative standards of the region.

Cardinal Roger Mahony of the Catholic Archdiocese of Los Angeles expresses opposition to the Border Protection, Antiterrorism, and Illegal Immigration Control Act that won U.S. House of Representatives approval, claiming that the legislation unfairly penalizes immigrants and those who might give them assistance.

Clifton Kirkpatrick, stated clerk of the Presbyterian Church (U.S.A.)'s General Assembly, expresses his concern about provisions of the immigration legislation that the U.S. House of Representatives has approved, commenting that the legislation will classify undocumented aliens as felons and subject them to deportation without a hearing, and could destabilize the U.S. economy because needed workers cannot enter the country.

In October the nine-member Judicial Council of the United Methodist Church, meeting at the First United Methodist Church in Houston, in a unanimous vote (with one member absent) defrocks Irene Elizabeth Stroud, a lesbian minister from Pennsylvania. The council's judgment overrules the decision of an appeals court, which reversed the original decision to defrock Stroud after she announced to the members of the First United Methodist Church of Germantown in Philadelphia, where she has served as an associate pastor, that she is a lesbian living in a committed relationship with another woman.

In another case, the UMC Judicial Council, in a five-to-three ruling (with one member absent) reinstates a pastor who was suspended because he denied church membership to a gay man. Bishop Charlene P. Kammerer of the Virginia Conference removed Edward H. Johnson as pastor of South Hill United Methodist Church, but the majority opinion of the Judicial Council states that a pastor has the duty to use judgment in deciding who may be accepted as a member of a local church. A dissenting council member writes that the decision violates the principle that the church is open to all. The two cases illustrate the divisions within the United Methodist Church over the issue of homosexuality.

In October the Catholic Archdiocese of Los Angeles releases summaries of files documenting the failure of diocesan leaders to deal with the many priests accused of sexually molesting children. Leaders failed to notify the police or church members, instead shifting suspected priests to other parishes or offering them counseling.

In October the North Texas Association of the United Church of Christ votes to accept as a member of the denomination the Cathedral of Hope in Dallas, a liberal church considered to be the world's largest gay congregation.

2005 (*cont.*)	In December U.S. District Judge John E. Jones III, a member of an Evangelical Lutheran Church in America congregation, rules in *Kitzmiller v. Dover Area School District* that the theory of intelligent design is simply repackaged creationism, lacks credibility as science, and therefore has no place in the public school curriculum of Dover, Pennsylvania.
2006	In January, Robert H. Schuller, noted pastor of the Reformed Church in America–affiliated Crystal Cathedral in Garden Grove, California, announces that his son, Robert A. Schuller, will succeed him. An installation ceremony for the younger Schuller is held on January 22.

In February, at the Ninth Assembly of the World Council of Churches (WCC) meeting in Porto Alegre, Brazil, delegates from the United States, including Michael Livingstone, president of the National Council of Churches of Christ in the U.S.A., and Sharon Watkins, general minister and president of the Christian Church (Disciples of Christ), present a letter of apology to the delegates on behalf of the U.S. Conference of the WCC for U.S. actions in the world, including the war in Iraq.

An Episcopal Church nominating committee announces the names of four candidates for presiding bishop, a position subject to election at the General Convention later in the year. Three of the four candidates voted in favor of ratifying V. Gene Robinson's selection as the bishop of New Hampshire. Conservative Episcopal spokespersons express dissatisfaction with all four candidates.

In March the Executive Council of the Episcopal Church asks denomination members to adhere to the "Baptismal Covenant" by alleviating the suffering of illegal immigrants even if federal legislation should make such assistance illegal.

Bishop Thomas Wenski, chairman of the United States Conference of Catholic Bishops Committee on International Policy, issues a statement expressing the moral concerns of the bishops regarding the U.S. military operation in Iraq. The bishops state that U.S.

military personnel should remain in Iraq only until a transition of power to Iraqis has occurred, and they urge the U.S. government not to rely solely on military methods to resist terrorism.

In March fifty-five Catholic lawmakers issue the document "Statement of Principles by Fifty-Five Catholic Democrats in the U.S. House of Representatives." This brief document expresses an obligation to care for the poor and disadvantaged and a commitment to reducing the number of unwanted pregnancies by adopting policies that assist women in carrying pregnancies to term.

In March the Vatican defrocks a former vice chancellor of the Boston Archdiocese of the Catholic Church, along with six other priests who have been accused of sexually molesting children. The Boston archbishop expresses sorrow for the harm the priests have done.

In April, in a nonbinding referendum, delegates of the American Baptist Churches in the Southwest vote to recommend leaving the Covenant of Relationships with the ABC.

A Presbyterian Church (U.S.A.) regional judicial commission, in a six-to-one vote, acquits Jane Spahr, a minister in San Rafael, California, of charges that she violated the denomination's constitution—which specifies that marriage is a union of a man and a woman—by marrying two lesbian couples. The court states that the constitution's reference to marriage is "a definition, not a directive."

Delegates to the June General Assembly of the Presbyterian Church (U.S.A.) revise a policy on Middle East investments that was ratified at the 2004 General Assembly. The previous policy, which called for selective divestment in multinational corporations conducting business in Israel, led to objections from church members and Jewish organizations. The new policy states that Presbyterian investments in both Israel and Palestinian territories should be limited to peaceful activities.

2006
(*cont.*)

Attempting to deal with the issue of homosexuality, delegates to the PCUSA General Assembly retain a church law stating that clergy, lay elders, and deacons must restrict sexual relations to marriage between a man and a woman, but they pass new legislation stating that local congregations may follow a more flexible policy when selecting clergy and lay officials if sexual orientation becomes an issue.

The PCUSA General Assembly creates controversy in the wider Christian community by asking the church to consider alternative formulations of the Trinity (Father, Son, and Holy Spirit), such as "Mother, Child, and Womb" and "Rock, Redeemer, and Friend."

In June delegates to the Episcopal Church General Convention elect Katharine Jefferts Schori as the denomination's presiding bishop–elect, who will take office in November.

On the last day of the Episcopal convention, Jefferts Schori, in a sermon, refers to "our mother Jesus" giving birth to a new creation, a statement that further upsets conservatives.

Following the urging of Presiding Bishop Frank Griswold and Presiding Bishop–Elect Katharine Jefferts Schori, Episcopal Church General Convention delegates agree to a resolution asking dioceses to refrain from consecrating gay bishops. Liberal as well as conservative delegates express their displeasure with the resolution. The resolution responds to the 2004 Windsor Report, a statement of the Lambeth Commission on Communion, chaired by Archbishop Robin Eames of Ireland.

The Episcopal Church publicly apologizes for slavery, promises to fight against racism, and initiates an investigation of possible compensation to African American church members for any historical involvement in slavery and the slave trade.

In June Archbishop of Canterbury Rowan Williams issues a statement proposing that the Episcopal Church in the United States either reject the investment of gay bishops and the blessing of same-gender unions or surrender full membership in the Anglican Communion. To be enacted, Williams's proposal must be considered by several major church meetings, a process that will take at least four years.

In June delegates to the General Synod of the Reformed Church in America instruct General Secretary Wesley Granberg-Michaelson to send letters to President George W. Bush, Secretary of State Condoleezza Rice, and U.S. Senate Majority Leader Bill Frist urging a relaxation of travel restrictions on church leaders traveling between the United States and Cuba.

In July the Episcopal dioceses of Springfield, Illinois, and Central Florida join four other dioceses (Pittsburgh; South Carolina; San Joaquin, California; and Fort Worth, Texas) in rejecting the authority of Presiding Bishop–Elect Katharine Jefferts Schori and seeking oversight from Anglican provinces in other countries.

In July President George W. Bush vetoes a bill that would expand federal funding for stem-cell research using surplus embryos from fertility clinics. Congress fails to override the veto.

In September the Episcopal Diocese of Newark avoids further controversy within the denomination by selecting a Massachusetts priest as the new bishop rather than an openly gay candidate.

In September Anglican Communion primates from Asia and Africa, meeting in Kigali, Rwanda, declare that the process of establishing a separate Anglican Communion structure in the United States should begin. The primates suggest that conservative Episcopalians choose a representative other than Presiding Bishop Katharine Jefferts Schori to attend the next meeting of Anglican primates scheduled for February 2007.

In October the Catholic Diocese of Davenport, Iowa, becomes the fourth diocese to file for bankruptcy. Bishop William Franklin states that the settlement of more than two dozen claims of sexual abuse against as many as eleven priests requires this action. The diocese has paid more than $10.5 million in settlements.

U.S. Representative Mark Foley (R-FL) resigns from Congress when it is revealed that he sent sexually suggestive e-mail messages to House pages. In October

2006
(*cont.*)

Foley reveals the name of the Catholic priest he claims sexually molested him when he was a teenage altar boy. The Archdiocese of Miami bars the priest, who is now sixty-nine years old and living in Malta, from functioning as a priest. Mary Ross Agosta, a spokeswoman for the diocese, offers an apology to Foley.

In October the United States Conference of Catholic Bishops drafts the document "Ministry to Persons with Homosexual Inclination: Guidelines for Pastoral Care." Although the bishops affirm the church's disapproval of same-gender sexual relationships, they recommend that parishes reach out to gay Catholics by, for instance, baptizing the adopted children of same-gender couples.

In November the Catholic Archdiocese of Los Angeles agrees to a $60 million settlement in a case involving forty-five individuals making claims of sexual abuse against twenty-five priests. Cardinal Roger Mahoney states that he and the church accept responsibility. More than 500 sexual abuse lawsuits against the archdiocese remain.

In November estimates are made that approximately 200 congregations have left the United Church of Christ after the denomination's 2005 General Synod affirmed the right of same-gender couples to marry.

In December the members of two large parishes and five additional smaller churches in Virginia vote to secede from the Episcopal Church and affiliate with the Nigerian Anglican Church and its archbishop, Peter J. Akinola, who is a strong opponent of the U.S. church's stand on homosexuality. Observers speculate that the secessions could lead to legal struggles over ownership of church property.

2007

In January several United Methodist Church bishops and ministers sign a petition objecting to the prospective establishment of a George W. Bush presidential library museum and public policy institute at Southern Methodist University in Dallas. The signers cite the war in Iraq, the alleged use of torture on prisoners, and the death penalty as reasons for their opposition. Methodists are asked to sign the petition online.

In February primates from thirty-eight Anglican national churches, meeting in Tanzania, demand that the U.S. Episcopal Church agree not to sanction any ceremony to bless same-gender unions and not to approve any candidate for bishop who is involved in a sexual relationship with a person of the same gender. The primates set a September 30, 2007, deadline for accepting these demands. In addition, the primates announce that they will establish a five-member pastoral council to manage U.S. congregations that object to the liberal sexual policies of the Episcopal Church.

In February Michael Webb, attorney for the Catholic Diocese of San Diego, announces that the diocese will file for bankruptcy protection. The announcement is made just before the first trial is to begin in a lawsuit alleging sexual abuse by diocesan priests. San Diego will become the fifth Catholic diocese to file for bankruptcy protection.

In February Robert Drinan, Catholic priest and liberal Democratic congressman (D-MA) from 1971 to 1980, dies. Drinan was the first member of Congress to call for President Richard M. Nixon's impeachment.

In February the disciplinary committee of the Evangelical Lutheran Church in America announces that a gay pastor involved in a same-gender relationship will be removed from the pastoral roster, effective August 15. However, committee members object to the policy barring practicing homosexuals from the clergy and urge church leaders to alter the policy at an August meeting. Mark Chavez, head of Word Alone Network, a group that supports the ban, comments that the current policy conforms to scripture.

In March Episcopal bishops, meeting in Navasota, Texas, reject the demands of Anglican primates, publicly announcing that "all God's children, including gay and lesbian persons, are full and equal participants in the life of Christ's Church." They also reject the proposal to establish a foreign pastoral council to oversee dissenting congregations.

5

Biographical Sketches

The individuals covered here either have played significant formal roles within the denominations or have been alternative voices within the mainline churches. Some are historical figures, such as Reinhold Niebuhr and Harry Emerson Fosdick, who helped to lay the present religious and ethical foundations of the mainline denominations. Others, such as Katharine Jefferts Schori, Sharon E. Watkins, and Roger Mahoney, currently hold leadership positions within mainline denominations. Yet others, including Joan Chittister and John Shelby Spong, represent voices of dissent within the mainline denominations. Together, the people selected for inclusion provide a broad sample of the beliefs, values, concerns, and social and political engagement within the mainline denominations.

Daniel Berrigan (b. 1921)

A Catholic priest, peace activist, and poet, Daniel Berrigan, along with his brother Philip, also a priest, gained widespread recognition in the 1960s for engaging in protests against the Vietnam War. Berrigan authored more than thirty books, including *The Trial of the Catonsville Nine* in 1970. Born in Virginia, Minnesota, to an Irish-Catholic family, Berrigan entered a Jesuit seminary after completing high school in 1939 and was ordained in 1952. He studied in France, where he became familiar with the worker-priest movement. Berrigan taught theology at Le Moyne College in Syracuse, New York, from 1957 to 1962, and from 1963 to 1965 he served as assistant editor of *Jesuit Missions*, after which he became associate director of United Religious Work. In the 1950s Daniel and Philip engaged in the civil rights movement, taking part in the protest marches in Selma, Alabama. In the 1960s, as the United States became more deeply involved in Vietnam, Berrigan took part in establishing an interfaith coalition to protest the war. In 1969 Berrigan traveled to Hanoi with Howard Zinn, a radical intellectual and professor at Boston University, to assist in the release of three American pilots imprisoned by the North Vietnamese government. Later that year Berrigan decided to engage in more radical protest. He joined a group of war protesters who entered the draft board office in Catonsville, Maryland, took nearly 400 draft files, and burned them outside the building. The group came to be known as the Catonsville Nine. Police arrested Berrigan and he was placed on trial, found guilty, and sentenced to three years in prison. However, he fled from custody and for four months was sheltered by supporters. During that time, he made brief appearances at public events. Federal Bureau of Investigation agents finally captured Berrigan, and he served eighteen months in prison. He was paroled in 1972.

In 1980 Daniel and Philip, along with six others, formed the Plowshares Movement to protest nuclear weaponry. The group, which came to be known as the Plowshares Eight, entered the General Electric plant in King of Prussia, Pennsylvania, which manufactured nose cones for nuclear warheads. They hammered on two nose cones—symbolic of the prophecy of peace in the Book of Isaiah (2:4): "He shall judge between the nations, and shall arbitrate for many peoples; they shall beat their swords into plowshares, and their spears into pruning hooks; nation shall not lift up sword against nation, neither shall they learn war any more"—and poured blood on files. Authorities arrested the group on felony and misdemeanor charges and in 1981 they were placed on trial in Norristown, Pennsylvania. After the jury convicted the group of various charges, including burglary, and sentenced them to prison terms, a lengthy appeal process began. After nearly ten years, the Pennsylvania Court of Common Pleas in Norristown sentenced the Plowshares Eight to parole for up to twenty-three and one-half months, taking into account time already served. More recently, Berrigan has participated in protests against the 1991 Gulf War, the U.S. invasion of Afghanistan, and the invasion of Iraq. On Good Friday in 2003 Berrigan, then eighty-three years old, was arrested at an antiwar protest at the USS *Intrepid* aircraft carrier in New York City.

Joan Chittister (b. 1936)

Joan Chittister, a member and former prioress of the Benedictine Sisters of Erie, Pennsylvania, has published more than thirty books and contributes a column for the *National Catholic Reporter*, a liberal publication. Her writings deal with such topics as justice, equality, the maintenance of peace, and the rights of women. An activist, she proclaims that human beings should be willing to bring needed changes to society. She has claimed that praying to God to eliminate nuclear weapons is a type of blasphemy because human beings made the weapons and, if they decide to do so, they can eliminate them. Within the Catholic Church, Chittister often has disagreed with official church policy and has received criticism from more conservative members for her advocacy of women's ordination as priests. In 2004 she spoke in Dublin, Ireland, at a conference supporting women's ordination even though the Vatican opposed her attendance. Chittister questions whether everything that is to be known about the Christian faith was available in the first century. She notes that Catholics learned from Protestants that people could read the Bible for themselves. Referring to Copernicus, Chittister comments that Catholics also learned that the telescope could reveal more about the cosmos than what is written in the book of Genesis, and they discovered that they could stop segregating churches, schools, and society in general.

Chittister contracted polio one month after entering a Benedictine convent at the age of sixteen. Initially, she lost the use of an arm and a leg and was confined to an iron lung. Recovery from the disease lasted four years, after which she was able to resume her religious training. She earned a master of arts degree in communication arts from the University of Notre Dame. From 1974 to 1990 Chittister served as president of the Conference of American Benedictine Prioresses and was for twelve years the prioress of the Benedictine Sisters of Erie. In addition, she has served as president of the Leadership Conference of Women Religious and as the co-chair of the Global Peace Initiative of Women, an organization associated with the United Nations. Chittister has attended various international conferences, including the Fourth UN Conference of Women in Beijing, China, in 1999, and the Pan-Asian Youth Summit in Hiroshima, Japan, in 2004.

In her *National Catholic Reporter* column, Chittister presents her views on current political events. With the U.S. invasion of Iraq, she commented frequently on U.S. foreign policy. In November 2003 she suggested that the Patriot Act, which granted increased powers to the federal government to combat terrorism, threatened democracy in the United States at the same time that the Bush administration proclaimed that the United States was attempting to spread democracy in the Middle East. Just over a year later, Chittister criticized the U.S. government for the continuing occupation of Iraq, referring to the failure to discover evidence that Saddam Hussein possessed weapons of mass destruction and to revelations of prisoner abuse at Abu Ghraib prison. She commented on the arrogance of the occupation and the quagmire into which the nation had become embroiled. By the end of 2005 Chittister urged the reestablishment of the constitutional system of checks and balances in the federal government, citing Congress's lack of will to investigate the Bush administration's intentions to invade Iraq at the same time that many in the rest of the world raised questions about the military action. She encouraged an investigation of why the checks and balances system failed to work. In March 2006 Chittister expressed her views on Iran's intention to proceed with a nuclear program, warning against committing the same policy mistakes and again criticizing the doctrine of preemptive war. She referred to the "blood spattered children" in Iraq who were being prepared for a future war. Chittister declared that while invading another nation, the U.S. government spied on its own citizens and fortified the borders against the poor, and she contrasted the existence of the poor with the nation's great wealth. She found fault with the new Iraqi constitution, claiming that it did not guarantee democracy for the women of the country.

Chittister has reproached the hierarchy of the Catholic Church on issues other than her call for the ordination of women. She defended Thomas Gumbleton, the auxiliary bishop of Detroit, who denounced the Conference of Catholic Bishops of Ohio for opposing legislation intended to extend the statute of limitations in child sexual abuse cases. She declared that the bishops had neglected the abused in an effort to avoid financial responsibility. Comparing Gumbleton with those in government—from Daniel Ellsberg, who released the Pentagon Papers, to Joseph Wilson, who criticized faulty intelligence prior to the Iraq invasion—Chittister wondered whether the church would treat a truth teller any better than did a secular institution.

William Sloane Coffin, Jr. (1924–2006)

From the civil rights movement of the early 1960s through the protest movement against the Vietnam War and on to the crusade to eliminate nuclear weapons, William Sloane Coffin, Jr., played an active role among mainline clergy pursuing political causes. Coffin was born into a New York family of privilege. His father was vice president of W. and J. Sloane, a furniture manufacturing company, and was also president of the board of trustees of the Metropolitan Museum of Art. Coffin's uncle, Henry Sloane Coffin, served as president of the Union Theological Seminary. After his father's sudden death in 1933, Coffin's mother moved the family to Carmel, California, where the three children attended public school. Coffin showed talent as a piano player, so his mother encouraged his musical ability, taking him to Europe in 1939 to study music in Paris. When the Second World War began, Coffin and his mother moved to Geneva, Switzerland, and then returned to the United States, where Coffin attended Phillips Academy in Andover, Massachusetts. After graduating from high school, he began to study music at Yale University, but in 1943 he joined the army, serving in military intelligence. After the war, Coffin returned to Yale and graduated in 1949. Coffin entered the Union Theological Seminary, but after a year, he joined the Central Intelligence Agency (CIA), at least partially because he regretted taking part in the forcible repatriation of Soviet citizens after the war and wanted to oppose the oppressive Stalinist regime. However, Coffin became disillusioned with the organization because of its involvement in the overthrow of the Iranian prime minister in 1953 and the coup d'état in Guatemala in 1954. After leaving the CIA, Coffin entered Yale Divinity School, where in 1956 he received a bachelor of divinity degree and was ordained a Presbyterian minister. In 1958 Coffin took the position of chaplain at Yale University, where he stayed until 1975. In 1961, at the request of Sargent Shriver, director of the Peace Corps at the beginning of John F. Kennedy's presidency, Coffin took a temporary leave from

Yale to develop a training program and to construct a Peace Corps camp in Puerto Rico.

During his tenure at Yale, Coffin became involved in political causes. He organized so-called freedom riders to travel by bus to Southern states to protest segregation policies. In 1963 he was arrested while participating in a demonstration at a segregated amusement park in Baltimore. An early critic of U.S. involvement in Vietnam, Coffin became active in the movement to oppose the military draft. In 1968 a federal grand jury indicted Coffin and four others, including Benjamin Spock, the noted pediatrician, for conspiring to help young men resist the draft. Coffin, Spock, and two other defendants were convicted, but the verdict was overturned on appeal. In 1977 Coffin left Yale to become senior minister at the Riverside Church in New York City, which was affiliated with the United Church of Christ and the American Baptist Churches in the U.S.A. While serving at Riverside Church, Coffin continued to advocate progressive causes—including gay rights, the needs of the poor, and nuclear disarmament—and remained engaged in current politics. In 1979 he participated in a mission to Iran to conduct Christmas services for the American hostages being held in Teheran. In 1987 Coffin left the New York church to become president of SANE/FREEZE (subsequently called Peace Action), an organization that advocated nuclear disarmament. He claimed that the United States and other nuclear nations were practicing nuclear apartheid by insisting on maintaining their own arsenals while attempting to keep other nations from developing such weapons. After becoming the organization's president emeritus in the early 1990s, Coffin continued to present lectures on the dangers of nuclear weapons and the need to develop peaceful ties with other nations. Although Coffin suffered a stroke in 1999, which slowed his activities somewhat, he continued to oppose U.S. military involvement around the world, speaking out against the Persian Gulf War in 1991 and the Iraq War in 2003.

John Claggett Danforth (b. 1936)

Throughout U.S. history, members of the Episcopal Church have played significant roles in the country's political, economic, and social life. John Danforth, a retired senator, a former U.S. ambassador to the United Nations, and an ordained priest in the

Episcopal Church, is an archetype of the influential mainline Episcopalian who believes in moderation, reasonableness, and compromise. While holding public office, his religious training and beliefs undoubtedly influenced his stands on political issues, and he gained a reputation for being a highly principled politician. In more recent years Danforth, generally considered a political moderate, has become a vocal critic of the religious right and the Republican Party's alliance with conservative Christian groups.

Born in St. Louis, Danforth is the grandson of William H. Danforth, who founded Ralston Purina, and son of Donald Danforth, who became chief executive of the company. Danforth graduated from Princeton University in 1958 and went on to attend both Yale University Law School and Yale Divinity School, receiving both a bachelor of divinity degree and a bachelor of laws degree in 1963. He was ordained in the Episcopal Church the same year. Danforth practiced law in New York City and St. Louis before running as a Republican for the office of Missouri attorney general in 1968. He ran successfully for reelection in 1972. In 1976 Danforth won the U.S. Senate election in Missouri, succeeding retiring Senator Stuart Symington. Danforth won reelection in 1982 and 1988. He gained wide attention during the 1991 confirmation battle of U.S. Supreme Court nominee Clarence Thomas for his strong support for Thomas. The two men had become friends when Thomas worked with Danforth in the Missouri attorney general's office and in the U.S. Senate as an aide.

Although Danforth never served as a full-time Episcopal priest, he has held numerous positions within the church, including membership on the governing board of Washington Cathedral; associate priest of the Church of the Holy Communion in University City, Missouri; assistant rector of the Church of the Epiphany in New York City; and assistant chaplain for New York's Memorial Sloan-Kettering Cancer Center. Danforth presided at the funerals of *Washington Post* owner Katharine Graham in 2001 and former President Ronald Reagan in 2004.

After leaving the Senate in 1995, Danforth resumed his private law practice. In 1999 Attorney General Janet Reno asked him to head an investigation of the Federal Bureau of Investigation's actions during the 1993 siege at the Branch Davidian compound in Waco, Texas. Although Danforth was rumored to be George W. Bush's choice as a vice presidential running mate in 2000, that position went to Richard Cheney. In September 2001 President Bush asked

Danforth to serve as special envoy to Sudan, a country devastated by civil war. Although he devoted himself to bringing peace to the war-ravaged country, his efforts to resolve differences among the warring factions ultimately proved unsuccessful. In July 2004 Danforth succeeded John Negroponte as the U.S. ambassador to the United Nations, where he continued to focus on ameliorating the violent conditions in Sudan. After just five months Danforth resigned from the U.N. position, stating that he wished to spend more time with his wife. Prior to President Bush's choice of Condoleezza Rice, some had speculated that Danforth might be the president's choice for secretary of state.

In March 2005 Danforth published an opinion column in the *New York Times* expressing his deep concern about the influence of the religious right in the Republican Party. He cited the party's support for a constitutional amendment to prohibit gay marriage and opposition to embryonic stem-cell research, and also referred to Republicans' efforts to pass a bill empowering the federal courts to hear an appeal from the Florida state court system over its ruling that a feeding tube could be removed from Terri Schiavo, a woman who had been in a vegetative state for more than thirteen years. In each case, Danforth claimed that Republicans had bowed to the wishes of conservative Christians. Although he opposed abortion, Danforth stated that he could not accept the claim that human cells are equivalent to human beings who are suffering from diseases that possibly could be treated through embryonic stem-cell research. To restrict such research, he argued, involved introducing religious doctrine into statutory law. Although recognizing that religious conservatives as well as religious liberals have a basic right to engage in political activity, Danforth faulted the Republican Party for adhering to the political agenda of a specific religious movement. The traditional agenda of the party, including limited government, limited regulation and taxation, judges who interpret the law and do not legislate, and maintaining a strong national defense, has been jeopardized by undue attention to the conservative Christian agenda. Danforth stated that while in the Senate, he worried about the size of the deficit but did not spend any time agonizing over the effect that gays might have on the institution of marriage. In fall 2006 Danforth published *Faith and Politics: How the "Moral Values" Debate Divides America and How to Move Forward Together*, in which he presented in detail his argument about the appropriate role of religion in democratic politics.

Dorothy Day (1897–1980)

Dorothy Day founded the *Catholic Worker*, a publication that advocated a combination of Catholic belief and a commitment to radical social reform to create a more just society. Born in Brooklyn, New York, Day spent most of her early years in Chicago. Her concern for the plight of the working class in the early twentieth century led her to embrace Communist ideology. In 1914 Day received a scholarship to the University of Illinois at Urbana, but she showed little interest in formal studies. She left college after two years and moved to New York City, where she became a reporter for *The Call* and *The Masses*, socialist periodicals. When the latter publication expressed opposition to U.S. involvement in the First World War, the U.S. Postal Service denied *The Masses* a mailing permit and raided its offices, seizing issues of the magazine and mailing lists. In 1917 Day moved to Washington DC, where she joined other women in picketing the White House in support of women's right to vote. Police arrested Day and she served thirty days in a workhouse.

In 1924 Day entered a common-law marriage with Forster Batterham, an anarchist who did not believe in religion or marriage. When she became pregnant in 1926, Day decided to have the child despite Batterham's objections. She previously had undergone an illegal abortion to terminate a pregnancy resulting from another affair and thought it was a miracle that she could become pregnant again. After the child was born in early 1927, Day had the girl baptized in the Catholic Church. With the end of her relationship with Batterham, Day joined the Catholic Church, and thus began her efforts to combine religious faith with radical social views. In late 1932 Day reported on a march in Washington DC for *Commonweal* and *America* magazines. The demonstrators were publicizing the need for jobs, unemployment insurance, old-age pensions, and health care. On her return to New York, Day met Peter Maurin, a French immigrant, who urged her to begin a newspaper based on Catholic social values and the need to transform society peacefully. In May 1933 Day and Maurin began publishing *The Catholic Worker*. They printed 2,500 copies of the first issue, which sold for a penny. Within a year they were printing 100,000 copies, and by 1936 they distributed 150,000 copies of each issue. In addition to starting *The Catholic Worker*, Day took more direct steps to aid the destitute, opening a house in New York to shelter the homeless. By 1936 the Catholic Worker movement had established thirty-three houses around the country. The movement also established farm communes, but they achieved only limited success.

Day advocated pacifism in the pages of *The Catholic Worker*. Her position on the Spanish Civil War, which began in 1936, stimulated opposition to the newspaper among Catholics as well as those on the political left. The fascist side, led by Francisco Franco, received support from American Catholics, while the American left backed the Republican faction. By refusing to support either side in the civil war, Day lost many newspaper subscribers. Concerned with the Nazi treatment of Jews in Germany, Day helped to found the Committee of Catholics to Fight Anti-Semitism. Even with American entry into the Second World War following the Japanese attack on Pearl Harbor, Day maintained a pacifist stance and urged movement members to provide assistance for the sick and wounded, help feed the hungry, and offer shelter to the homeless. Many men associated with the Catholic Worker movement were either imprisoned or served as medics in the military.

Following the Second World War, as fear of nuclear conflict gripped the nation, Day and the Catholic Worker community in New York refused to take part in a mandated yearly civil defense drill that began in 1955. Each year the group demonstrated against nuclear weapons instead of taking part in the drill. By 1961, the last year the drill was held, 2,000 people joined the protest. During the Vietnam War, Day and other members of the Catholic Worker movement protested U.S. military policy. Many in the movement again faced prison for refusing military service while other members entered alternative service. In 1973, at the age of seventy-five, Day was arrested for picketing with farm workers. That same year the Jesuit magazine *America* devoted an issue to Day, stating that over the previous forty years she had served as a model for the American Catholic community.

Robert (Bob) W. Edgar (b. 1943)

In January 2000 Robert W. Edgar became the general secretary of the National Council of Churches of Christ in the USA (NCC), the major U.S. organization of mainline denominations. The organization includes thirty-five Protestant, Anglican, Orthodox, and historically African American denominations. Edgar, a former member of Congress from Pennsylvania, expresses distinctly liberal positions on various political issues. Born in Philadelphia, Edgar graduated from high school in Springfield, Pennsylvania, and went on to Lycoming College in Williamsport, Pennsylvania, where he received a bachelor of arts degree in 1965. In 1968 he received a master of divinity degree from Drew University Theological School in Madison, New Jersey, and was ordained a minister in the United Methodist Church. In 1969 he earned a certificate in pastoral psychiatry from the Hahnemann Medical College and Hospital in Philadelphia. From 1971 to 1974 Edgar served as the chaplain of Drexel University in Philadelphia. In 1974 he entered politics, campaigning as a Democratic candidate for the U.S. House of Representatives in the Seventh Congressional District, which traditionally voted Republican. He won the election and went on to serve six terms. While in Congress, Edgar focused on several public policy areas, including improving public transportation, limiting questionable water projects, and protecting the environment. In 1986 Edgar decided not to run for reelection, and instead made an unsuccessful bid for a seat in the U.S. Senate, running against Senator Arlen Specter. Following his defeat, Edgar briefly served as a special assistant to Representative William H. Gray III before becoming president of the Claremont School of Theology in Claremont, California, a position he held from 1990 to 2000.

Edgar has been active in various organizations, including the National Coalition for Health Care, Common Cause, the National Religious Partnership for the Environment, and the Environmental and Energy Study Institute. As a member of the executive committee of the Leadership Conference on Civil Rights, he joined in sending a letter to members of Congress, urging them to oppose the 2004 Marriage Protection Act. In November 2005 he joined with other representatives of the NCC to call on Congress to increase the national minimum wage. A report issued by the NCC titled "A Just Minimum Wage: Good for Workers, Business and Our Future" noted that, despite inflation, the minimum wage, which was $5.15 per hour, had not been increased since 1997 and declared that this was not a fair wage either economically or ethically.

James A. Forbes, Jr. (b. 1935)

James Forbes, an ordained minister in the American Baptist Churches in the USA and the Original United Holy Church of

America, supports progressive causes in U.S. politics. In 1989 Forbes became the fifth senior pastor of the Riverside Church in New York City, succeeding William Sloane Coffin. Before assuming the pastorate of the Riverside Church, Forbes served from 1976 to 1985 as an associate professor of preaching at Union Theological Seminary and from 1985 to 1989 as the first Joe R. Engle Professor of Preaching at the seminary. When he accepted the position at the Riverside Church, the seminary named Forbes the first Harry Emerson Fosdick Adjunct Professor of Preaching. Forbes also serves on the teaching staff of Auburn Theological Seminary in New York City. He served as pastor at St. John's United Holy Church of America in Richmond, Virginia, from 1965 to 1973; at Holy Trinity Church in Wilmington, Delaware, from 1960 to 1965; and at St. Paul's Holy Church in Roxboro, North Carolina, from 1960 to 1969. From 1968 to 1970 Forbes served as campus minister at Virginia Union University in Richmond. He is a member of the board of directors of the Interfaith Alliance Foundation, an organization dedicated to helping communities achieve social justice.

In 2004 Forbes made several presentations, one at the Democratic National Convention, in which he used the theme of the United States returning to the original spiritual and moral values on which the nation was established, as expressed in the Declaration of Independence, the Constitution, and the Bill of Rights. Using the analogy of the prodigal son, Forbes urged the United States to return home. He noted that although the United States has never lived up to the ideals established in these documents, they still point to what the nation should be. However, in recent years, the nation has strayed from spiritual and moral values. He referred to the widening gap between rich and poor; a spirit of domination; and a culture of materialism, consumerism, rugged individualism, and intolerance.

Forbes advised his audience not to let the religious right determine their level of religious devotion. Frequency of church attendance should not be the measure of a person's worth in God's sight. He had harsh words for those who use government to benefit special interests while otherwise proclaiming that government is irrelevant and should be as small as possible. According to Forbes, such people make a prostitute out of that government. He urged citizens not to allow the terrorist events of September 11, 2001, lead to the abandonment of the high principles of the nation, and urged religious and progressive leaders to take part in returning the nation to the values of the past. Progressive voices, he declared, must speak against the "right wing madness."

Harry Emerson Fosdick (1878–1969)

In the 1920s and 1930s Harry Emerson Fosdick defended modernism in Christianity against fundamentalist beliefs. Fosdick questioned several of the major tenets of fundamentalism, including the virgin birth of Jesus, the literal inerrancy of the Bible, and the second coming of Christ, and embraced the social gospel, emphasizing the importance of human reason in religious faith and the responsibility of Christians to engage in social as well as personal betterment. He argued that the belief in scriptural infallibility had restricted biblical research, contributed to persecution, and delayed human progress. Fosdick emphasized direct religious experience in contrast to philosophical, theological, and cultural expressions of that experience that may vary over time. The controversies that Fosdick faced in the early twentieth century have repeatedly resurfaced in subsequent years within mainline denominations and between them and more evangelical and fundamentalist groups.

Born in Buffalo, New York, Fosdick graduated from Colgate University in 1900. In 1901 he entered Union Theological Seminary in New York City, where he was exposed to such influences as higher criticism of the Bible and the pragmatism of William James. As the result of working with the poor in the Bowery while at the seminary, Fosdick experienced a nervous breakdown. Following treatment at a sanitarium in Elmira, New York, he returned to Union Theological Seminary, receiving his degree in 1904. He was ordained a Baptist minister in 1903 and became a pastor of the First Baptist Church in Montclair, New Jersey. Fosdick remained at that church until 1915, when he became a professor of practical theology at Union Theological Seminary, where he had taught part-time since 1908. He taught students a method of preaching that emphasized personal counseling to a large group. In 1918 Fosdick became a minister at a Presbyterian church. Concerned about fundamentalist influence in the church, in 1922 he preached his famous sermon, "Shall the Fundamentalists Win?" in which he not only criticized fundamentalism but also expressed his own modernist beliefs. In 1923 delegates to the general assembly of the Presbyterian Church approved a resolution asking the New York church to require preaching and teaching that conformed with the denomination's confession of faith, including belief in biblical inerrancy, the virgin birth of Jesus, the physical resurrection, and the second coming of Christ. Unwilling to accept the requirements of the resolution, Fosdick resigned.

In 1931, with the financial assistance of John D. Rockefeller, Jr., Fosdick became the pastor of the newly constructed Riverside Church, which was affiliated with the Northern Baptist Convention. In fact, the church was interdenominational and open to all Christians of all races. Fosdick remained the pastor until his retirement in 1945. During his tenure as pastor, he developed a national radio ministry. Fosdick attempted to steer a course between fundamentalism on one hand and a radicalism that would deny what he considered the basic truths of the Christian faith on the other. He championed various social causes, including civil liberties and civil rights, and invited African Americans to preach from his pulpit. Consistent with his progressive social philosophy, Fosdick advocated birth control and planned parenthood, supporting the work of Margaret Sanger.

Wesley Granberg-Michaelson (b. 1945)

The 1994 General Synod of the Reformed Church in America selected Wesley Granberg-Michaelson as the denomination's general secretary. Granberg-Michaelson graduated from Hope College in 1967 and from Princeton Theological Seminary in 1968. From 1969 to 1975 he worked for Oregon Senator Mark O. Hatfield. While a member of the Church of the Saviour in Washington DC, Granberg-Michaelson became acquainted with the commitment a local congregation can make to social causes and the importance of small groups in the activities of a church. In 1976 Granberg-Michaelson became managing editor of the progressive Christian magazine *Sojourners*, a position he held until 1980. In 1981 he moved with his wife to Missoula, Montana, where he established the New Creation Institute, an organization concerned with the environmental responsibility of Christians as well as the church's role in maintaining the health of individuals. In 1982 he joined the staff of the World Council of Churches (WCC) as executive secretary of the section on Justice, Peace, and Creation, focusing his attention on environmental issues. He decided to complete an education in theology, and graduated from Western Theological Seminary in Holland, Michigan, in 1984. From 1992 to 1994 Granberg-Michaelson served as a staff member of the WCC in Geneva, Switzerland. He worked to solidify relations between the WCC and evangelical groups. In 1994 he accepted the position of general synod secretary of the Reformed Church in America. Among the books that Granberg-Michaelson has authored are *Leadership from Inside Out: Spirituality and Organizational Change*, published in 2004, and *Issues of Christian Conscience: Ecology and Life*, published in 1988.

Granberg-Michaelson has taken public stands on various political issues. For instance, in 1998 he called for President Bill Clinton's resignation, claiming that, due to the president's moral failure stemming from the Monica Lewinsky affair, the nation faced a political crisis. The president, he asserted, had inappropriately segregated personal morality from public responsibility. Among articles that Granberg-Michaelson published in *Sojourners*, "Our Gravest Temptation: Politicians Have Given the President a Military Blank Check" presented an initial reaction to the September 11, 2001, terrorist attacks. While recognizing the enormity of the assault on innocent civilians, Granberg-Michaelson cautioned against allowing the attacks to push the United States into extreme responses that could create more enemies for the nation around the world.

Wilton D. Gregory (b. 1947)

In 2001 Wilton D. Gregory was elected president of the United States Conference of Catholic Bishops (USCCB), thus becoming the first African American to hold that position. Gregory's major challenge as president of the USCCB was the sexual abuse scandal that has rocked the church. He attempted to face the scandal head-on, calling the instances of abuse crimes and apologizing publicly to the victims and the members of the church. Gregory called the sex scandal the worst crisis in the history of the church because it threatened the relationship of trust between church leaders and lay members. On social issues, Gregory has advocated the view that racism is a sin as serious as more generally recognized sins and has declared that Catholics have an obligation to take steps to eliminate racism. He identified racial profiling and white flight from inner-city schools as major social problems. Gregory has written in opposition to euthanasia, physician-assisted suicide, and the death penalty.

Born in Chicago to Protestant parents, Gregory was baptized at age twelve in the Catholic Church. He was educated at Quigley Preparatory Seminary South and Niles College of Loyola in Chicago, and St. Mary of the Lake Seminary in Mundelein, Illinois, where he received a master's degree in pastoral theology in 1973, the same year he was ordained a priest. He served for three years as the priest of a parish in Glenview, Illinois, and then began studies at the Pontifical Liturgical Institute of San Anselmo in Rome, earning a doctorate in sacred liturgy in 1980. Gregory then became a professor at St. Mary of the Lake Seminary. In 1983 Gregory was ordained a bishop, becoming at the time the youngest U.S. Catholic bishop. After serving for ten years as auxiliary bishop under Joseph Cardinal Bernardin in Chicago, he was appointed by Pope John Paul II as bishop of the Belleville, Illinois, Diocese. In 1998 Gregory was elected vice president of the National Conference of Catholics Bishops (now the United States Conference of Catholic Bishops). After three years in this position, he was chosen president of the conference.

Confronting the sexual abuse scandal, Gregory and USCCB Vice President William S. Skylstad met with Vatican officials, including Pope John Paul II, in 2002 to discuss the crisis. Returning to the United States, Gregory met with reporters to answer questions about the widening scandal. He admitted that the church had made mistakes in its handling of the issue. Although Gregory had been told that the Vatican would allow the U.S. Catholic Church to handle the situation, Vatican authorities subsequently called the thirteen U.S. cardinals and conference leaders to Rome for further discussions. At a meeting of the USCCB following the Rome convocation, Gregory targeted the bishops, not the offending priests, for blame because they allowed abusers to remain in the ministry and reassigned them to parishes where they continued to sexually abuse youth. The bishops adopted a zero-tolerance policy, declaring that any priest found to have sexually abused a minor would be expelled from the ministry, and agreed to inform civil authorities of any claim of abuse. However, the Vatican ordered the bishops to revise portions of the policy.

Frank T. Griswold (b. 1938)

In 1997 the General Convention of the Episcopal Church elected Frank Griswold to a nine-year term as presiding bishop. He was invested in the position in January 1998. Early in his tenure as presiding bishop, Griswold advocated ecumenism, supporting full communion with the Evangelical Lutheran Church in America and closer relations with the Catholic Church. However, the dissension within his own denomination led to fears of internal disintegration that tended to overshadow his efforts to achieve external alliances with other denominations. Therefore, the presiding bishop expended much effort attempting to maintain unity among liberal and conservative factions within the denomination. Griswold recommended eliminating nonessential features in the church and concentrating instead on the essential and the enduring.

In addition to serving as primate and chief pastor of the Episcopal Church and as the president of the House of Bishops, Griswold has held other positions within the denomination, including chief executive officer of the Domestic and Foreign Missionary Society. Within the Anglican Communion, Griswold has served as a member of the joint standing committee of the Anglican Primates and the Anglican Consultative Council. He was a member of the standing committee for the 1998 Lambeth Conference. Prior to becoming presiding bishop, Griswold served as bishop coadjutor (1985–1987) and bishop of Chicago (1987–1997). Before being elected a bishop, he served three parishes in Pennsylvania. In 1959 Griswold received a bachelor of arts degree in English literature from Harvard College (known at Harvard as an A.B., or artium baccalaureus, degree). In 1962 he received a bachelor of arts degree in theology at Oriel College, Oxford University, and was awarded a master of arts degree in 1966. He was ordained a priest in the Episcopal Church in 1963. In 2000 Griswold published a brief book, *Going Home: An Invitation to Jubilee*, an application to contemporary society of the Old Testament tradition of release from financial obligation.

With the dissension within the Episcopal Church over the choice of V. Gene Robinson, an openly gay priest, as the bishop of the New Hampshire Diocese, Griswold attempted to present a conciliatory stance, walking a perilous line between liberals who desire recognition of same-gender unions and the ordination of gay priests on the one hand, and on the other conservatives who emphasize biblical passages they claim condemn homosexual activity as sinful. In 2004 he commented that the focus on sexuality issues distracted the denomination's attention away from more serious questions that involve matters of life and death. Griswold's sympathies at times appear to reside with the more liberal elements within the Episcopal Church. For instance, he has commented that while some in the church find divorce and remarriage acceptable—a practice that Jesus condemned—they are not willing to accept the marriage of gays and lesbians—a topic about which Jesus never spoke. Griswold saw some congregations leave the denomination over the issue of homosexuality. In June 2006, at the last general convention for which he would serve as presiding bishop, Griswold, along with Katharine Jefferts Schori, the newly elected presiding bishop, engaged successfully in last-minute efforts to have the convention's House of Deputies and House of Bishops approve a resolution responding to the Anglican Communion's request that the Episcopal Church place a moratorium on the consecration of gay bishops.

Mark S. Hanson (b. 1946)

In 2001 delegates to the Churchwide Assembly of the Evangelical Lutheran Church in America (ELCA) elected Mark S. Hanson the denomination's presiding bishop, and in 2003 Hanson was elected president of the Lutheran World Federation. He also serves on the executive council of the National Council of Churches of Christ in the U.S.A. (NCC). Hanson received a bachelor's degree in sociology from Augsburg College in 1968, and in 1969 he became a Rockefeller fellow at the Union Theological Seminary in New York—a non-Lutheran school—where he received a master of divinity degree in 1972. After his ordination in 1974, Hanson served as pastor at Prince of Glory Lutheran Church in Minneapolis. In 1979 he moved to Edina Community Lutheran Church in Edina, Minnesota, and in 1988 he assumed the pastorate at University Lutheran Church in Hope, Minnesota. In 1995 Hanson was elected bishop of the Saint Paul Area Synod of the ELCA, and in 1998 he was chosen president of the Minnesota Council of Churches, serving in that position until 2000. Hanson authored *Faithful Yet Changing: The Church in Challenging Times*, published by the ELCA publishing house, Augsburg Fortress Books. In the book, Hanson dealt with such topics as prayer, love, social justice, and witnessing to the Christian faith.

Hanson has supported ecumenical efforts, including discussions with the Catholic Church that led to the Joint Declaration on the Doctrine of Justification, an agreement signed in October 1999 by representatives of the Lutheran World Federation and the Catholic Church. He has expressed his enthusiasm for further discussions between Lutherans and Catholics and has suggested that the 500th anniversary in 2017 of the Lutheran Reformation should be an occasion for further reconciliation between Lutherans and Catholics. However, Hanson has faced dissension within the denomination over the Churchwide Assembly's approval in 1999 of the agreement with the Episcopal Church, "Called to Common Mission," that established full communion between the two denominations. Objecting to the agreement, some pastors and lay members established the Word Alone Network, which has continued to increase in membership as other issues, most notably questions of sexuality, have arisen. Hanson defended the agreement with the Episcopal Church against charges that it was a deception perpetrated by the Lutheran Church hierarchy, noting that two drafts of the agreement had been circulated among congregations for study and discussion, and that nearly 70 percent of voting members of the Churchwide Assembly approved "Called to Common Mission." Some Lutheran congregations have left the ELCA and joined an alternative group called Lutheran Congregations in Mission for Christ. A major reason for disassociation with the ELCA has been objections to proposals to allow for the ordination of openly gay pastors.

For many years Hanson has been active in pursuing such issues as racial justice, welfare rights, immigration rights, and housing for the poor. He also has expressed his concern for the environment, warning against the possibility of "ecocide," the destruction of a livable environment. An antiwar activist during his student days at the Union Theological Seminary, Hanson has continued his critical stance toward U.S. military involvement around the world. In March 2003, in a letter to denomination members, although noting strong disagreements among Lutherans over involvement in Iraq, Hanson expressed deep concern about the Bush administration's decision to initiate preemptive military action. Hanson stated that the United States, because of its wealth and power, has the responsibility to pursue policies that will lead to the peaceful resolution of conflicts. In 2006 Hanson joined with other denomination leaders in urging the Bush administration to take a more active role in bringing peace to the Middle East.

Katharine Jefferts Schori (1954–)

In June 2006 delegates to the seventy-fifth General Convention of the Episcopal Church elected Katharine Jefferts Schori to be the denomination's presiding bishop. Jefferts Schori's tenure as presiding bishop promises to be as trying as her predecessor's, Frank T. Griswold. Although liberal church members applauded her election, more conservative factions within the denomination expressed their objection to the choice. For instance, Bishop Jack Iker of Fort Worth, Texas, stated that the election amounted to a "gesture of defiance" and would contribute to the movement toward division and separation. Jefferts Schori's election indicated to many that the disagreement within the Episcopal Church over the election of V. Gene Robinson, an openly gay bishop, and the question of same-gender unions would continue to divide the denomination. In 2003 Jefferts Schori voted in favor of Robinson's ordination, explaining that the General Convention should accept the decision of the members of the New Hampshire diocese who knew of Robinson's thirteen-year relationship with another man but did not regard it as grounds for disqualification. Jefferts Schori also supports the blessing of same-gender unions. She has stated that, as a woman who entered a traditionally male occupation, she identifies with those whom many consider on the margins of society.

Born in Pensacola, Florida, Jefferts Schori graduated from high school in New Jersey and received a bachelor of science degree in biology from Stanford University in 1974. She studied oceanography at Oregon State University, receiving a master of science degree in 1977 and a doctorate in 1983. After working for the National Marine Fisheries Service in Seattle, Jefferts Schori moved to Corvallis, Oregon, with her husband. At the urging of fellow church members at the Episcopal Church of the Good Samaritan in Corvallis, she decided to enter seminary studies and received a master of divinity degree from Church Divinity School of the Pacific in Berkeley, California, in 1994 and a doctor of divinity degree in 2001. She was ordained a priest in 1994. Following ordination, Jefferts Schori served for six years as assistant rector of the Episcopal Church of the Good Samaritan in Corvallis. In 2001 she became the bishop of the Episcopal Diocese of Nevada, where she actively pursued ecological issues related to past nuclear testing, the mining industry, and water quality.

In 2004 Jefferts Schori supported immigration reform, urging the two U.S. senators from Nevada to back fair reform measures. Referring to the Judeo-Christian tradition of caring for the stranger and to the nation's long history of immigration, she advocated legislation that would permit increased numbers of workers to enter the United States legally and allow them to achieve permanent residence status and ultimately citizenship. Jefferts Schori also urged a policy that would allow those already in the country to move toward citizenship. In 2005, expressing her concern for the less advantaged, Jefferts Schori appealed to the senators and members of the U.S. House of Representatives from Nevada to oppose the fiscal year 2006 Federal Budget Reconciliation Act. She argued that budget cuts for food stamps, Medicaid, child care, and children's health programs would harm the most vulnerable in American society.

Elizabeth A. Johnson (b. 1941)

An exponent of feminist theology and of new understandings of the traditional Catholic faith, Elizabeth Johnson is a professor of theology at Fordham University and a nun in the order of the Sisters of St. Joseph. Johnson has argued that the Bible and other Christian writings support the use of feminine as well as masculine language to describe God. Her theological writings question patriarchal ways of understanding God and the world and promote new religious perspectives based on the experiences of women.

Johnson was born in Brooklyn, New York, and became a nun in 1959. In 1964 she received a bachelor of arts degree in the classics from Brentwood College on Long Island, and in 1970 she completed a master's degree in theology at Manhattan College in the Bronx. In 1981 Johnson received a doctorate in theology from Catholic University of America in Washington DC, and from 1981 until 1991 she taught theology at Catholic University, after which she moved to Fordham University's Bronx campus. In 1990 Johnson published *Consider Jesus: Waves of Renewal in Christology*, in which she examined twentieth-century Catholic thought on Christ. In 1992 Johnson published *She Who Is*, in which she proposed a feminist theology, reinterpreting the doctrine of the Trinity in terms of the feminine Sophia (wisdom). Johnson initiated the discussion with the "Spirit-Sophia" of the Trinity rather than the Father, thus avoiding what she considered the traditional patriarchal, and thus finite, understanding of God. She argued that to speak of God in purely masculine terms implies that the masculine is preferable to the feminine. Fundamental to Johnson's discussion is the observation that the Catholic Church, in order to survive, must change with evolving societal conceptions of gender. Without such change, she claimed, social reality will move beyond the church.

In a 1993 lecture, "Women, Earth, and Creator Spirit," presented at Saint Mary's College in Notre Dame, Indiana, Johnson suggested correlations between the exploitation of natural resources and the exploitation of women. In 1996, in "Does God Play Dice? Divine Providence and Chance," published in *Theological Studies*, she investigated the relationship between the role of chance, which natural science affirms, and the Christian view of a providential God. Johnson attempted to preserve the individual as an autonomous creature acting within a divinely established structure that allows for unpredictable, random, natural processes to operate toward a divine end. She concluded that God uses chance in the working of his providence.

In 1998 Johnson published *Friends of God and Prophets: A Feminist Theological Reading of the Communion of Saints*, in which she criticized the traditional doctrine of the communion of saints, labeling it hierarchical and patriarchal, consisting of a group of primarily male intercessors between a masculine God and people on earth. Reinterpreting the doctrine, Johnson posited a community structure, based on feminine experience, that includes the living and the dead who together interact with God. The symbol of the communion of saints, Johnson claimed, should support women's efforts to achieve equal dignity and to assist the church in becoming a true community of equally valued "friends of God and prophets."

Barry W. Lynn (b. 1948)

An ordained minister in the United Church of Christ (UCC), Barry Lynn has served as the executive director of Americans United for Separation of Church and State (AU) since 1992. Lynn has gained wide recognition as a strong opponent of official religious involvement in the public sphere. On issues such as the display of the Ten Commandments, the words "under God" in the pledge of allegiance, and the teaching of intelligent design in the public schools as an alternative to the theory of evolution, Lynn is a vocal proponent of the wall of separation doctrine, advocating the removal of religious influence from government policy. According to Lynn, religious organizations have the right under the U.S. Constitution to practice their religious beliefs but do not have the right to impose those religious beliefs on others through official public policy. While Lynn has not served as a minister of a congregation for an extended period, he maintains his ministerial position within the UCC. This official status undoubtedly grants greater credibility to his pronouncements on church-state relations.

Born in Harrisburg, Pennsylvania, Lynn received a bachelor of arts degree from Dickinson College in 1970 and a master of theology degree from Boston University in 1973. From 1971 to 1974 he taught in the religious studies department of Cardinal Cushing Central High School in South Boston, Massachusetts, after which he served as the director of the To Heal a Nation program of the United Church of Christ. After receiving a doctor of laws degree from Georgetown University in 1978, Lynn served for two years as legislative counsel for the UCC's Office of Church and Society in Washington DC. From 1984 to 1991 he worked as legislative counsel for the American Civil Liberties Union (ACLU). While working with the ACLU, Lynn cowrote the organization's policy on church-state relations and led opposition to the 1986 Meese commission report on pornography.

In 1992 Lynn accepted the position of executive director of Americans United for Separation of Church and State, an organization established in 1947 to oppose state funding of religious schools. Although AU had fallen on hard times, Lynn used his contacts with the ACLU and his fund-raising abilities to revive the organization. AU had a staff of ten when Lynn arrived, but ultimately that number increased to thirty-five as the annual budget exceeded $4 million. In 1995 Lynn coauthored *Your Right to Religious Liberty: A Basic Guide to Religious Rights*, in which the authors discussed such topics as government aid to religious organizations, religion and public education, the role of chaplains in the military, conscientious objection, religion in the workplace, religious displays in public places, and "deprogramming" adherents to religious cults.

Lynn is a major media figure, appearing on such news programs as *Larry King Live*; *Meet the Press*; *CBS Morning News*; *Fox Morning News*; and the ABC, CBS, and NBC evening news programs. He also has written opinion pieces for newspapers and news magazines, including *USA Today*, the *Wall Street Journal*, and *The Nation*. Critics claim that Lynn is trying to remove Christianity from the public sphere, thus allowing Christians fewer rights than other people. However, Lynn argues that the U.S. religious tradition constituted in the First Amendment provides for a strict separation of religious practice from secular public policy and hence establishes a prohibition on coercive state-sponsored religious observance of any kind. In addition to the constitutional issue, Lynn claims that separation of church and state has practical implications. He holds that past attempts to impose religious observance in the public schools led to social unrest and violence. Lynn opposes voucher systems for education, claiming that this type of government involvement in religion creates competition among religious denominations for government favors. Although Lynn opposes government involvement on social and religious questions, he tends to take liberal positions on other issues regarding government action, rejecting the libertarian position on economic and social questions such as assistance to the less advantaged. He dismisses the basic doctrine of individualism, adhering instead to a belief in communal responsibility. Lynn has expressed concern for the rise during recent decades of the religious right, and in 2006 he published *Piety and Politics: The Right-Wing Assault on Reli-*

gious Freedom, in which he identifies the religious right as a major threat to First Amendment freedoms.

Roger Michael Mahoney (b. 1936)

Appointed archbishop of Los Angeles in 1985 by Pope John Paul II, Roger Mahoney has championed the cause of the less fortunate, especially Hispanics. Mahoney was born in Hollywood, California, and spent his early years in the San Fernando Valley. He attended St. John's Seminary in Camarillo and was ordained a priest in 1962. Two years later Mahoney received a master of arts degree in social work from Catholic University of America in Washington DC. He returned to California to become the diocesan director of Catholic Charities and Social Services as well as a faculty member at Coalinga College in Fresno. He began his ministry with Hispanic people by joining the Administrative Council of the Episcopal Committee for Hispanics and helping organize a committee for farm workers. Mahoney worked in cooperation with farm worker organizer Cesar Chavez. In 1975 Pope Paul VI appointed Mahoney auxiliary bishop of Fresno and titular bishop of Tamascani. In 1980 Pope John Paul II named Mahoney bishop of the Diocese of Stockton. That same year, Governor Jerry Brown appointed Mahoney the first chairperson of the California Agricultural Labor Relations Board, which became involved in resolving labor disputes between the United Farm Workers Union and growers. Upon the retirement of Cardinal Manning in 1985, the pontiff appointed Mahoney the new archbishop of Los Angeles, an archdiocese of 4 million Catholics in Santa Barbara, Ventura, and Los Angeles counties. In 1991 Mahoney was granted the title of cardinal.

Mahoney is generally considered one of the more liberal spokespersons for American Catholicism, supporting change within the church as well as progressive causes in society. He has been active in the larger community, serving on the Blue Ribbon Committee for Affordable Housing Los Angeles and the Federal Commission on Agricultural Workers. Following the riots resulting from the acquittal of police officers accused of the Rodney King beating in 1992, he was appointed to the Rebuild L.A.

Commission. He served on several commissions established by the Catholic bishops, including the Committee on Farm Labor, the Committee on Migration and Refugees, and the Committee on Pro-Life Activities, which deals with such issues as abortion, physician-assisted suicide, and capital punishment. Mahoney also has expressed his concern over violence in the United States. For instance, following the shooting at Columbine High School in Littleton, Colorado, in 1999, he referred to the various possible causes, including the breakdown of the family, the collapse of a sense of community, the loss of respect for life, the portrayal of violent acts in the media, and the ready availability of firearms and other weapons.

Mahoney's archdiocese has been involved in the sexual abuse scandal that shook the Catholic Church in the United States. In October 2005 the church released documents revealing that Mahoney had participated in the transfer from parish to parish of more than one hundred priests in his archdiocese who had been accused of the sexual abuse of young people. More recently Mahoney has become personally involved with the controversial issue of immigration. He has supported the legalization of undocumented immigrants and the establishment of guest-worker programs. Following the U.S. House of Representatives' passage of a strict immigration bill, Mahoney declared that anti-immigration feelings in the United States were the result of hysteria and he called the legislation inhumane. In March 2006 he stated that if the bill became law, priests in his diocese were to ignore its provisions. Some more conservative Catholics have distanced themselves from Mahoney's activist stance on immigration, especially his call for disobeying the law. For instance, William F. Buckley, Jr., suggested that the United States Conference of Catholic Bishops should rebuke Cardinal Mahoney's call for disobeying the law despite his humanitarian motives. Calling the writing of law a democratic exercise, Buckley declared that Mahoney was in the wrong for showing contempt for authority in a democratic community.

Martin E. Marty (b. 1928)

For fifty years Martin Marty has contributed to the understanding of the place of religion in American public life. Distinguished professor emeritus at the University of Chicago—where he taught for thirty-five years—and an ordained Lutheran pastor, Marty has written or edited more than fifty books on the history of religion and the contemporary significance of the religious experience of Americans. Marty served as the book review editor and was successively the contributing, associate, and ultimately senior editor of *Christian Century*, an influential mainline Protestant magazine. He continues to write the column M.E.M.O. for the magazine.

Born in West Point, Nebraska, Marty moved to Milwaukee, Wisconsin, when he was a teenager and attended Concordia University and Washington University. Marty received a master of divinity degree from Concordia Seminary and a master of sacred theology degree from the Lutheran School of Theology in Chicago. He went on to complete the doctorate in American religious and intellectual history from the University of Chicago. Ordained in 1952, Marty served as an assistant Lutheran pastor in River Forest, Illinois, from 1952 to 1956 and as a pastor in Elk Grove Village, Illinois, from 1956 to 1963, when he joined the faculty of the University of Chicago as professor of the history of modern Christianity. As a result of conflicts within the Lutheran Church–Missouri Synod in the 1970s, Marty left that denomination. In 1998 Marty became the Fairfax M. Cone Distinguished Service Professor Emeritus at the University of Chicago, and the university's Institute for the Advanced Study of Religion, which he founded and directed, was renamed the Martin Marty Center.

Marty has written an impressive series of books on the history of religion in the United States. In *Righteous Empire: The Protestant Experience in America*, published in 1970, Marty recounted the development of Protestant denominations and the influence that Protestants have had on the shaping of American values and beliefs as well as their impact on national events. His many other works include *Pilgrims in Their Own Land: Five Hundred Years of Religion in America*, published in 1984, which presents a history of American religious experience that contains accounts of many individuals who played prominent roles in religion. Beginning in 1987 Marty directed the seven-year Fundamentalism Project of the American Academy of Arts and Sciences and coauthored five volumes resulting from the research. From 1996 to 1999 he directed the Public Religion Project, funded by the Pew Charitable Trusts. In one volume resulting from this study, *Politics, Religion and the Common Good*, Marty examined the role religion plays in American public life. Although religion can be a divisive force, Marty argued that religious convictions can play many positive roles, including providing strength during a crisis, demonstrating an alternative to exaggerated individualism, and encouraging people to be politically active.

Some have criticized Marty for not taking stronger stands on such contemporary issues as abortion, sexuality, and U.S. foreign policy, particularly faulting him for failing to take up such issues in his *Christian Century* column. Nonetheless, throughout his career as a teacher and a scholar, Marty has been a model for the mainline denominations, presenting moderate views on the subjects he engages. As a historian, he has attempted to present the progression of various strains in the nation's religious history, recognizing the pluralistic nature of that development. Although formally retired, Marty has continued an active speaking agenda and, especially after the terrorist attacks of September 11, 2001, is often asked to help his audiences achieve a better understanding of Islam.

A. Roy Medley (b. 1948)

During his tenure as general secretary of the American Baptist Churches in the U.S.A. (ABC), A. Roy Medley has faced severe challenges to the unity of the denomination, which has lost members and financial support attributed to controversy over church policy regarding homosexuality. Born in Ringgold, Georgia, Medley received a bachelor of arts degree in psychology from the University of Chattanooga and a master of divinity degree from Princeton Theological Seminary. In 1972 and 1973 he attended the Ecumenical Institute of the World Council of Churches in Bossey, Switzerland. Early in his career Medley became associate pastor at First Baptist Church in Trenton, New Jersey, where he stayed from 1974 to 1977. He was ordained a Baptist minister in 1975. In 1977 and 1978 he served as interim pastor at Christ Congregation in Princeton, New Jersey. After this experience as a local pastor, Medley entered church administration, becoming the administrative assistant to the manager of American Baptist National Ministries' Operations and Program Resource Unit. From 1978 to 1985 he served as a member of the National Council of Churches of Christ working group on hunger and poverty and the Ecumenical

Development Cooperative Fund of the World Council of Churches, and became the director of the Neighborhood Action Program of American Baptist National Ministries. He was responsible for various programs, including development and recruitment.

In 1986 Medley became an area minister and minister of Mission Support for the ABC of New Jersey, one of the thirty-four regions within the denomination, where he was responsible for stewardship education and fund-raising. As area minister, Medley focused on such activities as pastoral recruitment and conflict management. In 1992 Medley became the executive minister for New Jersey. He emphasized renewing older congregations, developing new churches, and attracting minorities to the denomination. In 2001 the ABC General Board confirmed Medley as the denomination's new general secretary. As general secretary, Medley, along with the General Ministries office, has such responsibilities as executing the policies that the General Board determines, maintaining relations with other denominations, raising and administering funds to support the mission budget, managing the denomination's communication media, maintaining records, and scheduling the denomination's biennial meetings.

Medley has joined with the leadership of other denominations in attempting to influence public policy. In January 2005 Medley, along with fifty-six other denomination leaders, signed a letter addressed to President George W. Bush that was published in the *New York Times*. The letter urged the president to use his leadership to end the Israeli-Palestinian conflict and stated that bringing peace to Jerusalem is crucial to a defense strategy to combat terrorism. In September 2005 Medley met with leaders of the Interfaith Convocation on Hunger at the National Cathedral in Washington DC. The group issued a letter to members of Congress and the president, urging them to remain committed to the goal of eliminating hunger. The group asked that national leaders prevent budget cuts to the national food stamp program.

At the same time that Medley engaged in ecumenical activities to improve ties with other denominations, he faced the prospect of deep divisions within the ABC. At the 2005 denominational meeting, the delegates passed a resolution affirming a policy that allows congregations to join another geographical region or association of the ABC if the congregation and the region mutually agree to the move. The resolution was an attempt to deal with disagreements that arose in regional organizations over congregations that had established a welcoming policy toward gays and lesbians. Commenting on the question, Medley stated that although he was "still traditional" regarding issues of human sexuality, he did not wish to separate himself from those who held differing views on homosexuality, a position he called a "paradox." He noted that the ABC was established on the principle of regional and local autonomy, and therefore the General Board or general secretary could not usurp the rights of local congregations. Thus, the national organization could not require regional and local church organizations to abide by a resolution passed in 1992 opposing homosexual conduct.

In September 2005 the executive committee of the American Baptist Churches of the Pacific Southwest decided to initiate the process of withdrawing from the denomination. In October, Medley announced that the denomination was closing its communications department as part of a budget cut resulting from declining funds. Despite his concern over the ABC Pacific Southwest's intention to leave the denomination, Medley stated that speculation about the demise of the ABC was unfounded and that the denomination was moving ahead with establishing closer relationships with other Baptist groups. In April 2006 the members of the ABC Pacific Southwest voted to continue the process of ending the regional organization's relationship with the ABCUSA.

Reinhold Niebuhr (1892–1971)

Reinhold Niebuhr's political activism rivaled his theological work in contributing to his prominence as a major figure in mainline Christianity. In his early years, Niebuhr adhered to a liberal and even socialist political ideology, but ultimately offered an alternative to the optimistic premises of the Social Gospel movement as well as to the more conservative elements within mainline Christianity of the twentieth century. Today, many of the positions that Niebuhr voiced can be detected in the theological and social stands that the mainline denominations have taken. Born in Wright City, Missouri, the son of a German Evangelical pastor, Niebuhr decided to follow in his father's vocation. He graduated from Elmhurst College, the proseminary of the German Evangelical Synod, in 1910. Niebuhr then attended Eden Seminary in St. Louis, Missouri, where he received a bachelor of divinity degree and was ordained a pastor in 1913. He went on to study at Yale University, where in 1914 he earned another bachelor of divinity degree, and the following year he received a master of arts degree. While at Yale, Niebuhr was strongly influenced by liberal Protestantism.

Although the Yale faculty encouraged him to complete a doctorate, he decided to gain practical experience as a minister. He went to Detroit to serve as pastor of the Bethel Evangelical Church, a small congregation of less than a hundred members. As the automobile industry grew, so did the size of the congregation, reaching nearly 700 members by the time he left in 1928. While in Detroit, Niebuhr sided with the workers against Henry Ford, criticizing the working conditions in the automobile plants and allowing union organizers to speak at his church. The First World War and the cynical aftermath for which the victors were responsible led Niebuhr to embrace pacifist views. In 1922 he joined the Fellowship for a Christian Social Order and a year later became the organization's traveling secretary, giving lectures in the eastern and midwestern states. In 1925 Niebuhr became involved in the Detroit mayoral race, opposing a Protestant candidate who had accepted support from the Ku Klux Klan. The winning candidate, a Catholic, appointed Niebuhr to chair an interracial committee to investigate race relations in the city. In 1928 Niebuhr left Detroit to become a professor of practical theology at Union Theological Seminary in New York City.

Niebuhr's political experience convinced him that the liberal belief in reason and the basic goodness of human beings was flawed. He joined the Socialist party and became editor of the socialist publication *World Tomorrow*. In 1930 Niebuhr entered politics more directly by running as the Socialist candidate for the New York state senate, but received less than 5 percent of the vote. In 1932 he entered the political waters once more, running for a seat in the U.S. House of Representatives, but did no better. He remained a socialist during the 1930s, but no longer took an active role in politics. Soon after the 1932 election, Niebuhr published *Moral Man and Immoral Society*, in which he concluded that although love may guide individuals, for groups of individuals, justice must be the overriding consideration. Current events, he observed, demonstrated that the notion of original sin, so objectionable to humanists, influenced much of human action.

With the onset of the Second World War, Niebuhr altered his pacifist stance and became a strong advocate of the struggle against Nazism, which he concluded should take precedence over the class struggle. In 1940 Niebuhr left the Socialist party, and in 1941 he founded the publication *Christianity and Crisis*. He became the chair of the Union for Democratic Action, which in 1947 became Americans for Democratic Action. During the Second World War, Niebuhr was one of a few who expressed concern for the fate of Jews in Europe. In 1944 he published *The Children of Light and the Children of Darkness*, in which he defended democracy as the governing system that promoted equality and coincided most closely with Christian doctrine. Also in 1944 Niebuhr took part in the creation of the Liberal party of New York. Following the Second World War, Niebuhr remained active in public life. In 1948 he took part in the creation of the World Council of Churches, an association supported by mainline denominations. In 1949 he served as a delegate to the United Nations Educational, Scientific and Cultural Association conference in Paris. As Senator Joseph R. McCarthy increased his attacks on alleged Communists in the U.S. government, Niebuhr claimed that the senator in fact hampered the fight against communism. Observing the rise of evangelist Billy Graham, Niebuhr expressed his displeasure at the increase in religious fundamentalism in the United States. In 1964 President Lyndon Johnson presented the Medal of Freedom to Niebuhr. However, as Johnson increased U.S. military operations in Vietnam, Niebuhr became a vocal critic of the war. He also came to oppose nuclear deterrence, a policy that he previously had supported.

Sean Patrick O'Malley (b. 1944)

Six months after Bernard Cardinal Law's resignation in December 2002 as archbishop of Boston due to the sexual abuse scandal, Pope John Paul II appointed Sean Patrick O'Malley to lead the diocese through the crisis. O'Malley already had experience handling abuse cases when he served as archbishop of the Fall River, Massachusetts, diocese. After a priest had been accused of molesting more than 100 children, O'Malley reached settlements with victims, imposed a zero-tolerance policy regarding priests found to have abused minors, and instituted abuse-education classes. In 2002, as archbishop of the Palm Beach, Florida, diocese, he dealt again with allegations of sexual abuse. Two bishops before him had left due to sexual abuse charges. O'Malley promised to remove all priests who were guilty of sexual abuse and to report all abuse claims to civil authorities.

O'Malley was born in Lakewood, Ohio, and was raised in Herman, Pennsylvania, where he entered the St. Fidelis Seminary, a boarding school for those intending to enter the Capuchin order. The school specialized in languages, and O'Malley received training in Latin, German, Spanish, Greek, and Hebrew. In 1965, at the age of twenty-one, O'Malley joined the Capuchin-Franciscan order, which follows the teachings of St. Francis of Assisi, the thirteenth-century monk who led a life of poverty and devotion. In 1970 he was ordained a priest. O'Malley attended Capuchin College in Washington DC, and earned a master of arts degree in religious education and subsequently received a doctorate in Spanish and Portuguese literature from Catholic University, where he taught from 1969 to 1973. O'Malley became involved in social causes, including participation in the Catholic Church's annual rally in Washington DC against abortion and calling for a commitment to assisting those in poverty. When asked to take part in a ministry to the Latino population of Washington, O'Malley established Centro Catolico Hispano, which provided various services to the Hispanic population, including legal advice and instruction in English as well as employment, medical, and dental assistance. Engaging in social activism, O'Malley assisted tenants in a dilapidated tenement owned by Antioch Law School. He moved into the tenement, helped the residents to make improvements to the building, and guided them in establishing a cooperative that ultimately purchased the building.

In 1978 O'Malley became executive director of the Office of Social Ministry within the diocese, and in 1984 the Vatican appointed him coadjutor bishop of St. Thomas, the U.S. Virgin Islands. The following year he became bishop. While bishop, O'Malley established a hospice for AIDS patients and built living quarters for the homeless. Even after becoming the archbishop of Boston, O'Malley maintained a humble lifestyle, refusing to move into the archbishop's mansion, living instead in a small apartment.

Upon assuming the position of archbishop of Boston, O'Malley quickly replaced the church's lead counsel who had been handling the civil lawsuits against the diocese, and hired the attorney with whom he had worked in settling abuse charges in Fall River. Approximately one month after O'Malley came to Boston, the archdiocese reached a settlement with 550 people who claimed they had been sexually abused by officials in the church. The total cost of the settlement was $85 million. In addition to the monetary settlement, the church offered victims mental-health counseling. With regard to the abortion issue, O'Malley commented in 2004 that if politicians fail to vote "correctly" on issues such as abortion, they should not present themselves for communion in the Catholic Church. O'Malley also has taken a public stand regarding the issue of marriage and homosexuality. He objected to any proposal before the Massachusetts legislature that would link a definition of marriage as a union between one man and one woman with the legal recognition of same-gender civil unions, fearing that those who support the marriage definition would be coerced into accepting something they otherwise opposed.

Norman Vincent Peale (1898–1993)

Best known as the advocate of the doctrine of positive thinking and as an exponent of the small-town values of the nineteenth century in an increasingly urbanized society, Norman Vincent Peale had a profound effect on mainline Christian thinking during much of the twentieth century. Peale's father, originally a physician, became a Methodist minister who moved frequently from congregation to congregation. At the time of Norman's birth, his father was serving a church in Bowersville, Ohio. Peale graduated from high school in Bellefontaine, Ohio, and attended Ohio Wesleyan University, graduating in 1920. He initially worked as a journalist, but in 1921 he entered Boston University's school of theology, a Methodist school, and was ordained a Methodist minister in 1922. Beginning with his first congregation, King's Highway Methodist Church in Brooklyn, New York, Peale used sales techniques, including personal visits to the growing neighborhood and postcard mailings, to attract new members. In 1927 Peale moved to University Methodist Church in Syracuse, New York, and employed the same strategy to attract people to the church. In 1932 Peale changed his affiliation to the Reformed Church in America and became the minister of Marble Collegiate Church in Manhattan, a position he held for fifty-two years. His simple style of preaching, laced with stories taken from his personal experiences, attracted people to the church, and membership grew from 600 to more than 5,000.

In 1932 Peale was asked to broadcast a radio program, "The Art of Living," for the Federal Council of Churches. The program remained on the air for forty years, with a broadcast of Peale's Sunday sermons added in later years. Requests for printed copies of his sermons led to the establishment of the Foundation for Christian Living, located in Pawling, New York, to print and mail literature. In 1945 Peale, along with his wife and a Pawling businessman, founded *Guideposts*, a magazine containing Peale's inspirational stories. The magazine ultimately achieved a circulation of more than one million copies. Peale became a popular speaker, scheduling engagements around the country. In 1947 Peale, along with Kenneth Beebe, founded the Horatio Alger Association, which recognized those who had overcome difficult circumstances to achieve success.

In two books, *The Art of Living* (1947) and *A Guide to Confident Living* (1948), Peale used anecdotes to present principles for living a successful and happy life. In 1952 he published his most well-known book, *The Power of Positive Thinking*. Although originally he had titled the manuscript "The Power of Faith," his publisher suggested a title that would attract nonchurch members. In this and other writings, Peale emphasized the attainment of power from Christ in order to achieve success and happiness. He recommended basic principles of rational living that, if followed, would result in self-fulfillment and happiness, and illustrated these simple rules of living with personal stories. He maintained that prayer could be effective in assisting people in living their everyday lives and that churches must offer their members practical lessons to help them achieve success and happiness. Many criticized Peale's practical advice to achieve success, claiming that he had distorted the original Gospel message. They claimed that Peale presented a strategy that involved believing in oneself rather than in God. Others criticized Peale, who had opposed the New Deal programs of President Franklin Roosevelt in addition to socialism and communism, for his conservative political message and his friendships with conservative politicians. Peale was viewed as the conformist, asking his listeners to adjust themselves to a changing America in terms of a nineteenth-century sense of self-mastery rather than confronting serious social problems.

George F. Regas (b. 1930)

Those wishing to respond to the political challenge of the religious right look to liberal religious figures such as George F. Regas for inspiration. Rector of All Saints Episcopal Church in Pasadena, California, for twenty-eight years, Regas guided his congregation toward a liberal and activist stance on contemporary public policy issues. He constantly emphasized the themes of peace and justice. Regas retired from his position at All Saints in 1995, and three years later he became executive director of the Regas Institute, an organization dedicated to the study of progressive religion and to countering the influence of conservative Christian groups on public policy issues. Collaborating with the liberal group People for the American Way, Regas established the Progressive Religious Partnership, an organization of Christian, Jewish, Muslim, and Buddhist religious leaders that presents a progressive religious perspective on issues of justice in the areas of economics, race, and gender as well war prevention and the maintenance of a just peace.

Regas attended the Episcopal Divinity School in Cambridge, Massachusetts, and Cambridge University, and received his doctorate from Claremont School of Theology in Claremont, California. He became rector of All Saints Church in Pasadena in 1967. In 1970, during the U.S. government's bombing campaign against Cambodia, Regas spoke publicly against U.S. involvement in Vietnam, delivering a sermon titled "Mr. President, the Jury Is In." He criticized President Richard Nixon's war policies and proposed that the church support the establishment of a Peace Operation Center to oppose the war. Because of his outspoken comments, conservative members of his congregation attempted to have Regas removed. However, Regas stayed at the church, and All Saints ultimately became a major center for liberal political activism in the Los Angeles area. The church established the Center to Reverse the Arms Race, and during Ronald Reagan's presidency All Saints sent representatives to Central America to express opposition to U.S. Latin American policy.

In 1990, when the George H. W. Bush administration was planning the Gulf War, Regas spoke from his pulpit on Christmas Eve against U.S. military involvement. Following the terrorist attacks of September 11, 2001, Regas opposed U.S. military action against Afghanistan. In 2002, as the George W. Bush administration prepared for the invasion of Iraq, Regas, as the representative of the Progressive Religious Partnership, declared that preemptive action against Iraq, which he concluded would cost thousands of lives and billions of dollars and could encourage additional acts of terrorism, would violate the moral foundations of the nation. Regas, along with other members of the organization's executive committee, met with the leadership of the U.S. Senate to express his concern for the Bush administration's preparations for unilateral military action. Regas has proposed an alternative to both pacifism and just-war theory, which emphasizes conflict resolution processes and the investigation of the causes of conflict.

During Regas's tenure at All Saints, the church established such programs as an AIDS Service Center, medical assistance for uninsured children, homeless shelters, and the Coalition for a Non-Violent City. Regas supported the blessing of same-gender unions, and in 1991 the church began the practice of blessing such unions. In 2000 Regas responded to more conservative Christians regarding homosexuality, claiming that for those writing the Bible, homosexuality did not represent a major issue. He observed that both liberals and conservatives tend to be selective when interpreting scripture. For instance, those who profess to be biblical literalists are in fact selective literalists; they emphasize the antihomosexual pronouncements in the Old Testament Book of Leviticus, but ignore such rules as stoning an adulterer and not eating pork and the acceptance of slavery. Regas recognizes the Bible as the foundational document of Christian churches, but taking the Bible seriously involves taking into account what has been learned in the many years since the books of the Bible were written. For Regas, the real difficulty involves not attempting to place homosexuality into the context of biblical passages that condemn it, but to contrast the prejudice practiced against homosexuals with what the Gospels say about Christ's gracious love.

Robert H. Schuller (b. 1926)

Many people in the United States and around the world know Robert H. Schuller as the televangelist who broadcasts from the Crystal Cathedral, the 10,000-member megachurch in Garden Grove, California. The church has a $72 million budget, employs approximately 500 people, and broadcasts television programs to millions of viewers around the world. Schuller disseminates a positive religious message called "possibility thinking." His church is the most well-known congregation within the Reformed Church in America (RCA), although most of those who have viewed Schuller's church service on television undoubtedly are not aware of the Crystal Cathedral's affiliation with this mainline denomination that has no more than 300,000 members nationwide. A focus for criticism of Schuller, and possibly an ingredient in his great success, is that he does not speak out on major contemporary issues such as race and homosexuality.

Schuller was born in Alton, Iowa, to Dutch-American parents who adhered to the Dutch Reformed tradition. After graduating from high school in 1943, Schuller attended Hope College in Holland, Michigan, a small liberal arts college affiliated with the RCA. After receiving a bachelor of arts degree, Schuller enrolled at Western Theological Seminary, an RCA institution also located in Holland. In 1950 he received a master of divinity degree and became the pastor of the Ivanhoe Reformed Church in Riverdale, Illinois. During his tenure at the church, the congregation grew from forty to four hundred members.

In 1955 RCA leaders asked Schuller to establish a new congregation in Garden Grove, California. With few RCA members in the area, Schuller dropped the denominational affiliation from the church name, calling it the Garden Grove Community Church. With few assets to begin a church, he rented a local drive-in theater, where he preached from the refreshment stand roof and his wife Arvella played a portable organ. Attending a worship service in automobiles became so popular that when in 1961 Schuller built a church structure, he provided members the option of coming into the church or staying in their cars. In 1968 Schuller established New Hope, a twenty-four-hour counseling and suicide prevention telephone service. In 1970 the church opened the Robert H. Schuller Institute for Successful Church Leadership, which held four-day conferences at which Schuller presented practical advice to pastors and lay leaders. Rick Warren, the popular author of *The Purpose-Driven Church* (1995) and *The Purpose-Driven Life* (2002), attended the institute. Also in 1970, Schuller began a television ministry. Originally telecast on the West Coast, the "Hour of Power" program soon expanded to more than 150 stations. Influenced by Norman Vincent Peale, also a Reformed Church pastor, Schuller emphasized a positive message, calling on people to shed negative self-images and to develop self-esteem, which he considered a fundamental human need. Possibility thinking involves eliminating negative thoughts and encouraging more positive attitudes. Such a theme coincided with a more progressive view of Christianity and society that mainline denominations have tended to adopt. Although more traditional Christians criticized Schuller's approach to Christian doctrine, his optimistic message gained favor with many, including political leaders. U.S. presidents from Richard M. Nixon to George W. Bush spoke well of Schuller for his positive religious message.

As the church continued to grow, Schuller decided to build a new sanctuary, a star-shaped glass-and-steel structure that would seat nearly 3,000 people. Those who wanted to remain in their cars during the service could do so. With the dedication of the new building in 1980, the church was renamed the Crystal Cathedral of the Reformed Church in America. In 1992 Schuller opened the Fuqua International School of Christian Communications and became the school's chancellor. He has authored more than thirty books, among them *My Journey: From an Iowa Farm to a Cathedral of Dreams* (2002), an autobiography in which Schuller described various crises in his own life that ultimately ended well, and *Don't Throw Away Tomorrow*, published in 2005, in which Schuller focused on familiar themes, including optimism, positive values, maintaining a focus, and looking to an ultimate authority.

In January 2006 Schuller stepped down as the senior pastor of Crystal Cathedral, handing over that position to his son, Robert Anthony Schuller. However, Schuller planned to continue the weekly television program.

Fulton J. Sheen (1895–1979)

Fulton Sheen is best known for his television programs, *Life Is Worth Living* (1952–1957) and *The Bishop Sheen Program* (1961–1968), on which he presented nondenominational interpretations of current events as well as more personal musings. During the early years of his broadcasts, Sheen became perhaps the most well-known Catholic in the United States. In addition to radio and television broadcasts, Sheen wrote more than sixty books, beginning with *God and Intelligence in Modern Philosophy: A Critical Study in the Light of the Philosophy of St. Thomas* (1925) and ending with *Treasure in Clay* (1980).

Sheen was born in El Paso, Illinois. His parents moved to Peoria, where in 1913 Sheen graduated from the Spalding Institute, which was directed by the Brothers of Mercy. He graduated from St. Viator College in Bourbonnais, Illinois, and enrolled in St. Paul's Seminary in Minnesota. After his ordination in 1919, Sheen continued his studies in philosophy at the Catholic University of America in Washington DC, receiving doctor of sacred theology and bachelor of canon law degrees in 1920. He then enrolled at the Catholic University of Louvain in Belgium, receiving a doctorate in 1923 and the *agrege en philosophie* in 1925. In addition, Sheen studied at the Sorbonne in Paris and at the Angelicum and Gregorian in Rome, and taught at St. Edmund's College in Ware, England. After completing his studies, Sheen was called back to the United States to serve a parish in Peoria. However, he quickly moved on to the Catholic University where he first assumed the chair of apologetics and subsequently taught philosophy. He maintained his faculty position at the university until 1950.

In 1930 Sheen began a series of radio broadcasts for NBC titled the *Catholic Hour,* which continued until 1952. In addition to the radio broadcasts, he preached regularly at St. Patrick's Cathedral and conducted classes in Catholicism for those interested in converting. In 1952 Sheen applied his polished speaking skills to television, broadcasting first on the DuMont network from 1952 until 1957, when he shifted to ABC. Sheen became a well-known television personality. He appeared opposite the popular celebrities Frank Sinatra and Milton Berle, but held his own in the ratings, ultimately achieving an audience estimated at more than 20 million viewers. A popular theme that he pursued was criticism of communism. Sheen's broadcast in February 1953, which involved a mock funeral for Soviet leader Joseph Stalin, gained much attention when Stalin died the next month. Analysts note that, unlike many anti-Communists of the time, Sheen did not resort to character assassination and did not offer unqualified praise for the U.S. system, presenting criticisms of materialist aspects of American capitalism. In addition to his television ministry, Sheen served as auxiliary bishop of New York from 1951 to 1966 and as national director of the Society for the Propagation of the Faith from 1950 to 1966.

Following a dispute with New York Cardinal Francis Spellman, Sheen received an appointment as bishop of the Diocese of Rochester, New York. While serving as bishop, Sheen remained in the public eye, taking stands on racial questions and opposing U.S. involvement in Vietnam. Not as skilled with administration as he was with the mass media, Sheen resigned his position in 1969, at which time Pope Paul VI appointed him to the largely ceremonial post of archbishop of the titular See of Newport, Wales. Sheen's writings, although scholarly, are generally not considered very original. His efforts in the broadcast media brought him the greatest fame as a spokesman for the Catholic Church. In retrospect, he demonstrated that religious broadcasting can be conducted with high intellectual and ethical standards.

John Shelby Spong (b. 1931)

John Shelby Spong, retired Episcopal bishop of Newark, New Jersey, has published several books expressing ideas that more conservative Christians find objectionable but that also suggest where mainline Christian denominations may be heading. Striking at the heart of traditional Christianity, Spong has questioned the belief in Jesus as the "only son" of God and grouped the belief in the virgin birth of Jesus with similar accounts in various other cultures. Spong commented that with the early eighteenth-century discovery of the presence of the egg cell as a vital ingredient in conception, such virgin birth stories, including that of Jesus, lost all credibility. He concluded that such stories reflect the sexism of patriarchal cultures. Spong argued that Christians must surrender such beliefs in order to stay relevant in the modern world. Many who object to Spong's recommendations question whether in rejecting some of the fundamental beliefs to which Christians have adhered over the centuries, Christianity can continue to survive at all.

Spong was born in Charlotte, North Carolina, when racial segregation still dominated Southern culture. He graduated from the University of North Carolina at Chapel Hill in 1952, and in 1955 he received a master of divinity degree from the Protestant Episcopal Theological Seminary in Virginia. From 1955 to 1957 Spong served as the rector of St. Joseph's Church in Durham, North Carolina, which is located near Duke University. From there, he moved to Calvary Parish, Tarboro, North Carolina. During his stay in Tarboro, Spong first became involved in a controversial social issue. As the struggle over desegregation developed,

Spong announced from the pulpit that he expected African American children to be protected and that he would be with the children as they attempted to enter a previously segregated all-white school. In 1965 Spong moved to Lynchburg, Virginia, as rector of St. John's Church, where, to the displeasure of those with more fundamentalist beliefs, he began an adult Bible study class that engaged in textual criticism. In 1969 Spong left Lynchburg for Richmond, Virginia, where he became rector of St. Paul's Church. While in Richmond, he was elected to the executive council of the diocese of Virginia and became a deputy to the Episcopal General Convention. Spong also began a televised Bible class and subsequently published two books, *This Hebrew Lord* (1974) and *In Search of Jewish-Christian Understanding* (1975), both of which investigated the relationship between Judaism and Christianity.

In 1976 Spong was chosen to serve as bishop coadjutor of Newark, becoming diocesan bishop in 1978. He continued to focus on social issues, speaking out on such topics as affordable health care and access to high-quality education. In the mid-1980s Spong commissioned a task force within the diocese to study sexual relations in contemporary society, particularly the increasing number of unmarried young people living together, unmarried older people cohabiting for economic reasons, and people staying together in long-term homosexual relationships. The committee's controversial report supported the recognition of gay marriage. Spong subsequently published *Living in Sin? A Bishop Rethinks Human Sexuality* (1988), in which he dealt with the subject of the task force's report. The strong conservative response to the report and Spong's book led him to write *Rescuing the Bible from Fundamentalism: A Bishop Rethinks the Meaning of Scripture* (1991). In 1989 Spong continued to stir controversy within the Episcopal Church when he ordained a homosexual to the priesthood.

Spong's wife, Joan Ketner Spong, died of cancer in 1988. Joan had suffered from mental illness for fifteen years and had refused treatment for cancer. In January 1990 Spong remarried. Spong continued to write and speak on controversial subjects, urging his denomination to accept the changed world view of the modern era. He published additional controversial works, including *Why Christianity Must Change or Die* (1998) and *Here I Stand: My Struggle for a Christianity of Integrity* (2000). His book, *The Sins of Scripture* (2005), directly attacks the fundamentalist view of the Bible as the inspired and inerrant word of God. Spong focuses on morally unacceptable scriptural pronouncements, including the treatment of women and children and the anti-Semitism of the Gospels, and speculates that Paul, the author of many of the New Testament epistles, was a suppressed homosexual. In 2007 Spong published *Jesus for the Nonreligious,* in which he attempts to walk a delicate line between traditional Christians and those who completely reject a belief in God.

John H. Thomas (b. 1950)

In 1999 delegates to the General Synod of the United Church of Christ elected John H. Thomas the denomination's general minister and president. Thomas is one of five members of the Collegium of Officers, over which he presides. He graduated with a bachelor of arts degree from Gettysburg College in 1972 and received a master of divinity degree from Yale Divinity School in 1975, at which time he was ordained and began serving as the associate minister of the First Congregational United Church of Christ in Cheshire, Connecticut. In 1981 Thomas became the minister of the First United Church of Christ in Easton, Pennsylvania. In 1988 Thomas attended the Ecumenical Institute in Bossey, Switzerland, and in 1991 he joined the administrative staff of the UCC, becoming assistant to the president for ecumenical concerns. Thomas took part in developing full communion relationships with the Evangelical Lutheran Church in America, the Reformed Church in America, and the Presbyterian Church (U.S.A.). In 1998 the negotiations resulted in full communion among the denominations. Thomas also has represented the UCC in ecumenical organizations, including the World Council of Churches, the National Council of Churches, and the World Alliance of Reformed Churches.

Thomas personally reflects the more liberal stance of his denomination. For instance, when James C. Dobson, conservative Christian leader and founder of Focus on the Family, declared that the cartoon character SpongeBob Squarepants expressed inappropriate tolerance for homosexuality, Thomas responded that the UCC welcomed the SpongeBob character, proclaiming that Jesus did not turn people away, and neither does his denomination. He indicated that Dobson, rather than the cartoon character, had crossed a moral line by presenting the inaccurate message that Christians do not adhere to the important values of tolerance and diversity. Thomas added that people should be able to confront the cross not as judgment but as embrace. The UCC leader was photographed with a SpongeBob doll sitting in a chair across from his desk.

In June 2005 Thomas issued a statement to members of the denomination regarding same-gender marriage. Recognizing that church members held fundamentally differing positions on the issue, he called for continued dialogue and the creation of a "climate of respect" for differing theological and moral views. Thomas then presented his own view of the issue. Recognizing that the United Church of Christ welcomes all people, he recommended that the UCC General Synod adopt a resolution affirming that gay, lesbian, bisexual, and transgender persons have the same right of marriage as heterosexual couples. Noting that the United States has a history of limiting the citizenship rights of various groups, Thomas identified the limitation on marriage rights as one of the few remaining areas in which the nation restricts full citizenship status to people considered alien. He declared that the marriage amendments that several state legislatures have passed, while presented as affirmations of traditional views of marriage, actually demean homosexual persons.

Sharon E. Watkins (b. 1954)

In April 2005 the General Board of the Christian Church (Disciples of Christ) (CCDC) unanimously endorsed Sharon Watkins as the denomination's general minister and president, and in July the General Assembly, meeting in Portland, Oregon, unanimously elected her to the denomination's highest post. She became the first woman to assume the highest office in a U.S. mainline denomination. Watkins has had varied educational and professional experiences. In 1975 she received a bachelor of arts degree from Butler University in Indianapolis with a major in French and Economics. From 1977 to 1979 Watkins gained international experience working as a missionary and director of education in Kinshasa, Zaire, where she developed and tested an adult literacy program and taught reading, writing, and English as a second language. Returning to the United States in 1979, Watkins became a staff associate for the Africa Department, Division of Overseas Ministries of the CCDC.

In 1980 Watkins entered Yale Divinity School. While in Connecticut, in addition to pursuing a master of divinity degree, she remained active in church work, serving as a student associate with the Downtown Cooperative Ministry in New Haven, as a part-time assistant minister, and then as a full-time assistant minister. After receiving her degree in 1984, Watkins first became interim coordinator of the Downtown Cooperative Ministry, supporting such projects as a homeless shelter and providing assistance to senior citizens. From 1985 to 1989 she served as pastor of the Boone Grove Christian Church in Indiana. During this time, Watkins gained firsthand experience with the economic difficulties of farmers and the ecological problems that rural areas face, including the pollution of groundwater. In 1989 Watkins assumed the position of director of church relations at Phillips University, becoming assistant vice president for development in 1992 and associate vice president for university relations in 1993. In 1994 she became director of student services at Phillips Theological Seminary. From 1992 to 1996 Watkins studied theology at the seminary, receiving a doctor of ministry degree. In 1997 she became senior minister at the Disciples Christian Church in Bartlesville, Oklahoma. Watkins has held various offices within the CCDC, including moderator of the church organization in Oklahoma (2000–2002) and member of the Commission on Clergy (1995–1996) and the General Board and the Administrative Committee beginning in 2001.

As general minister and president, Watkins has affirmed the commitment the CCDC has made to combating racism and achieving reconciliation among various ethnic and racial groups in order to bridge racial, language, and class divisions. She has emphasized the role of the CCDC as a group seeking unity among Christians, noting that the denomination is concerned primarily with inclusiveness rather than the maintenance of specific doctrines or creeds.

6

Data and Documents

This chapter presents data gleaned from empirical studies and surveys of Christian denominations in the United States that highlight the basic demographic characteristics of mainline Christians compared with evangelical Protestants, the political attitudes of mainline Christians contrasted with those of evangelical Protestants, and the political behavior of members of these denominations. The second part of the chapter contains excerpts from documents issued by the nine denominations included in this investigation as well as statements from individual members. These selections present the policy positions of the denominations in the subject areas discussed in Chapter 2. In any attempt to assess the potential influence of such communications, we must keep in mind, given the discussion in Chapter 7 of several dissenting groups, that the denominational leadership may not speak for a certain segment, perhaps even a majority, within the denomination. In addition, there are some differences among the mainline denominations in their positions on some of the issues. On the question of abortion, the judgment of the Catholic Church differs significantly from that of the mainline Protestant churches, which, perhaps more accepting of the notion that moral dilemmas may occur, pitting one moral good against another, have expressed a greater willingness to accept abortion as an option for a woman, at least in certain circumstances such as rape or severe fetal deformities. James L. Guth et al. (1997, 14) have noted that progressive clergy in the mainline Protestant churches have emphasized social justice issues while conservative leaders in evangelical denominations have focused more on concern for moral reform. Following the lead of Martin Marty, Guth et al. (1997, 191) suggest the existence of a "two-party system" in American Protestantism. The mainline and evangelical churches are distinguishable from each other both theologically and politically, constituting two Christian "parties."

Data Overview of the Mainline Denominations

An important element in the political influence of any group is the number of members. Students of interest groups note that although large memberships can add to the clout a group may have on policy issues—representing greater voting strength, pool of financial resources, and opportunity for mass political mobilization—the larger a group, the more likely that differing perspectives will develop among members and supporters, thus diluting its impact on the external political environment. The denominations treated here vary widely in total membership and trends over the last ten years. Table 6.1 reports total membership and number of congregations for each of the nine denominations, comparing 1990 figures with those from 2000.

All the denominations except the Catholic Church lost membership between 1990 and 2000, and expectations were that these churches would continue to lose members. Several explanations are offered for the reductions, including the greater appeal of evangelical churches; the conflicts within the mainline churches over such matters as the acceptance of homosexual pastors, the status of gay members, and the willingness of the denominations' leadership to speak publicly on social and economic issues; a more rapid decline in birth rates among mainline denomination members; general population shifts away from areas where the mainline churches have been more dominant; and the decreasing appeal of denominational identification, which traditionally was frequently associated with ethnic origin. Mainline Protestant denominations appear to be caught between two opposing trends: the increasing attraction of more conservative evangelical churches along with an increasing number of people who have no religious affiliation at all.

TABLE 6.1
Number of Mainline Churches and Their Membership, 1990 and 2000

Denomination	Year	Churches	Percent Change	Members	Percent Change
American Baptist	2000	5,756		1,436,909	
Churches in the U.S.A.	1990	5,808	−0.9	1,535,971	−6.4
Catholic Church	1998	19,584		62,018,436	
	1990	23,685	−17.3	58,568,016	+5.9
Christian Church	2000	3,781		820,000	
(Disciples of Christ)	1990	4,069	−7.1	1,049,692	−21.9
Episcopal Church	2000	7,364		2,333,327	
	1990	7,354	+0.1	2,446,050	−4.6
Evangelical Lutheran	2000	10,816		5,125,919	
Church in America	1990	11,087	−2.4	5,240,739	−2.2
Presbyterian Church	2000	11,178		3,485,332	
(U.S.A.)	1990	11,501	−2.8	3,788,009	−8.0
Reformed Church in	2000	898		289,329	
America	1990	924	−2.8	326,850	−11.5
United Church of Christ	2000	5,923		1,377,320	
	1990	6,260	−5.4	1,599,212	−13.9
United Methodist	2000	35,469		8,340,954	
Church	1991	37,100	−4.4	8,789,101	−5.1

Corrections are marked on tables throughout to align the table column head, and to reduce space between last line of tables and rules. The spacing currently matches the specs for this job exactly. Please indicate specifically how many points you would like these measurements adjusted, so we can change the specs accordingly.

Source: Association of Religion Data Archives (http://www.thearda.com).

In contrast to the mainline denominations, A. James Reichley (2002, 263) notes, increasing Catholic Church membership can be attributed largely to the immigration of sizable numbers of Hispanics into the United States. Unlike the mainline Protestant denominations, the Catholic Church has continued to rely on ethnic loyalties to maintain its membership base. In contrast to expanding lay membership, the Catholic Church faces a major challenge in maintaining an adequate number of priests and nuns. Table 6.2 is derived from data presented by Peter Steinfels (2003, 29–30) in his discussion of the crises facing the church. As the membership in the Catholic Church continued to increase, the number of priests and other religious persons declined greatly. Sisters traditionally were the mainstay of Catholic schools. However, with the reduction in the number of nuns available to serve in the church's school system, the proportion of Catholic youth

TABLE 6.2
Number of Catholic Professionals and Institutions, 1965 and 2002

	1965	2002	Percent Change
Priests	58,132	45,713	−21.4
Ordinations	994	479	−51.8
Sisters	179,954	75,000	−58.3
Brothers	12,271	5,690	−53.6
Parishes	17,637	19,496	+10.5
Elementary Schools	15,000	7,000	−53.3

Source: Peter Steinfels (2003, 29–30).

educated in parochial schools declined from approximately 50 percent in 1965 to less than 25 percent in 2002 (Steinfels 2003, 30).

The Baylor Institute for Studies of Religion survey (Bader et al. 2006) provides a breakdown of the religious affiliation of Americans based on a random sample of Americans conducted in 2006. Table 6.3 presents the results. The present investigation combines mainline Protestant denominations with the Catholic Church. In the Baylor survey, these two groups together constitute 43.3 percent of the sample, the largest religious segment of the U.S. population. Evangelical Protestant denominations by themselves make up approximately one-third of the sample. To the extent that the policy positions of evangelical Protestant groups differ from those of mainline Protestants, they represent an important challenge in the policy-making arena.

Religious Beliefs
and Policy Preferences

The Baylor Religion Study offers revealing information about the religious beliefs of mainline Protestants in contrast to the beliefs of evangelical Protestants and those unaffiliated with any religious group. Table 6.4 provides findings from that study, presenting the two extreme responses in each category: beliefs about God, about Jesus, and about the Bible.

The findings indicate significant differences between evangelical Protestant and mainline Protestant respondents (African American respondents are not included in this table), with greater

TABLE 6.3
U.S. Religious Affiliation, 2006

Affiliation	Percentage of Sample
Evangelical Protestant	33.6
Mainline Protestant	22.1
Catholic	21.2
Black Protestant	5.0
Other	4.9
Jewish	2.5
Unaffiliated	10.8

Note: The percentages do not add to 100 percent due to rounding errors.
Source: Baylor Institute for Studies of Religion—American Piety in the 21st Century, selected findings (Bader et al. 2006, 8).

TABLE 6.4
Religious Beliefs of Evangelical Protestant, Mainline Protestant, Catholic, and Unaffiliated Respondents (percentage)

	Evangelical Protestant	Mainline Protestant	Catholic	Unaffiliated
Belief about God				
No doubts that God exists	86.5	63.6	74.8	11.6
Don't believe in anything beyond the physical world	0.4	0.7	1.1	37.1
Belief about Jesus				
Jesus is the son of God	94.4	72.2	84.9	11.0
Jesus is a fictional character	0.0	0.9	0.2	13.7
Belief about the Bible				
Literally true	47.8	11.2	11.8	1.0
Ancient book of history and legends	6.5	22.0	19.8	82.3

Source: Baylor Institute for Studies of Religion—American Piety in the 21st Century, selected findings (Bader et al. 2006, 14).

proportions of evangelicals expressing a strong belief in God, in Jesus as the son of God, and in the Bible as the literal truth. Catholics and mainline Protestants differed somewhat on the first two beliefs, with a higher proportion of Catholics expressing strong belief in God and Jesus as the son of God, but nearly identical small proportions of both groups registered a high confidence in the literal truth of the Bible, in contrast to a much larger proportion of evangelical respondents expressing this view. Not surprisingly, those respondents who were unaffiliated with any religious group expressed the lowest level of belief.

Paul A. Djupe and Christopher P. Gilbert (2003), in a survey of more than 2,400 Evangelical Lutheran Church in America and Episcopal Church clergy, determined the frequency of clergy involvement in various forms of political activity and their approval of each type of activity. Table 6.5 presents results from their study.

Assuming that this sample is at least to some extent representative not only of the ELCA and Episcopal Church clergy but of all mainline Protestant clergy in the eight denominations examined in this study, moderately large proportions of pastors engage in such political activities as offering prayer and taking a stand on an issue, either publicly or from the pulpit, and urging church members to register to vote. Higher proportions of clergy approve of such actions than actually engage in them, suggesting that although certain pastors personally prefer not to participate in certain forms of political activity, they regard such activity to be appropriate if others choose to take part. As activities become more partisan, the rate of engagement tends to decline, with just 11.4 percent and 6.1 percent of the sample, respectively, having engaged in publicly endorsing candidates and actively campaigning. Not surprisingly, the lowest level of activity as well as approval was endorsing candidates while preaching, which is prohibited for organizations such as churches that enjoy tax-exempt status. Nearly as low is engaging in civil disobedience, although nearly 50 percent of the sample approved of this form of political activity, perhaps in part a recognition of the importance and popularity of this form of political engagement during the days of the civil rights movement.

Djupe and Gilbert also report the percentage of ELCA and Episcopal Church clergy who addressed in some way sixteen public policy issues in 1998. Based on a factor analysis procedure, the authors divided the issues into two categories: social justice and moral reform. The results are presented in Table 6.6.

As Djupe and Gilbert note, ELCA and Episcopal Church clergy are more likely to voice their concerns about social justice issues than moral reform issues. This finding coincides with the general view that mainline church leaders and policy-making groups more often have taken public stands on these issues. As the authors observe, six of the seven issues receiving greater attention are in the social agenda category; at least two-thirds of both

TABLE 6.5
Clergy Participation in and Approval of Political Activities in 1998 (percentage)

Action	Performed Act in 1998	Clergy Approved of Act
Publicly offer prayer on an issue	55.8	80.9
Publicly take a stand on an issue	51.4	81.4
Take a stand on an issue while preaching	48.9	63.6
Urge church members to register and vote	46.3	87.2
Contact public officials	39.7	89.0
Contribute money to party, PAC, candidate	25.7	64.8
Organize an action group in church	23.7	57.0
Publicly offer prayer for candidates	20.4	39.1
Organize a study group in church	13.6	77.9
Join a national group	12.3	60.3
Publicly endorse candidates	11.4	25.9
Participate in a protest march	7.8	68.8
Actively campaign	6.1	35.5
Engage in civil disobedience	1.7	49.5
Endorse candidates while preaching	1.4	7.1

Note: PAC = political action committee.
Source: Djupe and Gilbert (2003, 30).

groups of clergy focused on issues in this area. The clergy in the two denominations tend to differ somewhat: although Episcopal clergy more often emphasized homosexuality and gay rights, ELCA clergy spoke more frequently about political scandals (specifically the Clinton impeachment proceedings), national defense, and gambling laws (Djupe and Gilbert 2003, 34). The authors note that the tendency of clergy to take stands on public policy issues has increased since the 1960s (Djupe and Gilbert 2003, 109).

Andrew Kohut et al. (2000) present results from the 1996 Pew Religion Survey regarding reports by those who attend worship services a minimum of once each month on the issues their clergy had discussed. These results are reproduced in Table 6.7. Respondents from all religious groups report their clergy discussing most often the hunger and poverty issue. As the authors note, evangelical and mainline Protestant churches differ most markedly on the issues of abortion (66 percent versus 35 percent), school prayer (71 percent versus 46 percent), and homosexuality (45 percent versus 24 percent), with evangelical clergy speaking

TABLE 6.6
Clergy Addressing Public Policy Issues
in 1998 (percentage)

	ELCA	Episcopal Church
Social Justice Issues		
Hunger and poverty	88.6	91.6
Environment	77.6	74.2
Education	77.6	75.7
Civil rights	74.6	80.4
Women's issues	73.8	71.0
Unemployment, economy	66.0	67.5
Gay rights	45.3	60.1
Government spending, deficits	36.5	34.2
Moral Reform Issues		
Family problems	86.4	79.0
Gambling laws	51.5	32.0
Homosexuality	51.3	64.3
Current political scandals	48.9	42.1
Capital punishment	48.9	50.1
Abortion	48.2	46.0
Prayer in public schools	42.1	43.0
National defense	38.5	32.2

Source: Djupe and Gilbert (2003, 33).

TABLE 6.7
Issues Discussed by Clergy at Place of Worship (percentage)

Issue	All	Evangelical Protestant	Mainline Protestant	Black Protestant	Catholic
Hunger and poverty	87	86	91	93	90
Abortion	60	66	35	56	75
World trouble spots	59	55	68	69	59
School prayer	56	71	46	73	40
Pornography	41	59	26	33	34
Homosexuality	36	45	24	51	19
Right-to-die laws	29	25	21	31	38
Death penalty	27	26	19	39	27
Health care reform	26	21	16	62	18
Candidates and elections	21	20	12	47	12

Source: 1996 Pew Religion Survey, presented in Kohut et al. (2000, 105).

on these issues far more frequently than mainline clergy. The only two issues that more than 50 percent of mainline Protestant respondents reported their clergy discussing were social welfare and troubled conditions around the world.

Whether or not clergy discuss particular issues publicly or from the pulpit, their public policy views may both reflect and influence the publicly stated policy positions of denominational decision-making bodies and leadership. Djupe and Gilbert (2003, 40) present the political opinions of ELCA and Episcopal Church clergy on several issues. Table 6.8 reproduces the results on a select number of issues, primarily those on which there was greater approval.

Although a majority of both ELCA and Episcopal Church clergy approve of the policy positions, a consistently greater proportion of Episcopal Church clergy agree with the statements that indicate a more liberal stance. On the two issues on which agreement likely indicates a more conservative position (school prayer and defense spending), a larger percentage of Episcopal Church than ELCA clergy agree. This result suggests that there is a higher

TABLE 6.8
Political Opinions of ELCA and Episcopal Church Clergy
(percentage of those who agree with the statement)

Issue	ELCA Clergy	Episcopal Clergy
Homosexuals should have all the same rights and privileges as other American citizens.	82.8	86.6
Public policy should discourage ownership and use of handguns.	72.7	73.9
More environmental protection is needed, even if it raises prices or cuts jobs.	71.2	74.2
The federal government should do more to solve social problems such as unemployment and poverty.	64.6	68.6
We need government-sponsored national health insurance so that everyone can get adequate medical care.	64.0	70.3
Capital punishment should be abolished.	59.7	68.2
Recent welfare reform laws are too harsh and hurt children.	52.6	60.7
Blacks and other minorities need special government help to achieve an equal place in America.	51.1	56.4
We need a federal law or amendment to permit prayer as a regular exercise in schools.	10.1	16.3
The United States should spend more on the military and defense.	8.0	12.3

Source: Djupe and Gilbert (2003, 40).

proportion of conservative clergy in the Episcopal Church than in the ELCA, which may help to explain the greater threat to denominational unity in the Episcopal Church since the election of V. Gene Robinson, an actively gay priest, as bishop of the New Hampshire Diocese.

Documents and Quotations

The following documents and quotations provide a sample of mainline denominations' expressions of concern on public policy issues that reflect basic value positions, focusing on the issues discussed in Chapter 2. Many of the statements are derived from the denomination's official documents, but some originated in the declarations of individuals.

Equality and Poverty

Extreme poverty binds more than one billion of God's children, depriving them of the abundant life God intends for all. The MDGs [Millennium Development Goals] are a set of eight targets for eradicating global poverty adopted by the 191 member states of the United Nations, including the United States, out of the conviction that humanity can build a better and safer world if it is willing to unite. The Goals reflect the reality that the resources, strategies, and knowledge to end global poverty exist if only the moral and political will can be built. Christians must play a key role building this will and holding governments accountable for promises made.

A world that meets the Goals would have 500 million fewer people living on less than a dollar a day, 70 percent of whom will be women. More than 400 million fewer people will go to bed hungry each night. The lives of 30 million children currently destined to die before their fifth birthday would be saved. The rise of HIV and AIDS, malaria and tuberculosis would be halted, and infection and death rates would begin to decline. The population of orphans in the world—currently numbered at more than 110 million—would begin to decline as well. In short, a world that has achieved the MDGs will be a world that more greatly reflects Christ's prayer that all be one as he and the Father are one.

—*Joint pastoral letter from Frank T. Griswold, Presiding Bishop and Primate, the Episcopal Church, and Mark S. Hanson, Presiding Bishop, Evangelical Lutheran Church in America (September 14, 2006)*

America has not felt at home a lot lately with the widening gap between the rich and the poor, with the new spirit of dominionism taking over in the name of God, America doesn't quite feel the same. The redevelopment of class preference, and the ignoring of the poor, or the kind of abandonment of the spirit of tolerance and inclusiveness, a growing spirit that serves the few and abandons the common good, America has not quite been feeling like herself, or itself, if the feminist critique would require me not to always use her in a negativity, using she. So, I say to you that I believe we ought to celebrate, because those of us who are in here, we just long for the time when America can say, lift it up citizens, I'm back. . . .

There are many who are allowing themselves to be hopelessly divided between the red and the blue, and that also includes between races and class. There are those who have lost a sense of mission, and who think that the primary existence of America is simply to fight terrorists. There are those who are now in a matter of what I call prostituted patriotism. . . .

Then there are those who, using the same image, prostitute government, use her when it's beneficial for what your special interests are, and the rest of your time you're talking about how irrelevant it is, the smaller the better, not being able to enjoy any benefits there from. Prostitution.

Well, I'm here to say, we don't need to spend too much time talking about who led her away, or how she drifted away, but the truth is, let's say, America is not quite herself, given the virus of hate that's spreading through the land, given the triumph of greed, given the pride that sometimes reaches supremacist dimensions, nationalism, imperialism, dominionism, rugged individualism that cares only about itself, privateism, consumerism, all of these others, somebody has led to the abandonment of the true American ideals. . . .

How can we find the way back? I want to suggest, let us remember those who inspired us to be at our best, our founding mothers and fathers, let us look again at the founding documents, and help citizens across the country to see that therein is the DNA of America, and anybody who acts in a way that thumbs a nose at the Constitution, at the Declaration of Independence, at the Bill of Rights, that you have had a strange shift in your DNA, a genetic mutation, making something real odd, and that's what's happening in America, a shift in the DNA. Those founding documents tell us who we are really supposed to be.

—*James Alexander Forbes, Jr., American Baptist Churches in the USA Ministry, and Pastor of Riverside Church (speech in Washington DC, June 3, 2004)*

Public Schools

While we acknowledge and affirm the contribution of private schools to the welfare of children and the nation, public schools are the primary route for most children—especially the children of poverty—into full participation in our economic, political, and community life. As a consequence, all of us, Christians and non-Christians alike, have a moral responsibility to support, strengthen, and reform the public schools. They have been and continue to be both an avenue of opportunity and a major cohesive force in our society—a society becoming daily more diverse racially, culturally, and religiously.

We welcome the fact that many public schools now teach about our nation's diversity and the role of religion in human life and history, and applaud the schools' efforts to promote those virtues necessary for good citizenship in a pluralistic democracy. . . . Just as we encourage schools to ensure that all religions are treated with fairness and respect, so we urge parents and others to refrain from the temptation to use public schools to advance the cause of any one religion or ethnic tradition, whether through curriculum or through efforts to attach religious personnel to the public schools.

—*National Council of Churches of Christ policy statement, "The Churches and the Public Schools at the Close of the Twentieth Century" (November 11, 1999)*

As a minister and a lawyer, I have learned over the years that few social issues spark more confusion and misunderstanding than school prayer. Despite common belief, the Supreme Court has not banned prayer in schools. The high court ruled that school-sponsored, mandatory programs of religious worship in public schools violate the First Amendment. A child's religious upbringing, the court declared, belongs to his or her parents, not school officials.

Children have the right to pray voluntarily in school whenever they like. They may also read the Bible or other religious books during their free time. All over the country, students meet freely in public schools after classes to study the Bible, Jewish scriptures or other religious and non-religious texts. Attendance at these "equal access clubs" is voluntary, and students—not school officials—run them. Clearly, there is a place for voluntary religious activity in public education. . . .

Our nation is a religiously diverse society where the government welcomes various religious expressions but officially endorses none. Our policy of separation of church and state has given America more religious freedom than any other country.

—*Barry W. Lynn, Executive Director of Americans United for Separation of Church and State (March 29, 2002)*

The scriptural witness that "the heavens are telling the glory of God, and the firmament proclaims [God's] handiwork" (Psalm 19:1) is a theological foundation for the empirical sciences in Western culture since the 16th century. Its implication has been that in order to know the world that God creates, it is necessary to look at the world and see what it is like. Presbyterians as members of the Reformed tradition have historically affirmed this view, and so have valued the pursuit of scientific knowledge and its dissemination through public education. . . .

Today efforts continue at state and local levels to undermine public science education by removing, reducing, or impugning references to biological evolution, Big Bang cosmology, the age of the earth, or the findings of anthropology with respect to human origins. Yet, the Presbyterian Church (U.S.A.) has not clearly delineated in its creeds, confessions, General Assembly resolutions and study papers, or educational materials developed by the church, the relationship of the findings of the sciences concerning the historical origins of the universe, the earth, life, and humanity to the affirmation of God as creator. The understanding of this relationship is essential for Presbyterians if they are to fulfill their responsibilities as credible witnesses to God as creator of a historical universe, and as Christian citizens in relation to public education.

— *Presbyterian Church (U.S.A.), 213th General Assembly (2001)*

Mainline Political Engagement

The temptation to try to fight fire with fire is understandable. Conservative religious thought has had such a long free ride in the media that it is presupposed to be the true expression of religious belief. Progressives who speak out get covered only when they are the man-bites-dog story. Witness the hurrahs and amazement that greeted an evangelical Christian coalition that took the remarkably benign step of accepting the overwhelming evidence of scientists that global warming is real. At the same time, religious leaders who speak out against the war in Iraq or against draconian budget cuts get very little coverage, since the media still believe religious advocacy for peace and the poor is to be expected and is thus not news.

But there is much that is new—and bears watching—in the way progressive religion is operating these days. Political progressives and just plain old garden-variety Democrats are so desperate to be saved that they seem willing to accept unthinkingly the notion that progressive religion is not only the antidote to right-wing religion but also that progressive God-talk is the best way to express moral values. . . .

In the end, religious leaders at their best are not policy wonks, message gurus or campaign consultants. They stand at the margins of power, with the powerless, seeking to change the status quo. Dorothy Day, Martin Luther King Jr., William Sloane Coffin and the Berrigan brothers did not have a seat at the table and did not want it. To the extent that today's progressive religious leaders act out of that tradition, there is hope. If, on the other hand, they play the ancient role of theological adviser to princes and kings, we may all get more than we bargained for.

    —*Frances Kissling, President of Catholics for a Free Choice* (The Nation, *April 24, 2006*)

The public conversation about religious and moral values now has the potential to be a serious and thoughtful discussion in America. The good news for religion and public life in America is that the word *religious* will no longer always be followed by the word *Right*.

    To move away from the bifurcating politics of liberal and conservative, left and right, would be an enormously positive change and would open up a new "politics of solutions." Right now, Washington responds to a problem or crisis in two ways. First, politicians try to make us afraid of the problem, and second, they look for somebody to blame for it. . . . But they seldom get around to actually solving the problem. The media make everything worse by assuming that every political issue has only two sides, instead of multiple angles for viewing and solving the problem. . . . The answer is to put values at the center of political discourse and, in every public debate, to ask what kind of country and people we really want to be. We would find new agreements across old political boundaries and new common ground among people who agree on values and are ready to challenge the special interests on all sides who are obstructing the solutions most Americans would support. Ideologies have failed us; values can unite us, especially around our most common democratic visions.

    —*Jim Wallis*, God's Politics *(2005)*

Sexuality Issues

The television evangelists are always talking about the sin of Sodom and Gomorrah and how homosexuality destroyed the city. I do not know one respectable Biblical scholar attributing the destruction of Sodom and Gomorrah to homosexuality. Yet the words sodomy and sodomite have come to mean the perversity of homosexuality. . . .

    The sin of Sodom and Gomorrah was the sin of inhospitality, the sin of hardness of heart in the presence of human need, the sin of injustice and neglecting the poor. That was the abomination to God. Those were the Sodomites. It is amazing how God's judgment upon a city for its corporate injustice has been transformed into a clarion call against private sexual behavior. . . .

    In no way do I discount the Bible. It is the foundational document, the foundation for all churches around the world. It is central to my life as a religious person. But if you take the Bible seriously, you can't read it literally and dismiss what we have learned in the centuries after the Bible was finished.

Today we know gay and lesbian couples who live deeply committed lives of love and integrity. This sexual orientation and its expression in an honorable relationship was not the subject matter of the biblical writers. The really serious problem for Christians who live by "The Book" is not how to square homosexuality with certain passages which on the surface condemn it—but rather how to reconcile rejection, prejudice, and cruelty toward gays with the gracious, unconditional love of Christ.

—*George Regas, Episcopal priest and Rector Emeritus of All Saints Church, Pasadena, California* (Los Angeles Times, *February 3, 2000*)

The state has an obligation to promote the family, which is rooted in marriage. Therefore, it can justly give married couples rights and benefits it does not extend to others. Ultimately, the stability and flourishing of society is dependent on the stability and flourishing of healthy family life.

The legal recognition of marriage, including the benefits associated with it, is not only about personal commitment, but also about the social commitment that husband and wife make to the well-being of society. It would be wrong to redefine marriage for the sake of providing benefits to those who cannot rightfully enter into marriage.

Some benefits currently sought by persons in homosexual unions can already be obtained without regard to marital status. For example, individuals can agree to own property jointly with another, and they can generally designate anyone they choose to be a beneficiary of their will or to make health care decisions in case they become incompetent. . . .

Marriage is a basic human and social institution. Though it is regulated by civil laws and church laws, it did not originate from either the church or state, but from God. Therefore, neither church nor state can alter the basic meaning and structure of marriage.

Marriage, whose nature and purposes are established by God, can only be the union of a man and a woman and must remain such in law. In a manner unlike any other relationship, marriage makes a unique and irreplaceable contribution to the common good of society, especially through the procreation and education of children.

The union of husband and wife becomes, over a lifetime, a great good for themselves, their family, communities, and society. Marriage is a gift to be cherished and protected.

—*United States Conference of Catholic Bishops, "Between Man and Woman: Questions and Answers about Marriage and Same-Sex Unions"* (*November 12, 2003*)

While not the most important discipleship issue in the New Testament, nor our highest priority of ministry lest we focus on one set of sins above others that afflict us such as racism, greed, sexism and gluttony, nonetheless, sexual concerns increasingly dominate our attention (Romans 1:28). We live in a culture obsessed with sex. We see evidence of sexual abuse every day. We are stunned at the reports of sexual impropriety by persons in caring professions (I Corinthians 6:18). Many persons have been victims of these abuses. The result is an environment of deep suspicion regarding the sexual integrity of persons in authority. In this context, the matter of homosexual practices continues to divide American Baptists.

The official position of the American Baptist Churches USA is that "the practice of homosexuality is incompatible with Christian teaching" and that marriage is intended to be "between a woman and a man" (Ephesians 5:31). This is my personal belief, as the General Secretary of ABCUSA, but more so, it is my responsibility to uphold this as the official position of the General Board of ABCUSA. This has been implemented in the admission of official exhibitors at the ABCUSA Biennial, chaplain endorsements, and in the staffing practices of the staff accountable to me. . . .

Finally, I call upon all American Baptists to practice a life of prayer, purpose (Philippians 1:21), and passion (Philippians 3:13) in our lives together. We must pray with and for one another, share our purpose in Christ, and practice passionate care and regard for one another. In this way we bear witness to Jesus Christ (Philippians 2:1–11).

—*A. Roy Medley, General Secretary of the American Baptist Churches in the U.S.A., letter titled "A Call for American Baptists to Live Lives of High Moral and Ethical Responsibility" (July 17, 2006)*

Immigration

As the Bishop of the Episcopal Diocese of Nevada, I feel compelled to call upon you and the other members of Congress to support the move toward fair and just immigration reform. The Episcopal Church has lent strong support to interfaith efforts to accomplish this goal. I trust that in the coming days you will join your fellow Senators in pressing for comprehensive immigration reform. . . .

I ask your support for legislation which will provide for a substantial increase in the number of workers who can enter the United States legally, and eventually work toward permanent residence and citizenship. I urge adoption of a system which would permit those already here to work toward permanent residence and eventual citizenship, recognizing that certain criteria must be met. I have the utmost concern that the ancient religious and humanitarian expectation of hospitality and care for the stranger not be delegitimized or legally sanctioned. The Episcopal Church and our interfaith partners are on record as strongly opposing any such action, and we urge the adoption of the language drafted by the Senate Judiciary Committee.

America is a nation of immigrants, and has been the rich beneficiary of their gifts and talents, for hundreds of years. We would not
exist, and we would not enjoy the global position we do today, without
the contributions of immigrants. I urge a just and equitable approach to
the urgent need for immigration reform.
  —*Katharine Jefferts Schori, Episcopal bishop of the Diocese of Nevada
(elected presiding bishop of the Episcopal Church in 2006). Letter to U.S. Senators Harry Reid and John Ensign (April 21, 2004)*

We call upon our elected officials to enact legislation that includes the
following:
  An opportunity for hard-working immigrants who are already
contributing to this country to come out of the shadows, regularize their
status upon satisfaction of reasonable criteria and, over time, pursue an
option to become lawful permanent residents and eventually United
States Citizens;
  Reform in our family-based immigration system to significantly
reduce waiting times for separated families who currently wait many
years to be reunited;
  The creation of legal avenues for workers and their families who
wish to migrate to the U.S. to enter our country and work in a safe,
legal, and orderly manner with their rights fully protected; and
  Border protection policies that are consistent with humanitarian
values and with the need to treat all individuals with respect, while
allowing the authorities to carry out the critical task of identifying and
preventing entry of terrorists and dangerous criminals, as well as pursuing the legitimate task of implementing American immigration policy.
  —*Institute on Religion and Public Policy, "Interfaith Statement in
Support of Comprehensive Immigration Reform" (October 14, 2005); support-
ing organizations include the Episcopal Church; Lutheran Immigration and
Refugee Service; Stated Clerk, Presbyterian Church (U.S.A.); United States
Conference of Catholic Bishops; General Board of Church and Society, United
Methodist Church; and Wider Church Ministries, United Church of Christ.*

Whereas, the Christian Church (Disciples of Christ) in the United States
and Canada, throughout its history, has fought for social justice and
advocated in favor of the poor and dispossessed . . . and
  Whereas, there are thousands of undocumented workers in the
United States, most of whom are hard working people who make
important contributions to our society, pay taxes and raise children . . .
  Therefore, be it resolved . . . that the General Assembly calls the
different expressions of the Christian Church (Disciples of Christ) to
develop initiatives to better serve undocumented workers and to help
undocumented ministers to secure ministerial licenses and religious
worker visas; and

Be it further resolved that Christian Church (Disciples of Christ) ministers, at local, regional and general levels, contact their political representatives asking them to address the plight of undocumented workers in the United States; and

Be it further resolved that the General Minister and President, on behalf of our Church as a whole, write a letter to the President of the United States of America, communicating our Church's interest and ministry on behalf of undocumented workers.

—*Christian Church (Disciples of Christ) General Assembly, "On Ministry to and with Undocumented Workers" (2005)*

Faith-Based Initiative

Resolved, that the Executive Council of the Episcopal Church, USA . . . support our longstanding practice of receiving public funding for faith-based social service programs so long as such programs:

1. Do not require those seeking services to receive religious instruction, worship or proselytizing as part of receiving services;
2. Do not discriminate against or give preference to any person applying for such services on the basis of religion, as well as race, national origin, sexual orientation, age, sex or disability;
3. Do not discriminate or give preference to any employee or applicant for employment on the basis of religion, as well as race, national origin, sexual orientation, age, sex or disability; and
4. Meet professional standards of accounting and conduct consistent with programs similar in scope and nature; and be it further

Resolved . . . that the Church strongly supports increased public funding for programs addressing critical human needs at the local, state, and federal level through both secular and faith-based providers, support proposals to use the tax code to create incentives for increasing charitable giving, and encourage Episcopalians to be active in supporting proposals through advocacy; and be it further

Resolved . . . that governments be encouraged to improve their delivery of assistance to faith-based and community service providers, including timely payment for services rendered, simplified paperwork requirements, and appropriate technical assistance. . . .

—*Episcopal Church, "Executive Council Resolution: Regarding Public Funding for Faith-Based Social Service Programs" (June 20, 2001)*

The USCCB [United States Conference of Catholic Bishops] has been supportive of President Bush's Faith-Based and Community Initiatives proposal because we believe it has potential to put new tools in the hands of those struggling daily to overcome the most difficult problems in our communities: persistent poverty, violence, substance abuse, inadequate housing, and obstacles faced by those entering the job market. . . .

Catholic social teaching and the principle of subsidiarity have long stressed the importance of small and intermediate-sized communities or institutions in exercising moral responsibility. We support increased resources for faith-based and community-based mediating institutions that are pursuing creative, responsive and effective solutions with the potential to help people gain independence from violence, addiction and poverty. Faith-based groups should be allowed to participate in federally funded programs to meet social needs on the same terms as other groups, without changing their fundamental nature or facing discrimination because of their religious identity.

—*United States Conference of Catholic Bishops Office of Social Development and World Peace, "Faith-Based Initiative" (October 2005)*

[We] support the principle that government funding should not compromise the identity or the integrity of religious organizations. We don't want this opportunity to distract churches from their basic mission. On the other hand, churches should not use these federal funds to pay for their worship services or catechesis. The money should be used for some broad social benefit that would serve the whole community. . . .

Some big questions remain. For example, will government dollars mean that religious organizations will not be free to give preference to members of their own faith groups when hiring employees? Will congregations have the staffing to handle the inevitable paperwork, or will that only be possible for more specialized organizations like Lutheran Social Services?

While the answers to these question are still unclear, we should put the most charitable construction on the idea and work to make it consistent with our understanding of the functional interaction of church and state.

—*H. George Anderson, ELCA presiding bishop, "Faith-Based Initiatives and the Church" (March 15, 2001)*

Iraq War

Most everyone seems to agree now that Iraq is a mess. But few with the power to make policy are saying that the U.S. is wrong. . . . What I fear is that there will be no fundamental change in a policy that is mistaken at its core, that becomes increasingly immoral, and that cannot succeed. That policy is to use military force to establish a democratic government capable of uniting Iraq's various factions, providing for its security, and acting sympathetically to U.S. interests in the region.

President Bush, especially in the mid-term elections, raised the rhetorical stakes in this war. *The credibility of the U.S. is on the line. We need to honor those who have already died. Most of all, we are engaged in the front lines of a global battle against terror where our most cherished ideals are at stake.* If the President believes this, as I'm sure he sincerely does, then why should we expect his administration to make any fundamental change in policy?

In 1968, with elections demonstrating growing discontent toward the nation's involvement in Vietnam, a basic change in direction would have been possible. But it would have required admitting that we were wrong—wrong in using military force to try to impose an internal political solution in Vietnam that was sustainable and to our liking. . . . Instead, [President Richard] Nixon made changes that were cosmetic, and the immoral tragedy endured.

It's hard, I guess, to ask nations to repent. Power breeds impunity. Yet, this is the word we need to speak and to hear at this window of national reassessment. This is the wrong war, in the wrong place, for the wrong reasons, at the wrong time.

Repentance, we know, always opens new possibilities. Admitting that we have been wrong is the most important step in deciding what we should do next. I wish the Iraq Study Group, and all the others offering advice to the President, would start there.

—*Wesley Granberg-Michaelson, general secretary, Reformed Church in America. "Bush, Vietnam, and Iraq—Déjà Vu All Over Again."* God's Politics—Jim Wallis blog *(November 21, 2006)*

Our bishops' Conference continues to dialogue with U.S. policy makers regarding Iraq. In statements, letters and meetings, we have expressed grave moral concern regarding "preventive war," noted the new moral responsibilities that our nation has in Iraq, worked to protect religious freedom in Iraq, supported firm resolve and effective strategies in the struggle against terrorism, condemned torture and called for efforts to address the abuse of prisoners and detainees, shared the moral elements of a "responsible transition," and sought to contribute to a serious and civil discussion regarding ways forward in Iraq.

We remain concerned for the safety of the men and women who serve generously in the U.S. military. We are grateful for their heroic sacrifices on behalf of the Iraqi people and affirm the extraordinary ministry of military chaplains among them. We are deeply concerned for the lives and dignity of the Iraqi people who are also our sisters and brothers and deserve our care and solidarity. . . .

At this critical time, our nation needs open and courageous dialogue to examine where things stand in pursuing justice and peace in Iraq, assess what is achievable there, and evaluate the moral and human consequences of alternative courses of action. Let us pray for the wisdom and courage needed to take steps along the difficult path toward a responsible transition that helps Iraqis build a better future. As President of our Conference of bishops, I make this appeal in the spirit of the Beatitudes, which assure us, "Blessed are the peacemakers, for they will be called children of God" (Matthew 5:9).

—*William S. Skylstad, president of the United States Conference of Catholic Bishops. "Call for Dialogue and Action on Responsible Transition in Iraq" (November 13, 2006)*

Our view of this war in Iraq is informed by our belief that war is contrary to the will of God, and an affront to God's creation (Genesis 6:11–12). Some member communions, therefore, including the historic peace churches, believe that all war is sin and never justified, and that participation by Christians in war cannot be sanctioned, even as others might consider it as engagement in a "lesser evil." Other member communions hold that war can sometimes be justified if certain criteria are met. The cause or case for military action must be just, the war must be sanctioned by recognized governments, the war must be carried out so as to minimize civilian casualties, the destruction and death must not exceed in proportion the potential gain of peace and/or justice, and the war must be clearly a last resort. Whether one views the war in Iraq from the peace church perspective, or from that of the churches informed by a "just war" tradition, it is clear to the member churches that this war violates the churches' clear ethical norms. . . .

We urge our government to give meaningful support to U.S. troops. . . . And we insist that our government begin a process of restoring trust in its conduct of foreign policy and multilateral engagement, damaged and undermined by a pattern of deception both in the arguments made by the Administration leading up to the war, as well as during the conduct of the war.

—*National Council of Churches USA, "Pastoral Message on the War in Iraq" (November 7, 2006)*

Science

We recognize science as a legitimate interpretation of God's natural world. We affirm the validity of the claims of science in describing the natural world, although we preclude science from making authoritative claims about theological issues. We recognize technology as a legitimate use of God's natural world when such use enhances human life and enables all of God's children to develop their God-given creative potential without violating our ethical convictions about the relationship of humanity to the natural world.

In acknowledging the important roles of science and technology, however, we also believe that theological understandings of human experience are crucial to a full understanding of the place of humanity in the universe. Science and theology are complementary rather than mutually incompatible. We therefore encourage dialogue between the scientific and theological communities and seek the kind of participation that will enable humanity to sustain life on earth and, by God's grace, increase the quality of our common lives together.

— *United Methodist Church,* The Book of Discipline *(2004)*

Abortion

Roe v. Wade has left a trail of broken hearts. Through Project Rachel and other ministries, we will continue to help the broken-hearted. Those who resort to abortion out of a sense of desperation often find the cruel reality of abortion too difficult to bear. But it is too difficult only in a world without God and therefore without hope. We must reach these hearts and give them hope. These are the converted hearts that will at last bring an end to abortion.

Roe v. Wade cannot stand as the law of this great nation, a nation founded on the self-evident truth that all people are created with an inalienable right to life. We are committed, no matter how long it may take, no matter the sacrifices required, to bringing about a reversal of this tragic Supreme Court decision. We will speak out on behalf of the sanctity of each and every human life wherever it is threatened, from conception to natural death, and we urge all people of good will to do likewise. For, as Pope John Paul reminds us, "it is impossible to further the common good without acknowledging and defending the right to life, upon which all the other inalienable rights of individuals are founded and from which they develop" (*The Gospel of Life,* no. 10). *Roe v. Wade* must be reversed.

— *Statement of the United States Conference of Catholic Bishops on the Thirtieth Anniversary of* Roe v. Wade *(November 12, 2002)*

Our belief in the sanctity of unborn human life makes us reluctant to approve abortion. But we are equally bound to respect the sacredness of the life and well-being of the mother, for whom devastating damage may result from an unacceptable pregnancy. In continuity with past Christian teaching, we recognize tragic conflicts of life with life that may justify abortion, and in such cases we support the legal option of abortion under proper medical procedures. We cannot affirm abortion as an acceptable means of birth control, and we unconditionally reject it as a means of gender selection.

We oppose the use of late-term abortion known as dilation and extraction (partial-birth abortion) and call for the end of this practice except when the physical life of the mother is in danger and no other medical procedure is available, or in the case of severe fetal anomalies incompatible with life. We call all Christians to a searching and prayerful inquiry into the sorts of conditions that may warrant abortion. . . . We particularly encourage the Church, the government, and social service agencies to support and facilitate the option of adoption.

Governmental laws and regulations do not provide all the guidance required by the informed Christian conscience. Therefore, a decision concerning abortion should be made only after thoughtful and prayerful consideration by the parties involved, with medical, pastoral, and other appropriate counsel.

—*United Methodist Church,* The Book of Discipline *(2004)*

We believe the Bible teaches the sanctity of human life. Men are given the precious gift of life from God and are created in the image of God. Therefore, we believe, in principle, that abortion ought not to be practiced at all. However, in this complex society, where many times one form of evil is pitted against another form of evil, there could be exceptions. It is our Christian conviction that abortion performed for personal reasons to insure individual convenience ought not be permitted. . . .

We call on our members to support efforts for constitutional changes to provide legal protection for the unborn.

—*Reformed Church in America, Statement of the General Synod of 1973 on Abortion*

Resolved, the House of Bishops concurring, That this 71st General Convention of the Episcopal Church reaffirms resolution C047 from the 69th General Convention which states . . .

We believe that legislation concerning abortions will not address the root of the problem. We therefore express our deep conviction that any proposed legislation on the part of national or state governments regarding abortions must take special care to see that individual conscience is respected, and that the responsibility of individuals to reach informed decisions in this matter is acknowledged and honored as the position of this Church; and be it further

Resolved, That this 71st General Convention of the Episcopal Church express its unequivocal opposition to any legislative, executive or judicial action on the part of local, state or national governments that abridges the right of a woman to reach an informed decision about the termination of pregnancy or that would limit the access of a woman to safe means of acting on her decision.

—*Episcopal Church General Convention, "Reaffirm General Convention Statement on Childbirth and Abortion" (1994)*

Embryonic Stem-Cell Research

[T]he 213th General Assembly (2001) of the Presbyterian Church (U.S.A.) affirms the use of fetal tissue and embryonic tissue for vital research. Our respect for life includes respect for the embryo and fetus, and we affirm that decisions about embryos and fetuses need to be made with responsibility. Therefore, we believe that the Presbyterian Church (U.S.A.) and other faith groups should educate their members in making these very difficult ethical decisions. With careful regulation, we affirm the use of human stem cell tissue for research that may result in the restoring of health to those suffering from serious illness. We affirm our support for stem cell research, recognizing that this research moves to a new and challenging frontier. We recognize the need for continuing informed public dialogue and equitable sharing of information of the results of stem cell research. It is only with such public dialogue and information sharing that our diverse society can build a foundation for responsible movement toward this frontier that offers enormous hope and challenge.

—*213th General Assembly of the Presbyterian Church (U.S.A.), "Ethical Guidelines for Fetal Tissue and Stem Cell Research" (2001; reaffirmed by the 216th General Assembly, 2004)*

Whereas, there are currently over 25,000 frozen embryos in IVF (in-vitro fertilization) clinics that probably will eventually be discarded, and Whereas, the NIH [National Institutes of Health] developed guidelines regulating federally funded research on stem cells, provided they were taken from frozen human embryos derived from in vitro fertilization and which would be discarded after the treatment of infertile couples . . . and,

Whereas, by banning the research, we foreclose the possibility of doing all we can to improve the lot of the living, and in many cases giving them new life,

Therefore, be it resolved that the Twenty-third General Synod of the United Church of Christ supports federally funded embryonic stem cell research within ethically sound guidelines (including concern for justice, privacy, access to the benefits of the research for all) and the limitations set forth by the National Institutes of Health, and

Be it further resolved that the Twenty-third General Synod requests the General Minister and President of UCC to send a letter to the President of the United States urging approval of federal funding for embryonic stem cell research with NIH guidelines. . . .

—*United Church of Christ 23rd General Synod, "Support for Federally Funded Research on Embryonic Stem Cells" (2001)*

End-of-Life Decisions, the Right to Die, and Euthanasia

When death is judged to be certain and imminent, we affirm that grave injustice to the respect and memory of persons is rendered if extraordinary technology is applied. Our highest concern is for the total person rather than technological curiosity and mechanical performance. We are confronted with values of human and personal life in the face of every death. . . .

Christianity has long taught that suffering can have meaning. Through it God can work his grace for the one who suffers and for others. Redemptive suffering is meaningful pain. This is markedly different from the dehumanizing and mindless suffering of the artificially maintained terminally ill. . . .

We affirm that direct intervention to aid the irremediably deteriorating and hopelessly ill person to a swifter death is wrong. While direct intervention in many cases may appear "humane," deliberate injection of drugs or other means of terminating life are acts of intentional homicide. This deliberate act is far removed from decisions which allow people to die—like shutting off a life-supporting machine or even withholding medication. Permission for the normal process of death is an act of omission in the spirit of kindness and love within limits of Christian charity and legal concerns. Direct intervention to cause death, known as direct euthanasia, cannot be permitted. We affirm there is a distinct moral difference between killing and allowing to die.

—*Evangelical Lutheran Church in America, "Death and Dying: An Analysis Offered by Task Force on Ethical Issues in Human Medicine, ALC" (1977)*

The church affirms life and has a perspective both on living and on dying that is in contrast to that of much of society. Because of that difference in perspective, the church is called to be prophetic. As always, to be a prophet is to speak and act on behalf of the powerless and in a way that calls Christians individually and as communities to live the costly life which a Christian perspective demands.

With regard to physician-assisted suicide, the commission is convinced that the prophetic task of the church is to create a Christian community of care as described in this paper. The one who suffers and those who give care to the sufferer most need a community in which people are united by grace, people who affirm that one has the right to stay alive without justifying his or her existence and who can understand the deep humanity of situations in which people are tempted to take their own lives as an end to suffering. To decry physician-assisted suicide

without offering the loving, caring community which takes away the occasion for suicide is to offer law when grace is needed.
  —*Reformed Church in America, Commission on Christian Action,*
"Perspective on Physician Assisted Suicide" (1994)

By euthanasia is understood an action or an omission which of itself or by intention causes death, in order that all suffering may in this way be eliminated. Euthanasia's terms of reference, therefore, are to be found in the intention of the will and in the methods used.

It is necessary to state firmly once more that nothing and no one can in any way permit the killing of an innocent human being, whether a fetus or an embryo, an infant or an adult, an old person, or one suffering from an incurable disease, or a person who is dying. Furthermore, no one is permitted to ask for this act of killing, either for himself or herself or for another person entrusted to his or her care, nor can he or she consent to it, either explicitly or implicitly.

Nor can any authority legitimately recommend or permit such an action. For it is a question of the violation of the divine law, an offense against the dignity of the human person, a crime against life, and an attack on humanity.

It may happen that, by reason of prolonged and barely tolerable pain, for deeply personal or other reasons, people may be led to believe that they can legitimately ask for death or obtain it for others. Although in these cases the guilt of the individual may be reduced or completely absent, nevertheless the error of judgment into which the conscience falls, perhaps in good faith, does not change the nature of this act of killing, which will always be in itself something to be rejected. The pleas of gravely ill people who sometimes ask for death are not to be understood as implying a true desire for euthanasia; in fact, it is almost always a case of an anguished plea for help and love. What a sick person needs, besides medical care, is love, the human and supernatural warmth with which the sick person can and ought to be surrounded by all those close to him or her, parents and children, doctors and nurses.
  —*United States Conference of Catholic Bishops, Sacred Congregation for the Doctrine of the Faith, "Declaration on Euthanasia" (1980)*

Environment

Within the United States, public policy should assist industrial sectors and workers especially impacted by climate change policies, and it should offer incentives to corporations to reduce greenhouse gas emissions and assistance to workers affected by these policies.

We encourage all parties to adopt an attitude of candor, conciliation, and prudence in response to serious, complex, and uncertain challenges. We hope the continuing dialogue within and among the diverse disciplines of science, economics, politics, and diplomacy will be guided by fundamental moral values: the universal common good, respect for God's creation, an option for the poor, and a sense of intergenerational obligation. Since religious values can enrich public discussion, this challenge offers opportunities for interfaith and ecumenical conversation and cooperation. . . .

As people of religious faith, we bishops believe that the atmosphere that supports life on earth is a God-given gift, one we must respect and protect. It unites us as one human family. If we harm the atmosphere, we dishonor our Creator and the gift of creation. The values of our faith call us to humility, sacrifice, and a respect for life and the natural gifts God has provided.

—*United States Conference of Catholic Bishops, "Global Climate Change: A Plea for Dialogue, Prudence, and the Common Good" (June 15, 2001)*

Resolved, that the Executive Council . . . calls on the U.S. Congress and Administration to pass meaningful conservation-based energy legislation consistent with the long-standing belief that we are stewards of God's creation, responsible for its care and preservation; and be it further

Resolved, that the Church urges government and industry to consider raising vehicle fuel economy for all vehicles in the United States, increasing funding for mass transit, investing in renewable energy research and development, regulating carbon dioxide, increasing energy efficiency for consumer products and increasing funds for the Low Income Home Energy Assistance Program, and be it further

Resolved, that the Episcopal Church strongly opposes drilling or mining in our nation's dwindling wild lands and places important to the traditional cultures of indigenous peoples, including oil and gas exploration and drilling in the Alaska National Wildlife Refuge that threaten the life and culture of the Gwich'in people

—*Executive Council, Episcopal Church, "Calling for Responsible Energy Policy and Protection of Creation" (February 22–25, 2002)*

Capital Punishment

Whereas, the General Assembly of the Christian Church (Disciples of Christ) has often spoken in opposition to the death penalty . . . and has called for a moratorium on the death penalty . . . and

Whereas, a high percentage of people on death row are poor and powerless and have often received inadequate defense at their trials; and

Whereas, a disproportionate number of people on death row are people of color reflecting the presence of systemic racism with[in] the U.S. criminal justice system; and

Whereas, the use of the death penalty does not reduce the rate of violent crimes in our communities and may encourage additional violence; and

Whereas, an increasing number of nations of the international community have condemned and abolished the death penalty as cruel and unusual punishment . . .

Therefore, be it resolved that the General Assembly of the Christian Church (Disciples of Christ) . . .

1. Calls upon elected officials to abolish the death penalty in the United States; and
2. Encourages Disciples of Christ members and congregations in the US and Canada to become advocates for the abolishment of the death penalty; and
3. Invites members, congregations, regions and general units of the Christian Church (Disciples of Christ) to share resources for education and advocacy. . . .
4. Calls upon congregations to create ministries to support and nurture those who have lost loved ones to violent criminal action as well as for families with loved ones on death row.

—*Christian Church (Disciples of Christ), "Resolution on the Death Penalty" (October 2003)*

Resolved, that the Executive Council commit ourselves, and call upon all members of the Church, to strengthen efforts to abolish the death penalty, and at the same time find the sensitive capacity to stand with the friends and families of murder victims as they struggle to redeem this tragedy in their lives, and it is further

Resolved, that just as we commit ourselves to work vigorously in this effort as we go back to our communities, we call upon the Episcopal Church to pursue and work vigorously for an immediate moratorium and the subsequent abolition of the death penalty in all states and the federal system. . . .

The Episcopal Church in the United States of America has long opposed capital punishment, and at the most recent General Convention (2000) reaffirmed the Church's opposition to the death penalty. In our baptismal covenant, we respect the dignity of every human being, and commit ourselves to strive for justice and peace among all people. The Church will continue to decry the revenge of state-sanctioned homicides. We abhor the racism and economic injustices evident in our criminal justice system.

—*Episcopal Church Executive Council, "Recommitment to Abolish the Death Penalty" (June 20, 2001)*

The United Methodist Church declares its opposition to the retention and use of capital punishment and urges its abolition. . . .

The death penalty falls unfairly and unequally upon marginalized persons including the poor, the uneducated, ethnic and religious minorities, and persons with mental and emotional illnesses. . . .

The United Methodist Church cannot accept retribution or social vengeance as a reason for taking human life. It violates our deepest belief in God as the Creator and Redeemer of humankind. . . .

We call upon United Methodists . . . to:

work in collaboration with other ecumenical and abolitionist groups for the abolition of the death penalty in those states which currently have capital punishment statutes, and against efforts to reinstate such statutes in those which do not;

speak out against the death penalty to state governors, state and federal representatives;

develop educational materials on capital punishment; and

oppose all executions through prayer and vigils.

—*United Methodist Church*, Book of Resolutions *(2000)*

References

Bader, Christopher, Kevin Dougherty, Paul Forese, Byron Johnson, F. Carson Mencken, Jerry Z. Park, and Rodney Stark. 2006. *Selected Findings from the Baylor Religion Survey, American Piety in the 21st Century: New Insights to the Depth and Complexity of Religion in the US.* Waco, TX: Baylor Institute for Studies of Religion.

Djupe, Paul A., and Christopher P. Gilbert. 2003. *The Prophetic Pulpit: Clergy, Churches, and Communities in American Politics.* Lanham, MD: Rowman and Littlefield.

Guth, James L., John C. Green, Corwin E. Smidt, Lyman A. Kellstedt, and Margaret M. Poloma. 1997. *The Bully Pulpit: The Politics of Protestant Clergy.* Lawrence: University Press of Kansas.

Kohut, Andrew, John C. Green, Scott Keeter, and Robert C. Toth. 2000. *The Diminishing Divide: Religion's Changing Role in American Politics.* Washington DC: Brookings Institution Press.

Reichley, A. James. 2002. *Faith and Politics.* Washington DC: Brookings Institution Press.

Steinfels, Peter. 2003. *A People Adrift: The Crisis of the Roman Catholic Church in America.* New York: Simon and Schuster.

7

Directory of Organizations

This list of organizations represents the wide variety of associations within the mainline denominations. Many are associated officially with the denominations and focus on serving the members of the church as well as attempting to benefit the wider society and to encourage public policy changes to bring about social, economic, and political reform. Others are dissenting associations that disagree with official church positions on values and doctrine, disapprove of some aspect of church policy, or attempt to encourage the church to alter its agenda and assume new responsibilities. Given the recent push on sexuality issues in many denominations, several of the organizations listed here have developed around the status of homosexuals in the church. The organizations provide online versions of many of the publications listed here.

Affirmation: United Methodists for Lesbian, Gay, and Bisexual Concerns (AUMLGBC)
P.O. Box 1021
Evanston, IL 60204
www.umaffirm.org

This organization, established in 1976, encourages the opening of the United Methodist Church to all people on an equal basis, independent of sexual orientation. The group supports the church's ministry to all persons regardless of race, social standing, age, gender, or sexual orientation. Affirmation attempts to inform church members about the organization's concerns, encourages ecumenical contacts with other denominations, and assists those who claim to be experiencing discrimination. It publishes a quarterly newsletter, *Affirmation Newsletter*.

American Anglican Council (AAC)
2296 Henderson Mill Road NE, Suite 406
Atlanta, GA 30345-2793
(800) 914-2000
(770) 414-1518 (fax)
http://www.americananglican.org

In June 1996, 75 members of the Episcopal Church, including nine bishops, met in Techny, Illinois, to affirm the authority of scripture and to renew their commitment to the traditional beliefs of the Christian faith and the Anglican Communion. The attendees elected a board of trustees and subsequently incorporated as a 501c(3) organization in the District of Columbia. The AAC holds that biblical imperatives and Christian ethical principles play an essential role in maintaining a well-ordered society. The group supports the sanctity of life and chastity in sexual relations. The organization cooperates with other renewal groups within the Episcopal Church to oppose any teachings or policies of the church that they believe contradict scripture and historic Anglicanism. The council publishes *Encompass*, a monthly newsletter.

American Baptist Women's Ministries (ABW)
P.O. Box 851
Valley Forge, PA 19482-0851
(800) 222-3872
(610) 768-2275
www.abwministries.org

The members of this organization, established in 1951, are women in the American Baptist Church U.S.A. Participants attempt to reach beyond the formal church structure, supporting the various mission goals of the church, including local, national, and international social concerns. The ABW seeks to determine the needs of communities in which congregations are located and develop programs to meet those needs, cooperating with other community organizations. The organization works to integrate women into the various activities of the church and assist women to attain leadership skills. ABW publishes *Vital Woman Magazine* three times each year.

American Baptists Concerned (ABC)
P.O. Box 3183
Walnut Creek, CA 94598
(925) 439-4672
www.rainbowbaptists.org

Clergy and lay members of the American Baptist Church in the U.S.A. established this organization in 1972 to encourage gay persons and their families in the church to unite for mutual support. The organization lobbies the ABCUSA to take steps to meet the needs of the denomination's homosexual members. The organization publishes *Voice of the Turtle*, a quarterly newsletter.

Anglican Communion Network (ACN)
535 Smithfield Street, Suite 910
Pittsburgh, PA 15222
(412) 325-8900
www.acn-us.org

The Anglican Communion Network, more formally known as the Network of Anglican Communion Dioceses and Parishes, was established in January 2004 following the election of V. Gene Robinson, an openly gay priest, as bishop of New Hampshire. The organizational meeting, which included twelve Episcopal bishops, elected Robert Duncan, bishop of the Pittsburgh diocese, to a three-year term as moderator and selected a twelve-member steering committee. The ACN, which advocates a traditional interpretation of biblical mandates, provides a dissenting voice within the Episcopal Church. The organization includes approximately 800 congregations representing 200,000 members. Fourteen primates in other countries around the world have expressed their support for the ACN. The network is committed to missionary activities in North America and in other parts of the world and to establishing partnerships with Christians in other churches and with other Anglican associations in North America. Although the ACN remains within the Episcopal Church, it ultimately may prove to be a way station on the path toward ultimate separation.

Anglicans United (AU)
P.O. Box 763217
Dallas, TX 75376-3217

(972) 293-7443
www.anglicansunited.com

The AU was established in 1987 as Episcopalians United for Reformation, Renewal and Revelation (EU) to perpetuate the traditional doctrines of the Episcopal Church. The group has focused much of its efforts on maintaining traditional church policy on sexuality. In 1988 the organization mounted a successful effort at the Episcopal General Convention to oppose a resolution that would have permitted the ordination of practicing homosexuals. At the 1994 General Convention, EU strongly objected to what its members considered a biased sexuality study that the church hierarchy had commissioned. In 1993 the organization established Latimer Press to provide Christian educational materials for youth and adults. Various splinter groups of the Episcopal Church met in 2002 and 2003, and the name of the organization was changed to the Anglican Union to reflect a broader membership both within and outside the United States. The AU publishes *United Voice*, a bimonthly newspaper.

Association for Church Renewal (ACR)
1110 Vermont Avenue NW, Suite 1180
Washington DC 20005
(202) 682-4131
(202) 682-4136 (fax)
www.ird-renew.org

The Association for Church Renewal, closely connected to the Institute on Religion and Democracy, is composed of representatives from more than thirty church renewal groups from mainline denominations in the United States and Canada. The organization asserts that the leadership of mainline denominations as well as the World Council of Churches are excessively liberal and out of touch with the orthodox beliefs of many of their members. The ACR estimates that its mailings regularly reach 2.4 million people in the mainline denominations. The association, formed in 1996, supports church members in promoting orthodox Christian doctrine and traditional notions of marriage and the family. The organization advocates freedom of religion in the United States and around the world, evangelism efforts, and the sanctity of life. Those in the association resist trends toward revising traditional

Christian doctrines and any compromise with non-Christian religious beliefs.

Association for the Rights of Catholics in the Church (ARCC)
P.O. Box 85
Southampton, MA 01073
(413) 527-9929
(413) 527-5877 (fax)
www.arcc-catholic-rights.org

This organization of Catholics advocates fundamental reforms within the Catholic Church, including shared decision making and greater accountability within the church, the recognition of the basic rights of all baptized Catholics through the creation of a Charter of the Rights of Catholics in the Church, acceptance of the ordination of women and married people, the right of ordained persons to choose either celibacy or marriage, and the right of persons who have remarried to receive the sacraments of the church. ARCC publishes *ARCC Light*, a bimonthly newsletter.

Biblical Witness Fellowship (BWF)
P.O. Box 102
Candia, NH 03034
(800) 494-9172
www.biblicalwitness.org

This organization, composed of dissenting clergy and lay members of the United Church of Christ, was established in 1978 as the United Church People for Biblical Witness. The group assumed its present name in 1984. Members of the BWF adhere to the beliefs of traditional Christianity as set forth in the Dubuque Declaration formulated at a 1983 meeting held in Dubuque, Iowa. Pointing to the denomination's loss of members and congregations since the 1960s, the organization claims to offer an alternative to what are considered the radical social positions of the UCC leadership. The BWF proclaims the sacredness of human life from the moment of conception and believes that God determined that sexual intimacy can be expressed legitimately only in the bond of heterosexual marriage. The organization supports local church autonomy from the national organization and assists congregations in obtaining pastors who are faithful to traditional biblical principles. BWF publishes a newspaper, *The Witness*, two or three times each year.

Catholic League for Religious and Civil Rights
450 Seventh Avenue
New York, NY 10123
(212) 371-3191
(212) 371-3394 (fax)
www.catholicleague.org

Established in 1973, the Catholic League is a lay organization that focuses on defending the rights of Catholics to express their faith openly without experiencing discrimination and denigration. The league monitors the mass media for possible examples of biased portrayals of Catholics and the Catholic Church and encourages boycotts against companies that sponsor television programs that the organization determines to contain unfair content. The group responds to alleged discrimination against Catholic applicants to universities or employees and may take part in litigating such cases. The league lobbies legislative bodies to ensure that Catholic interests are protected in any public policy initiatives. The league publishes *Catalyst*, a monthly journal.

Catholic Legal Immigration Network (CLINIC)
McCormick Pavilion
415 Michigan Avenue NE
Washington DC 20017
(202) 635-2556
(202) 635-2649 (fax)
www.cliniclegal.org

Established in 1988, the CLINIC provides support for the legal immigration programs of Catholic dioceses and charities. The organization administers legal services projects; manages diocesan immigration programs; and assists congregations in attaining foreign-born priests, nuns, and other religious workers to meet the needs of immigrant communities in the United States. Members assist dioceses in providing legal services to low-income and impoverished immigrants who wish to attain the reunification of families, citizenship, and safety from persecution or violence. The organization supports the improvement of U.S. government immigration policies and publishes *In the Balance*, a quarterly newsletter.

Catholic Worker Movement (CWM)
Peter Maurin Farm

41 Cemetery Road
Marlboro, NY 12542
(845) 236-4774
www.catholicworker.org

More than 185 communities make up the Catholic Worker Movement, each of which provides food, clothing, and shelter for the homeless and abandoned. The movement has no central administrative structure and each community operates independently of the others. The address provided above is for one of the communities, situated just north of New York City, which is named for one of the movement founders. Dorothy Day, a socialist journalist who converted to Catholicism, and Peter Maurin, an immigrant from France, established the CWM in 1933. They began publishing *The Catholic Worker*, a newspaper that the organization still distributes. Members of the group voluntarily accept a life of poverty in order to transcend simply providing charity to engage in sharing the experience of the poor. Members may seek employment outside the community or a community may engage in small economic enterprises, but donations contribute the major share of financial support. The communities support labor unions, human rights, and nonviolence. During periods in which the United States had a military draft, members became conscientious objectors and several were imprisoned for their refusal to serve in the military. During the Vietnam conflict, the movement played a role in stimulating opposition to the war.

Catholics for a Free Choice (CFFC)

1436 U Street NW, Suite 301
Washington DC 20009-3997
(202) 986-6093
www.catholicsforchoice.org

Established in 1973, Catholics for a Free Choice supports the right of individuals and couples, as moral agents, to make family planning decisions and have access to contraception and safe, legal abortion. The organization advocates legal rights for gays and lesbians; freedom from sexual abuse in the family; social and economic justice, including access to reproductive health services; equal rights for women in government, society, and churches; and public policies based on objective research. Among CFFC's campaigns are Condoms4Life, an effort to persuade the Catholic Church to lift the ban on condom use; See Change, which calls for the Catholic Church to have the same status at the United Nations as other religions; and Catholic Vote, an initiative to analyze the influence of the Catholic hierarchy on Catholic voters—especially regarding pro-choice elected officials. The organization publishes a quarterly journal, *Conscience*, which covers such topics as child care, fighting poverty, gender equality, and electoral politics.

Christian Alliance for Progress

P.O. Box 40495
Jacksonville, FL 32203-0495
(888) 381-0108
www.christianalliance.org

The Christian Alliance for Progress, composed of individuals from various denominations and religious viewpoints, strives to emphasize the core beliefs and values of Christianity in response to the contemporary involvement of Christian groups in the search for political influence and power. The Christian Alliance affirms the separation of church and state, not wanting to control government, but to communicate a message of Christian conscience to the public realm. Referring to the Gospel message expressed in the life of Jesus, the organization calls for compassion for the hungry, the poor, and the sick; opposes human injustice; supports equal treatment for all; and invites Christians to become responsible stewards of the natural environment.

Christian Churches Together in the U.S.A. (CCT-USA)

4500 60th Street SE
Grand Rapids, MI 49512
(616) 698-7071
www.christianchurchestogether.org

All nine of the denominations included in this investigation took part in establishing Christian Churches Together. In March 2006 representatives from thirty-four evangelical Protestant, mainline Protestant, African American Protestant, Orthodox, and Catholic churches and religious organizations met in Atlanta to adopt bylaws and officially establish CCT-USA. Wesley Granberg-Michaelson, general secretary of the Reformed Church in America, became the organization's interim moderator. The principal goals of the newly formed organization are to encourage increased interaction and understanding among the member churches and Christian groups, to facilitate common action, and to communicate a unified message to society in promoting the common good. Christian Churches Together plans to sponsor national and regional forums on various topics, including public policy issues.

Churches Uniting in Christ (CUIC)
475 East Lockwood
Webster Groves, MO 63119
(314) 252-3160
www.cuicinfo.org

In 2002 nine denominations, including the Christian Church (Disciples of Christ), the Episcopal Church, the Presbyterian Church, the United Church of Christ, and the United Methodist Church, formed Christians Uniting in Christ. The CUIC became the successor to the Consultation on Church Union, which for forty years engaged in discussion among mainline denominations regarding possible future collaboration. The participating denominations in CUIC reached agreement on such basic doctrines as the sacraments of baptism and communion, the incarnation of Jesus, and the inspirational role of the Holy Spirit. The organization emphasized that the member denominations will combat racism and discrimination within the church and in the larger society and will oppose any exclusionary policies based on race, age, gender, class, disability, or sexual orientation.

Conference for Catholic Lesbians (CCL)
P.O. Box 436, Planetarium Station
New York, NY 10024
(718) 680-6107
www.cclonline.org

Formed in 1982 by Catholic women who identified themselves as lesbians but also affirmed the significance of the Catholic tradition in their lives, the CCL attempts to support lesbian women who wish to remain within the Catholic faith. The organization advocates just treatment of women within the church and the larger society. The CCL promotes conferences and lectures espousing the policy positions of the group and publishes *Images*, a quarterly newsletter.

Disciples Justice Action Network (DJAN)
1040 Harbor Drive
Annapolis, MD 21403 (East Coast office)
(410) 212-7964
www.djan.net

In 1996 approximately 100 individuals, meeting at a church in Chicago, formed the Disciples Justice Action Network to express concerns that members of the Christian Church (Disciples of Christ) have regarding issues of peace and justice. Among its members, the organization has 450 individuals and families as well as 42 congregations and other organizations. DJAN has taken stands on various issues, including stem-cell research, the rights of women, sexuality, poverty, food stamps, budget cuts, immigration, the crisis in Darfur, and the Middle East conflict. DJAN officials participated in the debate over the proposed Federal Marriage Amendment, expressing their religious- and constitution-based concerns. On the issue of abortion, the organization joined pro-choice groups in signing an amicus brief in a case before the U.S. Supreme Court (*Gonzales v. Planned Parenthood*) arguing that the Partial-Birth Abortion Ban Act of 2003 did not contain an exception for the health of the woman. DJAN distributes *Call To Justice!*, a quarterly newsletter containing information about the personnel and activities of the organization.

Earth Ministry (EM)
6512 23rd Avenue NW, Suite 317
Seattle, WA 98117
(206) 632-2426
(206) 299-3339 (fax)
www.earthministry.org

Established in 1992, Earth Ministry is composed of more than 1,400 individual members and 100 congregations located primarily in the northwestern United States. The organization supports the position of the National Council of Churches that a major contemporary moral issue is environmental degradation. Christians are asked to communicate with policy makers, assist friends and other church members to become more knowledgeable about environmental issues, write opinion pieces for local newspapers, and encourage local congregations to pass resolutions on topics such a global warming. EM urges Christians to support the poor, the hungry, and others in need and to oppose warfare and human greed.

Ecumenical Advocacy Days (EAD)
c/o Office of Public Life and Social Policy
United Church of Christ
100 Maryland Avenue NE, Suite 330
Washington DC 20002
(202) 470-0127
www.advocacydays.org

Beginning in 2003 Ecumenical Advocacy Days has held an annual four-day conference in Washington DC to encourage support for social welfare agendas. The conference participants include theologians, policy experts, politicians, and grassroots religious activists. In 2003 EAD focused on U.S. foreign policy in Africa and the Middle East; in 2004 the organization expanded the agenda to include the poor of the Middle East and Latin America; in 2005 it added treatment of the disadvantaged in the United States; and in 2006 the conference, titled "Challenging Disparity: The Promise of God— The Power of Solidarity," investigated the possible contributions that a progressive religious viewpoint could make to U.S. foreign and domestic policy. The theme of the March 2007 conference was "And How Are the Children?" Following training sessions where more than 1,000 people received instruction on advocating policies in the interest of children, participants visited Capitol Hill to speak with congressional representatives. Those religious groups sponsoring the conferences include Catholic Relief Services, the Christian Church (Disciples of Christ), the Episcopal Church, the Evangelical Lutheran Church in America, the Presbyterian Church (U.S.A.), the Reformed Church in America, the United Church of Christ, and the United Methodist Church.

Episcopal Church Office of Government Relations
110 Maryland Avenue NE, Suite 309
Washington DC 20002
(800) 228-0515
www.ecusa.anglican.org

The Government Relations Office of the Episcopal Church acts as an advocate for those policies set by the church's General Convention, which is held every third year. With a staff of four people, the organization follows the progress of legislation that is of concern to the church, lobbies elected officials, and organizes local support for and against proposed legislation. The office took part in developing President George W. Bush's faith-based initiative for funding religious organizations that offer social services, opposed oil drilling in the Arctic National Wildlife Refuge, and supported passage of an international religious freedom bill. In addition, the organization supported debt relief for poor nations and has advocated assistance for the poor in the United States, including child care services and health insurance. The Washington office works in cooperation with the Episcopal Public Policy Network, which activates members by sending green postcards alerting them to pending votes on legislation and related events.

Episcopal Peace Fellowship (EPF)
637 South Dearborn
Chicago, IL 60605
(312) 922-8628
www.epfnational.org

The Episcopal Peace Fellowship is an independent organization affiliated with the Episcopal Church that works to attain peace with justice in communities, the church, and the world by promoting a Christian response to violence. The EPF began in 1939 as the Episcopal Pacifist Fellowship, a group that supported conscientious objection to military service. In 1966 the organization assumed its present name, hired a full-time staff person, and altered its goal to supporting all those who seek peace, whether or not they are pacifists. The EPF has attempted to establish local chapters and encouraged discussion of such subjects as the death penalty, gun control, nuclear weapons, and conscientious objection. The membership elects the members of the national executive committee, which serves as the organization's governing board. The committee meets twice each year to establish policy and maintains contact with the Episcopal Church and other church organizations.

Episcopal Urban Caucus (EUC)
Park West Station
P.O. Box 21182
New York, NY 10025
(212) 699-2998
www.episcopalurbancaucus.org

Founded in 1980, the Episcopal Urban Caucus works with the Episcopal Church to achieve social justice, including taking action to oppose racism, promote peace, and ameliorate the conditions of poverty and hunger. The EUC holds an annual assembly at which bishops, clergy, and lay members attend workshops, participate in forums, and visit actual examples of urban ministry, which is the major focus of the group's activities. Assembly participants may approve resolutions that are recommendations to the Episcopal Church's General Convention. EUC participants engage in advocacy outside the organization's members. For instance, at the 2002 assembly in Los Angeles, members demonstrated along with hotel and restaurant union workers in support of higher wages, and in 2005 members visited Ellis Island in New York to highlight concern about immigration issues. A quarterly newsletter, *The Urban Networker*, presents information about assembly events and the issues of concern to the EUC.

Faithful America
110 Maryland Avenue NE, Suite 108
Washington DC 20002
(202) 544-2350
(202) 543-1297 (fax)
www.faithfulamerica.org

Faithful America, a program of the National Council of Churches in the USA, is an interfaith electronic advocacy group dedicated to influencing government priorities and creating just and compassionate public policy. Members include adherents of various faiths, including Christians, Jews, Buddhists, Hindus, and Muslims. The organization claims a membership of more than 100,000. Faithful America sends e-mail messages to members offering detailed information about public policy issues and provides the opportunity to send messages to elected officials and to sign petitions. The organization encourages communication among members and with others in their faith community. Members have the opportunity to discuss issues through the group's Weblog (www.faithfulamerica.blogspot.com).

Gay, Lesbian, and Affirming Disciples Alliance (GLAD)
P.O. Box 44400
Indianapolis, IN 46244-0400

(301) 528-4927 (capital area)
www.gladalliance.org

This organization within the Christian Church (Disciples of Christ) strives to have the denomination become more accepting of lesbian, gay, bisexual, and transgendered people and calls for full inclusion of the organization's members in the life of the church. The organization urges congregations to declare that they are "open and affirming" and that gays and lesbians are welcome in the denomination and its leadership. Members of the GLAD are organized into seven ministry teams to facilitate the work of the group. The alliance holds an annual meeting, which is scheduled at the Disciple's General Assembly in the years that the denomination convenes. Local chapters of the organization also meet periodically. The organization publishes *Crossbeams,* an occasional newsletter.

General Board of Church and Society (GBCS), United Methodist Church
100 Maryland Avenue NE
Washington, DC 20002
(202) 488-5600
www.umc-gbcs.org

The General Board of Church and Society, located on Capitol Hill in the nation's capital, has the responsibility of implementing the social policy statements of the United Methodist Church's General Conference. The board's Washington headquarters was opened in 1924 to represent the views of the Methodist Episcopal Church. The Board of Temperance, Prohibition and Public Morals moved to the site to influence the fight for prohibition. However, when prohibition came into effect, the Methodists found other social causes to pursue, such as opposition to gambling and obscenity in publications and films. In the following decades, the board's headquarters building became the focus for various social causes such as the civil rights movement, opposition to the war in Vietnam, support for equal rights for women, and advocacy of environmentalism. Among current issues on which the board advocates public policy positions are juvenile justice and the development of the concept of restorative justice; maintenance of basic freedoms of speech, religion, assembly, and privacy; the right to basic human needs such as food, clothing, shelter, education, and health care; elimination of the death penalty; and the use of peaceful means to resolve international conflicts. In addition to the Washington headquarters, the GBCS maintains a church center for the United Nations in New York City.

Good News
P.O. Box 150
308 East Main Street
Wilmore, KY 40309
(859) 858-4661
(859) 858-4972 (fax)
www.goodnewsmag.org

This organization revolves around the magazine *Good News*, which was first published in 1967. The organization and magazine advocate the basic beliefs of evangelicals within the United Methodist Church. Good News held its first annual convention in 1970. In the late 1960s members of Good News criticized the church's adult study materials, asserting that the curriculum lacked a theologically sound biblical foundation. The organization has opposed "theological pluralism," calling for biblically based doctrine, and expressed concern for liberal trends in theological education within the denomination's seminaries. The group encourages laypeople within the church to become involved in the church's legislative process from the local level to the national General Conference in order to maintain the voice of conservatives in the UMC and to elect conservatives to key positions in the church organization, including the Judicial Council. Good News opposes what the organization considers theological fads and objects to attempts to enact a liberal political agenda, including alterations of church policy on human sexuality.

Institute on Religion and Public Policy
1620 I Street NW, Suite LL10
Washington DC 20006
(202) 835-8760
(202) 835-8764 (fax)
www.religionandpolicy.org

Those associated with the Institute on Religion and Public Policy, recognizing that many Americans have deep religious convictions, believe that religion, ethics, and morality can play a positive role in the policy-making process at the local, state, national, and international levels. The institute is an interreligious organization that encourages cooperation between policy makers and faith-based organizations. In a context of cultural pluralism, the institute promotes "the cooperation of civilizations." The organization focuses on such issues as care for seniors, national security, international religious freedom, business practices, and community renewal. The institute conducts research on domestic and international policy questions, holds lectures and conferences, and publishes materials to facilitate communication between the religious community and policy makers, including weekly reports for members on Institute activities and concerns.

Integrity
620 Park Avenue, Number 311
Rochester, NY 14607-2943
(800) 462-9498
www.integrityusa.org

Integrity, an organization of gay, lesbian, bisexual, and transgendered people in the Episcopal Church that was established in 1974, strives to achieve full acceptance and participation of gay persons in the church and the larger society. Integrity encourages the study of human sexuality within the church and provides educational materials to the clergy and members of the Episcopal Church. The organization provides counseling and an AIDS ministry. It also publishes *The Voice of Integrity*, a quarterly magazine; *Integrity Handbook*, a biannual publication, and *Integrity—Directory*, annual publication.

Interfaith Alliance
1331 H Street NW, 11th Floor
Washington DC 20005
(202) 639-6370
www.interfaithalliance.org

The Interfaith Alliance, claiming a membership of 185,000 people representing more than 75 religious traditions as well as those with no religious affiliation, was founded in 1994 to provide an alternative voice to that of the religious right. The alliance states that the organization promotes a positive role for religion in public life, encourages citizens to participate in the public realm, assists individuals in becoming politically active in their communities, and responds to the political claims of those on the religious right. In 2006 the alliance organized an election-year program, One Nation, Many Faiths, Vote 2006, to provide a deeper understanding of the role that religion plays in elections and to foster a relationship between religious groups and government that maintains the independence of churches from the interests of political candidates. Local alliance organizations work in voter registration drives, attend candidate forums, write letters to newspapers, and encourage leaders to take to heart the message of the group. The Alliance publishes *The Light*, a quarterly newsletter, and offers political guides, including *Religion and Politics: A Guide for Political Candidates*, which provides advice about respecting all religions and warnings about the misuse of religion for partisan gain; and *Religion and Politics: A Guide for House of Worship*, which assists religious leaders regarding appropriate political activity in the church.

Lutheran Services in America (LSA)
122 C Street NW
Washington DC 20001
(202) 626-7932
www.lutheranservices.org

Lutheran Services in America represents the Evangelical Lutheran Church in America and the Lutheran Church–Missouri Synod and associated health and human services groups that provide such assistance as health care, disaster relief, and care for children and the elderly. The organization engages in lobbying activities, meeting with members of Congress and the executive branch. LSA represents the member organizations before the federal government, informing Congress and the Department of Health and Human Services about the Lutheran services funded through Medicaid. LSA advocates the provision of affordable housing for low-income families through the Department of Housing and Urban Development. The organization has opposed any policy to reduce the size of the federal budget that focuses primarily on cutting entitlement programs intended to assist the poor. The organization encourages political participation in support of its objectives and offers guidelines regarding the types of political activity in which nonprofit organizations may engage under Internal Revenue Service regulations. Approximately eight times each year, LSA distributes

LSA Washington, a periodical containing reports on the organization's public policy priorities.

Lutherans Concerned/North America (LC/NA)
P.O. Box 4707
St. Paul, MN 55104-0707
(651) 665-0861
(651) 665-0863 (fax)
www.lcna.org

This organization of Lutherans, established in 1974, encourages the church to welcome gay, lesbian, bisexual, and transgendered people into full participation in the church and the larger society. LC/NA is organized into forty local chapters throughout the nation. The organization supports the passage of legislation at the national level to prohibit discrimination in employment based on sexual orientation. LC/NA publishes *The Concord*, a quarterly newsletter.

Methodist Federation for Social Action (MFSA)
212 East Capital Street NE
Washington DC 20003
(202) 546-8806
(202) 546-6811 (fax)
www.mfsaweb.org

The Methodist Federation for Social Action, established in 1907, is composed of clergy and lay members who work to attain various social reforms, including the rejection of warfare, the elimination of nuclear weapons, the development of democratic social and economic planning to encourage the formation of a society devoid of discrimination, and the defense of civil rights and civil liberties. The organization supports human rights as presented in the Bible and the United Nations Declaration of Human Rights. MFSA also publishes *Social Questions Bulletin*, a bimonthy newsletter that contains discussions of religious, social, and political issues.

**More Light Presbyterians for Lesbian, Gay, Bisexual,
and Transgender Concerns**
P.M.B. 246
4737 Country Road
Minnetonka, MN 55345-2634

(505) 820-7082
(505) 820-2540 (fax)
www.mlp.org

Established in 1974, More Light Presbyterians strives to voice the interests of gay, lesbian, bisexual, and transgendered individuals within the Presbyterian Church. The organization seeks to achieve full membership rights in the church, including marriage and ordination, and publishes the *More Light Update*, a bimonthly newsletter.

National Council of Churches USA (NCC)

110 Maryland Avenue NE
Washington, DC 20002
(202) 544-2350
www.ncccusa.org

Member organizations of the NCC are drawn from Protestant, Anglican, Orthodox, evangelical, and African American denominations representing 45 million people and 100,000 local congregations. All the mainline Protestant denominations discussed in this book are members of the National Council of Churches. The NCC was established in 1950, supplanting the Federal Council of Churches. The NCC's Justice and Advocacy Commission, one of five commissions, has the responsibility of pursuing the issue agenda of the organization, including racial justice, the rights of women, environmental protection, and the problems faced by urban areas. Each year, representatives of the member denominations meet at the General Assembly to consider policy statements. Between meetings of the General Assembly, the governing board carries out the policies of the organization. The NCC publishes its annual *Yearbook of American and Canadian Churches*, a directory of information about member denominations, and *EcuLink*, a quarterly newsletter containing information about the organization's public policy advocacy.

National Ministries, American Baptist Churches USA (NM)

P.O. Box 851
Valley Forge, PA 19482-0851
(800) 222-3872, extension 2455
(800) 768-2470 (fax)
www.nationalministries.org

National Ministries, an organization within the American Baptist Churches USA, has the mission of disseminating the Christian faith, working for social justice, and training Christian leaders. The organization maintains an office in Washington DC, which encourages church members to become active politically and advocates the public policy preferences of the denomination. Members are encouraged to translate their Christian faith into political activism, sharing their views with others in the community and with legislators. National Ministries supports programs that benefit those who are less advantaged economically. NM administers Judson Press, the denomination's publishing outlet. Among the publications distributed are *The Christian Citizen*, a magazine published three times each year that focuses on issues of justice; *Mission in America*, a bimonthly publication covering American Baptist home mission activities; and *The Pebble*, a quarterly newsletter that provides information about the needs of children in the church and the wider community.

Network: A National Catholic Social Justice Lobby
25 E Street NW, Suite 200
Washington DC 20001-1630
(202) 347-9797
(202) 347-9864 (fax)
www.networklobby.org

In 1971 a group of forty-seven Catholic sisters formed Network as a means of communicating with government officials about the attainment of justice for all people. The organization represents the Catholic community in the nation's capital, attempting to influence Congress in policies related to peace and social and economic justice. Network membership includes both individuals and groups. Network claims a total of 100,000 people associated with the organization. When the Washington office decides to take a stand on legislation, members are contacted to send letters and e-mails to senators and representatives. Among the issues the organization has placed on its agenda are immigration policy, the provision of affordable housing, universal health care, wage equity, the attainment of peace in Iraq, fair international trade, a just system of taxation, and retirement security.
Network publishes *Connection*, a bimonthly magazine that provides analyses of issues, legislative updates, and the voting records

of congressional members; monthly legislative updates; weekly e-mail legislative updates.

Pax Christi–U.S.A. (PC–USA)
532 West 8th Street
Erie, PA 16502
(814) 453-4955
(814) 452-4784 (fax)
www.paxchristiusa.org

This Catholic organization, established in the United States in 1972, is dedicated to Christian nonviolence. The Pax Christi movement began in Europe after the Second World War in France and Germany and spread to other countries, including Italy, Spain, Austria, Switzerland, and Belgium. Pax Christi advocates the idea of Christian nonviolence, beginning with personal relationships, with the ultimate intent of establishing peace in the community and transforming society. The organization rejects warfare and other forms of violence and domination and advocates economic and social justice and an environmentally sustainable world. The United Nations recognizes Pax Christi as a nongovernmental organization with advisory status. PC–USA publishes *Catholic Peace Voice*, a bimonthly newspaper.

Presbyterian Washington Office
100 Maryland Avenue NE
Washington DC 20002
(202) 543-1126
www.pcusa.org/washington

The Washington Office of the Presbyterian Church (U.S.A.) opened in 1946 and acts as an advocacy arm for the denomination's General Assembly and the social policies dealing with justice and peace issues it has enacted. Washington Office personnel contact national policy makers by phone, by letter, and in person. They are available to testify before congressional committees and to assist church leaders who may be invited to testify. The office calls on denomination members to contact their congressional representatives on such issues as education, the federal minimum wage, the Middle East conflict, and immigration reform. The organization's Web site provides advice to church members who wish to contact their public officials about a public policy issue. In election years, the office encourages members to discuss issues with candidates and to become familiar with the church's stand on these issues. When Congress is in session, the office holds a two-hour briefing the second Tuesday of every month to update the status of bills related to subjects about which previous General Assemblies have made recommendations.

Presbyterian Women (PW)
100 Witherspoon Street
Louisville, KY 40202
(888) 728-7228
(502) 569-8600 (fax)
www.pcusa.org/pw/index.htm

Presbyterian Women was established in 1988, the successor to 200 years of women's organizations within the Presbyterian Church. The organization provides the opportunity for women to participate effectively within the Presbyterian Church (U.S.A.). The organization focuses its activities on the rights of the economically and politically disadvantaged, including the subjects of child abandonment, rape, and divorce, and takes stands on issues of justice, peace, and world hunger. PW engages in the educational ministry of the denomination and takes part in training church leaders by conducting workshops at the local, regional, and national levels, and publishes *Justice and Peace Links*, a newsletter issued three times per year.

Presbyterians for Renewal (PFR)
8134 New La Grange Road, Suite 227
Louisville, KY 40222-4679
(502) 425-4630
(502) 423-8329 (fax)
www.pfrenewal.org

A group of ministers and elders of the Presbyterian Church (U.S.A.) met in 1988 to consider the formation of a renewal organization within the denomination. The following year, a conference was held in St. Louis to establish Presbyterians for Renewal, the successor to two previous renewal organizations: Presbyterians United for Biblical Concern and Covenant Fellowship of Presbyterians. The conference members committed themselves to recognizing the Bible as the authority for their faith. In addition, they pledged to pursue social justice and to oppose racism and sexism. PFR is involved in the governance of the PCUSA, emphasizes the training of lay members for ministry within the church, and conducts renewal events for individuals and congregations. PFR publishes *ReForm*, an annual journal.

Presbyterians Pro-Life (PPL)
3942 Middle Road
Allison Park, PA 15101
(412) 487-1990
(412) 487-1994 (fax)
www.ppl.org

Objecting to the position of the Presbyterian Church (U.S.A.) on the issue of abortion and the church's membership in the Religious Coalition for Reproductive Choice, Presbyterians Pro-Life, composed of pastors and lay members of the PCUSA, is dedicated to protecting the right to life from the moment of conception until natural death. PPL holds that the Bible must be accepted as the sole and infallible guide for faith and conduct. Organization members oppose any action, including abortion, infanticide, and euthanasia, that they believe devalues human life. In addition to a pro-life stand, the organization takes the position that the church should support a biblical understanding of sexual relationships as restricted to one man and one woman in the covenant of marriage.

Progressive Christians Uniting (PCU)
1501 Wilshire Boulevard
Los Angeles, CA 90017
(213) 989-1630
www.progressivechristiansuniting.org

George F. Regas and John Cobb, Jr., established Progressive Christians Uniting in 1996 to provide an alternative to conservative Christian groups and individuals such as Jerry Falwell and Pat Robertson and to assist progressive Christian congregations and individuals in their work in such areas as labor rights, criminal justice reform, affordable housing, immigration reform, and fair economic and environmental policy. Originally known as the Claremont Consultation, the organization was given its present name in 2003. PCU's activities are limited primarily to Southern California, offering resources to congregations, clergy, and peace and justice activists. Among the organization's projects are Eyes on the Future, an educational program to help high school students make their concerns known in the wider community, and the Sustainability Project, an effort by Christian organizations to work for environmental sustainability and ecological justice.

Protestants for the Common Good (PCG)
77 West Washington Street, Suite 1124
Chicago, IL 60602
(312) 223-9544
(312) 223-9540 (fax)
www.thecommongood.org

This organization, active primarily in the Chicago area, was established in 1995 out of a concern that religious right organizations had given the mistaken impression that they spoke for all Protestants on public policy issues. PCG advocates an understanding of the common good that promotes the conditions for community flourishing. The organization's areas of activity include promoting democracy and economic justice, decreasing the poverty rate, improving public education, providing affordable housing for the poor, reforming the criminal justice system, lobbying for campaign finance and election reform, and enhancing environmental protection. Among the group's specific initiatives are support for an amendment to the Illinois Human Rights Act to ban housing and employment discrimination on the basis of sexual orientation, advocacy of a fair tax system to support public education and human services, and opposition to funding reductions for Medicare and Medicaid. PCG publishes *The Common Good*, a monthly journal.

Religious Coalition for Reproductive Choice (RCRC)
1025 Vermont Avenue NW, Suite 1130
Washington DC 20005
(202) 628-7700
www.rcrc.org

Founded in 1973, the RCRC supports the right of the individual to reproductive choice (including the right to abortion) without government involvement and religious freedom generally. The RCRC receives significant support from groups in mainline churches, including the Episcopal Church, the Presbyterian Church (U.S.A.), the United Church of Christ, and the United Methodist Church. The movement began in 1967 when Howard Moody, pastor of Judson Memorial Church, an American Baptist congregation in New York City, led pro-choice clergy in the formation of the Clergy Consultation Service on Abortion. In response to the Catholic Church's pledge to overturn the 1973 *Roe v. Wade* decision that legalized abortion, mainline Protestant and Jewish leaders met in Washington DC to plan the formation of the Religious Coalition for Abortion Rights. Twenty years later, the organization's name was changed to the Religious Coalition for Reproductive Choice, indicating the greater breadth of policy concerns, including sex education, AIDS, family planning, and contraception. The RCRC has supported the *Roe* decision in the political and legal realms. In 2005 the RCRC opposed the nomination of John Roberts as the U.S. Supreme Court chief justice.

Society of Catholic Social Scientists (SCSS)
1235 University Boulevard
Franciscan University of Steubenville
Steubenville, OH 43952
(740) 284-5377
(740) 283-6401 (fax)
www.catholicsocialscientists.org

This organization, composed of scholars, professors, researchers, and other Catholics engaged in the social sciences, encourages cooperation in the investigation of political, social, and economic systems in order to develop knowledge that can aid the mission of the Catholic Church, assist in the protection of human life, and promote recognition of the fundamental rights of human beings. The organization's journal, *Catholic Social Science Review*, has published articles on many subjects relevant to public policy, including natural law and American politics, the Catholic study of political institutions, the morality of affirmative action, social welfare, dealing with social change, corporate downsizing, Christianity and democracy, and political economy.

Sojourners/Call to Renewal
3333 14th Street NW, Suite 200
Washington DC 20010
(800) 714-7474
www.calltorenewal.org

Each headed by Jim Wallis, Sojourners and Call to Renewal decided in 2006 to unite their efforts to reduce poverty in the United States. The newly united organization plans to place the issue of poverty on the political agenda in future election campaigns. Sojourners/ Call to Renewal has invited individuals and religious organizations to endorse A Covenant for a New America, a commitment to provide families with economic security, to end poverty among children, and to support government and economic policies to reduce poverty in other nations. Religious organizations are encouraged to organize delegations to visit elected officials and to write letters to the editor of local newspapers expressing a moral obligation to fight poverty. Among the organizations that have endorsed the Covenant are the Evangelical Lutheran Church in America, the Christian Church (Disciples of Christ), the Presbyterian Church (U.S.A.), the United Methodist Church, and the National Council of Churches U.S.A. The organization publishes *Sojourners*, a monthly magazine, and *The Call*, an occasional newsletter.

Survivors Network of those Abused by Priests (SNAP)
P.O. Box 6416
Chicago, IL 60680-6416
(877) 762-7432
www.snapnetwork.org

Barbara Blaine established the Survivors Network in 1989 as a support group for those claiming to have been sexually molested by priests and others in the Catholic Church. The organization has no affiliation with the Catholic Church or its officials. SNAP offers people counseling in self-help group meetings in local chapters, over the phone, online, and at national meetings held twice each year. The network urges people to write to state legislators and members of Congress asking them to support proposed legislation to enhance sexual abuse laws in order to provide just settlements for all victims of sexual abuse.

Target Earth International
P.O. Box 10777
Tempe, AZ 85284
(610) 909-9740
(443) 284-2399 (fax)
www.targetearth.org

Target Earth is a Christian movement composed of individuals, churches, and college groups dedicated to the care of the environment and service to the poor. The organization works for the development of a sustainable planet that offers justice for all human beings. Target Earth engages in environmental activities in fifteen countries. The organization has sponsored a summer institute on sustainable development to provide participants with theoretical and practical understanding of economic development that does not threaten the ecosystem, and the opportunity to participate in a local community development project. Target Earth also supports the Global Stewardship Study Program, based at Jaguar Creek, an education center located in the rain forest of Belize. Participants combine the study of environmental subjects with Christian discipleship.

United Church of Christ Justice and Peace Action Network (JPANet)
100 Maryland Avenue NE, Suite 330
Washington DC 20002
(202) 543-1517
www.ucc.org/justice/jpan.htm

The Justice and Peace Action Network informs and activates members of the United Church of Christ to advocate public policy in accord with the values of the church community. Areas of concern for the JPANet include racial and economic justice, peacemaking, civil and human rights, global poverty, violence against women, stem-cell research, the minimum wage, and setting policy priorities in the federal budget. The organization cooperates with the Christian Church (Disciples of Christ) in its various activities. Each week that Congress is in session, JPANet provides online descriptions of legislation that can be used in local church bulletins and urges members to contact their representatives. JPANet also distributes an annual issues briefing book, which contains summaries of policy priorities. The organization presents sample letters that can guide members in writing to the appropriate decision makers. JPANet supports Our Faith Our Vote (OFOV), a Web-based campaign to encourage church members to register to vote, attend campaign activities, and plan "get out the vote" activities. Noting that recent congressional legislation has followed paths contrary to those that the UCC General Synod recommended, OFOV offers resources that explain the legal limits of church involvement in political activity.

United States Conference of Catholic Bishops (USCCB)
3211 Fourth Street NE
Washington DC 20017
(202) 541-3000
www.usccb.org

This assembly of the bishops of the Catholic Church is the highest church authority in the United States and is responsible for relating church doctrine to the present circumstances in the overall society. In 1917 the U.S. bishops established the National Catholic War Council, the precursor of the conference. In 1919, at the urging of Pope Benedict XV, the bishops established the National Catholic Welfare Council, with headquarters in Washington DC, to address questions of social need and justice. In 1922 the National Catholic Welfare Conference was established to deal with such social issues as education and immigration. In 1966, on the recommendation of the Vatican, two separate organizations were established: the National Conference of Catholic Bishops (NCCB), composed exclusively of bishops, and the United States Catholic Conference (USCC), with bishops as well as laypeople as members. In 2001 the NCCB and the USCC combined to form the United States Conference of Catholic Bishops. The USCCB has established several departments, many of which deal with questions of public policy, including environmental justice, international peace and justice, science and human values, and pro-life efforts. The bishops have issued statements on various issues, including criticizing the death penalty and opposing the construction of a fence along the U.S. border with Mexico.

United States Conference of the World Council of Churches
475 Riverside Drive, Room 1370
New York, NY 10115
www.wcc-usa.org

The United States Conference of the World Council of Churches functions as a communication channel between the WCC and the member churches in the United States. All of the mainline Protestant churches that are the focus of this book are members of the WCC. U.S. churches join with other member organizations to speak out on such issues as nuclear proliferation, racism, the

AIDS pandemic, and economic and social justice. In 2001 the WCC began a program titled the Decade to Overcome Violence (DOV) as a means to deal with violence within countries and internationally. In 2005, the DOV theme "The Power and Promise of Peace" focused on the United States. The conference publishes *Ecumenical Courier*, a quarterly newsletter. At the Ninth Assembly of the WCC in 2006, representatives from the United States presented a formal letter of apology on behalf of the U.S. conference that stated the United States "has done much . . . to endanger the human family and to abuse the creation." The letter declared that the United States responded to the terrorist attacks of September 11, 2001, by "raining down terror on the truly vulnerable among our global neighbors." Among those supporting the statement were Sharon Watkins, president of the Christian Church (Disciples of Christ) and John Thomas, president of the United Church of Christ.

Voice of the Faithful (VOTF)
P.O. Box 423
Newton Upper Falls, MA 02464
(617) 558-5252
(617) 558-0034 (fax)
www.voiceofthefaithful.org

Voice of the Faithful focuses its efforts on the sexual abuse controversy in the Catholic Church. VOTF claims that American bishops and the Vatican failed to deal adequately with the crisis and instead became involved in attempts to prevent news of the abuse from becoming public. The group serves the needs of sexual abuse victims, supports priests who are faithful to their vows, and strives to effect structural change within the church in order to prevent future abuse. The organization monitors the performance of dioceses, including financial management and clergy-laity communication. In Boston, VOTF has supported the establishment of a fund that will allow contributors to support Catholic programs without the possibility that the church hierarchy will use the resources for legal settlements and fees. The organization continues to accept the authority of the Catholic Church on other matters, declining to take stands on proposals that other groups within the church have made. For instance, it refuses to support an end to the celibacy of priests and does not advocate the exclusion of nonpracticing homosexuals from the priesthood or the ordination of women.

Witherspoon Society
1418 Clarendon Drive
Wayzata, MN 55391-2103
www.witherspoonsociety.org

Members of the Witherspoon Society are Presbyterians who advocate peace, justice, the preservation of the environment, and the involvement of church members in social issues. The society produces a quarterly newsletter, *Network News*, which includes commentary on issues of concern to the Presbyterian Church and the broader community. The society, which was founded in the 1970s, attempts to promote the activity of the Presbyterian Church toward biblically faithful engagement with society. Among the issues about which the group has become concerned and to which they wish to bring a biblical perspective are the Palestinian-Israeli conflict, immigrant rights, the use of torture, and the war in Iraq.

Word Alone Network
2299 Palmer Drive, Suite 220
New Brighton, MN 55112
(651) 633-6004
(651) 633-4260
www.wordalone.org

Clergy within the Evangelical Lutheran Church in America (ELCA) who were concerned about certain elements of the proposed agreement with the Episcopal Church decided to communicate primarily via the Internet to express more effectively their understanding of Lutheranism. Although the 1997 ELCA Churchwide Assembly rejected the agreement, the 1999 assembly approved a revised proposal titled Called to Common Mission. Among the concerns of this group of pastors was the Episcopal tradition of granting to bishops alone the authority to ordain new pastors. The organization has continued to act as a dissenting voice in the ELCA, focusing on such issues as the ordination of actively gay pastors and the blessing of same-gender unions. At the 2004 annual convention, network members approved a resolution that affirmed what they considered biblical teaching on sexuality and marriage and rejected any revision that contradicted that teaching. Other dissenters decided to move further away from the ELCA by establishing Lutheran Congregations in Mission for Christ.

8

Resources

These resources include books about the mainline denominations and their traditions, beliefs, organization, and current
concerns—including internal controversies over the denominations' value positions on key policy issues. More general works
about the policy concerns of these religious organizations are also
described. Nonprint resources, including videos, DVDs, and Web
sites, provide additional information about the mainline churches
and their various value positions on current issues.

Books

**Albright, Madeleine. 2006. *The Mighty and the Almighty: Reflec-
tions on America, God, and World Affairs*. New York: Harper
Collins.**

Albright, secretary of state under President Bill Clinton, reveals
that the Clinton administration followed a foreign policy guided
by political realism that largely ignored religious convictions. With
the rise of militant Islamist groups, she recommends that realism
be tempered by religious convictions and values while maintaining tolerance of others' religious beliefs. Albright urges the State
Department to nurture among its employees greater knowledge
of religious movements.

Alexander, J. Neil. 2003. *This Far by Grace: A Bishop's Journey through Questions of Homosexuality.* **Lanham, MD: National Book Network.**

Writing shortly after the Episcopal Church General Convention ratified the election of V. Gene Robinson, an openly gay priest, as a bishop, Alexander describes his personal transformation, through theological and scriptural exploration, from opposition to acceptance of homosexuals in the church.

Allen, Charles L. 1998. *Meet the Methodists: An Introduction to the United Methodist Church.* **Revised ed. Nashville, TN: Abingdon.**

This brief introduction to the United Methodist Church provides information about the beliefs of United Methodists, including the creeds to which the denomination adheres. Allen describes the historical development of the denomination and its governing structure and discusses the church's value positions and social concerns, including stands on education, warfare, and racial discrimination.

Anglican Communion Office. 2004. *Windsor Report 2004: Lambeth Commission on Communion.* **Harrisburg, PA: Morehouse.**

Archbishop of Canterbury Rowan Williams established the Lambeth Commission to investigate the theological and legal consequences of the decision of the Episcopal Church in the United States to select an actively gay bishop and the new policy of the Canadian Diocese of New Westminster to authorize the blessing of same-gender unions. This report presents the findings of the commission, which takes a conciliatory position on the continued association of the various provinces in the Anglican Communion.

Armentrout, Don S., and Robert Boak Slocum, eds. 2005. *An Episcopal Dictionary of the Church: A User-Friendly Reference for Episcopalians.* **New York: Church Publishing.**

This reference work provides extensive information about the Episcopal Church, including the denomination's history, organizational structure, theology, and worship practices. The dictionary offers additional information about the Anglican Church around the world.

Ayala, Francisco J. 2006. *Darwin and Intelligent Design.* Minneapolis: Fortress.

Ayala, a biologist, examines the idea of intelligent design, which involves the claim that the theory of evolution cannot explain the complex development of individual species. The existence of human beings therefore must be the result of a designer, or God. The author describes the theory of evolution and its success at explaining biological development, examines intelligent design as its contemporary proponents present the idea, and offers what he considers both its scientific as well as theological weaknesses as an explanation of the complexities of life.

Balmer, Randall. 1996. *Grant Us Courage: Travels Along the Mainline of American Protestantism.* New York: Oxford University Press.

Balmer describes his visits to twelve mainline Protestant churches that originally were the subjects of a series of articles published in *Christian Century.* The individual depictions suggest possible explanations for the membership losses that such churches have suffered at the hands of more fundamentalist and evangelical movements.

Balmer, Randall, and John R. Fitzmier. 1994. *The Presbyterians.* Westport, CT: Greenwood.

Balmer and Fitzmier present the history of the Presbyterian Church, including its European origins and its development in North America from the colonial period to the denomination's current participation in the ecumenical movement. The authors describe the historical divisions within the denomination over such issues as church doctrine and slavery. The book includes biographical sketches of prominent Presbyterian leaders and a chronology of important events.

Balmer, Randall, and Mark Silk, eds. 2006. *Religion and Public Life in the Middle Atlantic Region: The Fount of Diversity.* Lanham, MD: Alta Mira.

The contributors to this volume emphasize the religious pluralism in this region of the country, which began in seventeenth-century colonial America with such groups as the Quakers in Pennsylvania and the Catholics in Maryland. Individual essays investigate such topics as the relative influence of Protestants and Catholics and the religious identification of new immigrants.

Barlow, Philip, and Mark Silk, eds. 2004. *Religion and Public Life in the Midwest: America's Common Denominator?* **Lanham, MD: Alta Mira.**

This volume of essays investigates religious affiliation in the midwestern states. The editors note that the beliefs, attitudes, and values of residents in these states tend to mirror the overall religious perspectives of the nation. Individual essays treat such subjects as Methodism, the prevalence of Lutheranism in the region, and religious affiliation in Chicago.

Barrera, Albino. 2001. *Modern Catholic Social Documents and Political Economy.* **Washington DC: Georgetown University Press.**

Barrera focuses on Catholic social teaching on political economy, investigating its transformation from more traditional thinking about the just price for goods to the application of social and economic theory to postindustrial issues. Among various topics, the author discusses resolving conflicts between labor and management.

Bass, Diana Butler, and Joseph Stewart-Sicking, eds. 2006. *Mainline Church Transformation, from Nomads to Pilgrims: Stories from Practicing Congregations.* **Herndon, VA: Alban Institute.**

This work provides different accounts of mainline congregations that have reversed decline and now are active and growing. Success is attributed to discovering, and welcoming, the stranger and providing him or her with a connection to the community and to worshiping God.

Bates, Stephen. 2005. *A Church at War: Anglicans and Homosexuality.* **London: Hodder and Stoughton.**

Bates discusses the controversy over homosexuality—the ordination of homosexual priests and the blessing of same-gender unions—within the Anglican Communion. Although there are an estimated 77 million Anglicans around the world, it is the 2.3-million-member Episcopal Church in the United States that most clearly generated the conflict with the election of V. Gene

Robinson, an openly gay priest, as bishop of New Hampshire. Bates, a journalist, presents an in-depth look at the historical roots and the contemporary circumstances of this controversial topic.

Bayer, Charles. 1997. *The Babylonian Captivity of the Mainline Church.* **Atlanta, GA: Chalice.**

Bayer observes that the mainline churches are situated between the secular society on one side and conservative evangelicals on the other. The author discusses whether and how the mainline denominations can endure in such an unfavorable climate.

Beed, Clive, and Cara Beed. 2006. *Alternatives to Economics: Christian Socio-Economic Perspectives.* **Lanham, MD: University Press of America.**

Beed and Beed explore a Christian understanding of the economy using a biblical perspective. The authors propose an alternative to secular social science based on Christian values as a method to develop socioeconomic policies.

Benedetto, Robert, Darrell L. Guder, and Donald K. McKim. 1999. *Historical Dictionary of the Reformed Churches.* **Lanham, MD: Scarecrow.**

Beginning with a chronology, the authors include entries on the geographical areas where the Reformed tradition is strongest, significant figures within the Reformed tradition from the Reformation to the present, theological terms, church governance, education, and commitment to social activism.

Bequette, John P. 2004. *Christian Humanism: Creation, Redemption, and Reintegration.* **Lanham, MD: University Press of America.**

Bequette, writing from a Catholic perspective, investigates the origins of the Christian humanist world view. The author examines the importance of Christianity in such areas as literature, race relations, economic justice, politics, the rights of women, and the sanctity of human life.

Billingsley, Andrew. 1999. *Mighty Like a River: The Black Church and Social Reform.* **New York: Oxford University Press.**

Billingsley discusses the influence that black churches have had on shaping American society, particularly as they struggled with social, economic, and political problems in the African American community. The book contains accounts of black men and women who helped to found activist African American churches.

Black, Amy E., Douglas L. Koopman, and David K. Ryden. 2004. *Of Little Faith: The Politics of George W. Bush's Faith-Based Initiatives.* **Washington DC: Georgetown University Press.**

Using interviews with key political and governmental figures in Washington DC, the authors describe the development of President George W. Bush's faith-based initiative from the 2000 presidential campaign through the various congressional votes during Bush's first term. The authors focus on the reasons the initiative failed to win wide support in Congress, including conflict among competing interests and poor communication.

Blankman, Drew W. 2004. *Pocket Dictionary of North American Denominations: Over 100 Christian Groups Clearly and Concisely Defined.* **Downers Grove, IL: InterVarsity Press.**

Blankman provides descriptions of various churches in the United States, including mainline, evangelical, Pentecostal, and African American, as well as less orthodox groups.

Bloomquist, Karen L., and John R. Stumme, eds. 1998. *The Promise of Lutheran Ethics.* **Minneapolis: Fortress.**

This work contains contributions from ten Lutheran ethicists who investigate the role of a Lutheran approach to ethics in the contemporary world as a guide to Christian witness for justice. In an exchange, the contributors discuss the possible insights this ethical approach has for such issues as homosexuality that Evangelical Lutheran Church in America members currently are debating.

Booty, John. 1990. *What Makes Us Episcopalians?* **Harrisburg, PA: Morehouse.**

In this brief volume, Booty presents a synopsis of the history of the Episcopal Church in the United States, focusing on the four foundational principles of the denomination: tradition, experience, reason, and scripture.

Brackney, William H. 2005. *Human Rights and the World's Major Religions.* **Volume 2. Westport, CT: Praeger.**

In this second volume of a five-volume set, Brackney, professor of religion and director of the Baptist Studies Program at Baylor University, examines the idea of human rights in the Christian tradition from its origins to the present. The author provides insights into how Christian beliefs can contribute to a contemporary understanding of human rights.

Brondos, David. 2005. *The Letter and the Spirit: Discerning God's Will in a Complex World.* **Minneapolis: Augsburg Fortress.**

Brondos explores the biblical principles that can assist Christians in dealing with complex ethical problems in the contemporary world. Addressed primarily to Lutherans, the book attempts to guide readers in meeting human needs by consulting biblical mandates.

Brubaker, Pamela K., Rebecca Todd Peters, and Laura A. Stivers, eds. 2006. *Justice in a Global Economy: Strategies for Home, Community, and World.* **Louisville, KY: Westminster John Knox.**

The contributors to this volume, including ethicists and theologians, examine such social issues as land use, immigration, business accountability, environmental protection, and economic justice. The authors critically evaluate contemporary political and economic institutions and provide examples of communities that are trying to initiate societal reform.

Brugemann, Walter, ed. 2001. *Hope for the World: Mission in a Global Context.* **Minneapolis: Fortress.**

The authors of the articles in this collection investigate the ministry of the church in the global context, maintaining that in order to deal successfully with the crises resulting from political and military conditions as well as the globalization of the world economy, the church must modify the traditional ways in which it conducts its ministry and adjust that ministry to specific contemporary circumstances.

Bruggink, Donald J., and Kim N. Baker. 2004. *By Grace Alone: Stories of the Reformed Church in America.* **Grand Rapids, MI: W. B. Eerdmans.**

Bruggink and Baker present a history of the development of the Reformed Church in America from its roots in the sixteenth-century Reformation to the establishment of a church in New Amsterdam (ultimately New York) in 1628 and its mission in the new nation. The authors discuss the growth of the church, conflicts that arose, and its missionary efforts. The book contains a wealth of photographs and the stories of past and current members of the Reformed Church, including popular author Norman Vincent Peale and Robert Schuller, long-time pastor of the Crystal Cathedral in Garden Grove, California.

Bullock, Robert H., ed. 2006. *Presbyterians Being Reformed: Reflections on What a Church Needs Today.* **Louisville, KY: Westminster John Knox.**

The contributors to this volume, representing various theological perspectives, investigate the present status of the Presbyterian Church (U.S.A.), the values of the denomination, and what each author considers to be its most significant commitments.

Campolo, Tony. 1995. *Can Mainline Denominations Make a Comeback?* **Valley Forge, PA: Judson Press.**

Although many have concluded that the mainline denominations are becoming obsolete, Campolo argues that if these churches can adjust to past and future social changes, they may arrive at a satisfactory equilibrium between their traditional religious mission and an appropriate response to the nation's social problems.

Campolo, Tony. 2003. *Revolution and Renewal: How Churches Are Saving Our Cities.* **Louisville, KY: Westminster John Knox.**

Campolo recounts the experiences of men and women of faith who did not leave urban communities but instead remained committed to renewing the social and religious life of cities.

Campolo, Tony, and Michael Battle. 2005. *The Church Enslaved: Spirituality for Racial Reconciliation.* **Minneapolis: Fortress.**

Campolo and Battle urge Christian churches to take the lead in rectifying the effects of racial segregation. The authors examine racial divisions within churches and call for black and white churches to prevail over past conflicts. They argue that churches that have resolved such racial issues can help to bring about needed change in the larger society.

Carey, Patrick W. 1993. *The Roman Catholics.* **Westport, CT: Greenwood.**

Carey presents a summary of the history and development of the Catholic Church in the United States from the colonial period to the post–Vatican II events that brought significant change to the denomination. The author includes biographical sketches of leaders and other significant Catholic figures and a chronology of important events.

Carey, Patrick W. 2004. *Catholics in America: A History.* **Lanham, MD: Praeger.**

Carey examines the history of the Catholic community in America, discussing Catholics' involvement in civic, political, social, and cultural activities. The author identifies the people and events that helped determine the basic characteristics of Catholicism in the United States.

Carroll, Jackson W. 2000. *Mainline to the Future: Congregations for the 21st Century.* **Phoenix, AZ: Westminster John Knox.**

Carroll focuses on the success of nontraditional churches and proposes ways in which mainline denominations might learn from these churches and apply their tactics in order to reverse the downward trend in membership. The author recommends that a balance must be struck between the value of tradition and the reality of change.

Chalker, William H. 2006. *Science and Faith.* **Louisville, KY: Westminster John Knox.**

Although distinguishing the different truth claims that science and religion make, Chalker explains how the two realms can be seen to be compatible. The author argues that scientific knowledge and religious knowledge speak to different human needs and therefore there is no necessary conflict between the two ways of thinking.

Chestnut, Robert A. 2000. *Transforming the Mainline Church: Lessons in Change from Pittsburgh's Cathedral of Hope.* **Phoenix, AZ: Westminster John Knox.**

Chestnut, who became pastor of East Liberty Presbyterian Church in Pittsburgh in 1988, describes how the church reversed a long decline, increasing membership, expanding the church's ministry, and improving finances. The author suggests that other churches can do the same by accepting diversity, supporting innovative leadership, and paying attention to the religious concerns of a younger generation rather than focusing on narrow denominational issues.

Childs, James M., Jr., ed. 2003. *Faithful Conversation: Christian Perspectives on Homosexuality.* **Minneapolis: Fortress.**

In the five essays contained in this volume, the authors discuss the various issues of homosexuality that have intensified controversy in the church, including proposals for the ordination of gays and lesbians and the blessing of same-gender unions. The contributors engage in a forum to discuss how these questions are affecting churches.

Cimino, Richard, ed. 2003. *Lutherans Today: American Lutheran Identity in the 21st Century.* **Grand Rapids, MI: W. B. Eerdmans.**

The authors of this group of essays chart the territory established by the various Lutheran denominations in the contemporary American Christian landscape and speculate about the future of Lutheranism. Individual chapters deal with the "Lutheran left," the Word Alone movement within the Evangelical Lutheran Church in America, megachurches in the ELCA, the social theology of Lutheran pastors, and multiculturalism in the church.

Cleary, Edward L., and Allen D. Hertzke, eds. 2005. *Representing God at the Statehouse.* **Blue Ridge Summit, PA: Rowman and Littlefield.**

The nine essays in this volume examine the lobbying activities of Christian churches and other religious groups at the state level. Each essay focuses on the motivations of different denominations to engage in political activity and the varying interests involved, particularly those related to welfare policy.

Cnaan, Ram A., with Stephanie C. Boddie, Charlene C. McGraw, and Jennifer Kang. 2006. *The Other Philadelphia Story: How*

Local Congregations Support Quality of Life in Urban America. **Philadelphia: University of Pennsylvania Press.**

The authors present findings of a study of 1,392 congregations in the Philadelphia area, examining the churches' involvement in providing social services and support for other organizations. The authors conclude that nearly every congregation takes part in providing care for others, indicating the presence of an ethic of responsibility to help others in the community.

Cobb, John B. 1997. *Reclaiming the Church: Where the Mainline Church Went Wrong and What to Do About It.* **Phoenix, AZ: Westminster John Knox.**

Describing the decline of the mainline denominations from their once influential position, Cobb argues that in order to survive, these churches must engage the present social conditions, moving away from the margins of society.

Cobb, John B. 2003. *Progressive Christians Speak: A Different Voice on Faith and Politics.* **Phoenix, AZ: Westminster John Knox.**

Cobb argues that religion should play a crucial role in solving major social problems, urging Christian churches to become active in confronting such issues as hunger, the burgeoning world population, the welfare system, illegal drug use, human rights, immigration, pollution, and abortion.

Cochran, Clarke E., and David Carroll Cochran. 2003. *Catholics, Politics, and Public Policy: Beyond Left and Right.* **Maryknoll, NY: Orbis.**

The authors examine various issues from the perspective of Catholic social teaching, including education and welfare, health care policy, warfare and nuclear weapons, the criminal justice system, and protection of the environment and the sanctity of life.

Cooey, Paula M. 2006. *Willing the Good: Jesus, Dissent, and Desire.* **Minneapolis: Fortress.**

Recognizing that traditional Christian groups have tended to disapprove of dissent, Cooey argues that disagreement has been an important aspect of Christianity from the beginning and played an important role in the Reformation. The author claims that a willingness to dissent can benefit the church and contribute to a more relevant Christian theology and ethics.

Crew, Louie, compiler. 2003. *101 Reasons to Be Episcopalian.* **Harrisburg, PA: Morehouse.**

Crew, a member of the Executive Council of the Episcopal Church, compiled this list of reasons for being an Episcopalian from the responses he received from his online invitation to Episcopalians to answer the question, "What do you like about the Episcopal Church?" The responses, although not the result of a scientific poll, provide insights into the beliefs, customs, and disagreements among members of the Episcopal Church.

Cromartie, Michael, ed. 2005. *Religion and Politics in America: A Conversation.* **Lanham, MD: Rowman and Littlefield.**

This series of conversations, which grew out of six conferences hosted by the Ethics and Public Policy Center beginning in 1999, touches on various aspects of religious involvement in the public realm. Individual chapters focus on such topics as the social and political status of Catholics in the United States, the voting behavior of the faithful, and the effects of religion on public discourse.

Cummins, D. Duane. 2003. *A Handbook for Today's Disciples in the Christian Church (Disciples of Christ).* **3rd ed. Atlanta: Chalice.**

This brief volume contains basic information about the Christian Church (Disciples of Christ), including a history of the denomination from its formative years from 1800 to 1830 to its establishment as a more formal denomination in the 1960s, the beliefs of denomination members, sacraments and worship practices, denomination positions on moral and ethical issues, and the structure of the church.

Curran, Charles E. 2006. *Loyal Dissent: Memoir of a Catholic Theologian.* **Washington DC: Georgetown University Press.**

A Catholic priest and theologian, Curran recounts his disagreements with the Vatican over such issues as contraception, homosexuality, divorce, and abortion that led in 1986 to his losing the right to teach as a Catholic theologian—he was fired from his teaching position at the Catholic University of America. Curran also describes his disagreements with the Vatican over the permissibility of dissent and with the Catholic University of America over academic freedom.

D'Antonio, William V., Dean R. Hodge, and James D. Davidson. 2001. *American Catholics: Gender, Generation and Commitment.* **Berkeley, CA: Alta Mira.**

Using survey results from 1987, 1993, and 1999, the authors investigate the attitudes of U.S. Catholics toward the church hierarchy, the priest shortage, and the basic teachings of the church, as well as toward such social and political issues as capital punishment and military spending. The authors note that gender and generation differences, as well as different levels of commitment to the Catholic Church, tend to influence attitudes on such issues.

Davies, Susan E., and Sister Paul Teresa Hennessee, eds. 1998. *Ending Racism in Church.* **Cleveland, OH: Pilgrim.**

This work contains four case studies of church and community organizations that have worked to ameliorate racism. The contributors discuss the ways in which racism influences behavior, promotes hatred, and distorts the gospel message.

De Gruchy, John W. 2002. *Reconciliation: Restoring Justice.* **Minneapolis: Fortress.**

De Gruchy argues that Christianity can contribute to the reconciliation of people and nations torn by conflict and violence. He claims Christians have a role to play in maintaining the environment, achieving justice, encouraging interreligious ecumenism, and establishing international peace.

Dionne, E. J., Jr., Kayla Meltzer Drogosz, and Jean Bethke Elshtain, eds. 2004. *One Electorate Under God? A Dialogue on Religion and American Politics.* **Washington DC: Brookings Institution.**

The contributions to this volume focus on two essays, one written by former New York Governor Mario Cuomo, a liberal Catholic, and Marc Souder, a congressman from Indiana and a conservative evangelical. Contributors present their understanding of how religious convictions influence the political views of public figures and contribute to the democratic process.

Djupe, Paul A., and Laura R. Olson. 2003. *Encyclopedia of American Religion and Politics.* **New York: Facts on File.**

This book contains more than 600 entries dealing with religion and politics in the United States, from the nation's founding to the recent rise of the conservative Christian movement. Entries treat such topics as religious leaders, historical events, court cases, religious denominations, and political issues such as prayer in the public schools and abortion.

Dorrien, Gary. 2006. *The Making of American Liberal Theology: Crisis, Irony, and Postmodernity, 1950–2005.* **Louisville, KY: Westminster John Knox.**

While observing that liberal theology has been in dire straights for the last fifty years, Dorrien claims that its supporters have brought about a recent creative renewal. Liberal theology in all its diversity and complexity, he contends, offers an alternative perspective to orthodoxy as well as secularism.

Dreisbach, Daniel, Mark David Hall, and Jeffry H. Morrison, eds. 2004. *The Founders on God and Government.* **Lanham, MD: Rowman and Littlefield.**

The essays in this volume investigate nine of the founders of the nation and the relationship between their religious convictions and political views. Among those treated in individual essays are George Washington, John Adams, Thomas Jefferson, and James Madison, as well as lesser-known figures such as John Witherspoon, John Carroll, and James Wilson.

Edgar, Robert. 2006. *Middle Church: Reclaiming the Moral Values of the Faithful Majority from the Religious Right.* **New York: Simon and Schuster.**

A former member of Congress and an ordained elder in the United Methodist Church, Edgar urges more moderate Christians and adherents of other faiths to take part in shifting the political agenda away from such religious right issues as homosexuality and abortion and emphasize instead eliminating poverty, achieving peace, and protecting the environment—issues he considers central to Jesus's ministry.

Ellingson, Stephen. 2007. *The Megachurch and the Mainline: Remaking Religious Tradition in the Twenty-first Century.* **Chicago: University of Chicago Press.**

Ellingson examines the efforts of several mainline Lutheran churches in the San Francisco Bay Area to alter basic worship practices, blending the evangelical character of megachurches with the contemporary focus on pragmatism and consumerism. The author describes the changes congregations have introduced, including the substitution of traditional hymns with rock music and clerical robes with casual clothing.

Ellison, Marvin Mahan. 2004. *Same-Sex Marriage? A Christian Ethical Analysis.* **Cleveland, OH: Pilgrim.**

Ellison examines the arguments for and against same-gender marriage and makes proposals for updating Christian sexual ethics. The author calls for basic justice in the way the contemporary culture regards varied sexual relationships.

Fackre, Gabriel. 2005. *Believing, Caring, and Doing in the United Church of Christ.* **Cleveland, OH: United Church Press.**

Fackre, an ordained minister in the United Church of Christ, emphasizes three aspects of the UCC mission: the beliefs of denomination members, including the 1913 Kansas City Statement of Faith; ecumenical outreach to other denominations, including the Evangelical Lutheran Church in America; and the activities of the church in such areas as education and evangelism.

Fahey, Joseph J. 2005. *War and the Christian Conscience: Where Do You Stand?* **Maryknoll, NY: Orbis.**

Fahey examines the various traditional Christian stands on war, including pacifism, just war doctrine, the ethics of nuclear warfare, and the possibility of world community. The author offers guidelines for anyone attempting to decide which approach to accept.

Felder, Cain Hope. 2002. *Race, Racism, and the Biblical Narratives.* **Minneapolis: Fortress.**

Felder investigates the notion of race as expressed in the Bible, identifying subsequent misuses of biblical passages such as the "curse of Ham," which was used to support slavery and racial discrimination. The author urges church members to reexamine scripture in order to come to a deeper understanding of racial attitudes.

Fialka, John J. 2002. *Sisters: Catholic Nuns and the Making of America.* **New York: St. Martin's.**

Fialka argues that Catholic nuns, as the nation's first group of professional women, were also feminists. The author recounts the contributions nuns made to shaping the nation during the nineteenth century, including establishing hospitals and schools and providing assistance to the needy. Fialka notes that although there were over 180,000 nuns in the United States in the late 1960s, the total number today is less than 81,000.

Fisher, James T. 2000. *Catholics in America.* **New York: Oxford University Press.**

Beginning with the first Spanish exploration of Florida in 1528, Fisher surveys the Catholic experience in American history and the organization's involvement in the political process, including local politics and the abortion controversy. The author focuses on the roles that various Catholics have played, including Cardinal John J. O'Connor, Father Charles Coughlin, Dorothy Day, and Philip and Daniel Berrigan.

Flinders, Carol Lee. 2006. *Enduring Lives: Portraits of Women and Faith in Action.* **New York: Penguin.**

Flinders examines the lives of four women of faith who have ministered to others. Each had mystical experiences that led them to take active roles in the larger society. Helen Prejean, a Catholic nun who has worked with prison inmates, calls for the elimination of the death penalty; Jane Goodall, a primatologist, has led efforts to protect the habitat for chimpanzees and to preserve the general environment; Tenzin Palmo, a Buddhist nun, has called for the ordination of other Buddhist nuns; and Etty Hillesum, a Jewish woman killed by the Nazis in 1943, in her journals rejected the Nazi doctrine of hatred.

Fowler, Robert Booth, Allen D. Hertzke, Laura R. Olson, and Kevin R. den Dulk. 2004. *Religion and Politics in America: Faith, Culture, and Strategic Choices.* Jackson, TN: Westview.

The authors deal with the general nature of the relationship between religion and politics in the United States, examine in greater detail the major religious traditions, and investigate the conflicting constitutional understandings of the role of religion in public life.

Fryer, Kelly A. 2003. *Reclaiming the "L" Word: Renewing the Church from Its Lutheran Core.* Minneapolis: Augsburg Fortress.

This book, meant for Evangelical Lutheran Church in America congregations, is intended to assist church members in renewal efforts by focusing on the basic principles and teachings of the church. The author attempts to identify just what it means to be a Lutheran and stresses the importance of being a member of the denomination.

Gingerich, Ray C., and Ted Grimsrud, eds. 2006. *Transforming the Powers: Peace, Justice, and the Domination System.* Minneapolis: Fortress.

The contributors to this volume, theologians and students of ethics, examine such subjects as economics, politics, war and peace, ecological problems, and the attainment of social justice.

Griffin, David Ray. 2006. *Christian Faith and the Truth Behind 9/11: A Call to Reflection and Action.* Louisville, KY: Westminster John Knox.

Employing various accounts of the September 11, 2001, terrorist attacks, Griffin analyzes the events from a Christian perspective. The author compares the ancient Roman Empire to contemporary America and uses the teachings of the gospel to evaluate the present administration in Washington DC. He recommends what he considers appropriate responses of Christian churches to the terrorist threat.

Griffin, David Ray, John B. Cobb, Jr., Richard A. Falk, and Catherine Keller. 2006. *The American Empire and the Commonwealth of God: A Political, Economic, Religious Statement.* **Louisville, KY: Westminster John Knox.**

The authors offer a critique of the expansion of U.S. power around the world. Considering U.S. international action imperialistic, they claim the United States is responsible for ecological damage, destructive economic policies, the misuse of military force, and the unfair distribution of wealth.

Gritsch, Eric W. 1994. *Fortress Introduction to Lutheranism.* **Minneapolis: Fortress.**

Recognizing that Lutherans themselves have differing understandings of their identity, with some focusing on its origins as a reform movement, others emphasizing the primary importance of denominational theology, and yet others accentuating the strains of conflict, Gritsch presents an overview of the history and basic beliefs and teachings of Lutheranism.

Hamm, Richard L. 2007. *Recreating the Church: Leadership for the Postmodern Age.* **Atlanta: Chalice Press.**

Hamm, past general minister and president of the Christian Church (Disciples of Christ), discusses the origins of the crisis mainline denominations presently face and offers advice to the churches for adapting to a postmodern culture.

Hart, D. G., and Mark A. Noll, eds. 1999. *Dictionary of the Presbyterian and Reformed Tradition in America.* **Phillipsburg, NJ: P & R Publishing.**

This volume contains entries on a wealth of various topics relevant to the Presbyterian and Reformed tradition, including information about historical and contemporary figures, church organizations and movements, denominational controversies and agreements, worship practices, and significant events such as the American Revolution and the Civil War.

Hayes, Jeffrey, ed. 2005. *The Politics of Religion—A Survey.* **Florence, KY: Routledge.**

This work deals with the relationship between religion and politics in various cultures around the world and contains lengthy entries on such topics as the separation of church and state, religious fundamentalism, religion and democracy, and religion and terrorism. The book provides a context in which to study the role religious denominations in the United States play in public policy making.

Heclo, Hugh, and Wilfred M. McClay, eds. 2003. *Religion Returns to the Public Square: Faith and Policy in America.* Washington DC: Woodrow Wilson Center.

The contributors to this volume explore the ways in which religious institutions traditionally have engaged in American politics and their current activity in such policy areas as abortion, school prayer, the death penalty, and stem-cell research. They investigate the prospects for future interaction between religion and politics.

Hein, David, and Gardiner H. Shattuck. 2003. *Episcopalians.* Westport, CT: Greenwood.

Hein and Shattuck provide a history of the Episcopal Church from its roots in the sixteenth century to the formation of the Anglican Church in the colonies, the establishment of the Episcopal denomination following the American Revolution, expansion during the nineteenth century, and the issues and conflicts that arose during the twentieth century. The authors investigate the Episcopal Church's interaction with other denominations and the changing status of women and minorities within the church.

Hessel, Dieter T., and Larry L. Rasmussen, eds. 2001. *Earth Habitat: Eco-Injustice and the Church's Response.* Minneapolis: Fortress.

This volume contains the presentations of theologians who participated in the 1998 conference, "Ecological Earth," which was held at Union Theological Seminary. The contributors investigate ways in which Christians can transform their thinking and their churches, becoming justice oriented in order to deal more effectively with the ecological crisis.

Hoge, Dean R., Benton Johnson, and Donald A. Luidens. 1994. *Vanishing Boundaries: The Religion of Mainline Protestant Baby Boomers.* Phoenix, AZ: Westminster John Knox.

Employing the results of a survey of 500 respondents as well as forty in-depth interviews, the authors investigate the decline of mainline Protestant denominations since the 1960s. The respondents were members of the Presbyterian Church classified as part of the baby-boomer generation (those between thirty-three and forty-two years of age in 1989). The authors examine the respondents' religious faith and the reasons they offer for either leaving or remaining in the church.

Holmes, David L. 1994. *A Brief History of the Episcopal Church*. Harrisburg, PA: Continuum International.

Holmes traces the history of the Episcopal Church in North America from Jamestown, Virginia, in 1607 to the late twentieth century. The author describes the development of the church after the American Revolution, including such topics as evangelizing efforts among Native Americans, the religious beliefs of slaves and slave owners, the development of the social gospel, debates over the ordination of women, and the effects of immigration on the church.

Inskeep, Ken, and Bob Bacher. 2005. *Chasing Down a Rumor: The Death of Mainline Denominations*. Minneapolis: Augsburg Fortress.

Responding to claims that the mainline denominations continue a nonstop decline, the authors argue that these denominations play a significant role in American society and have the opportunity to continue doing so.

Jacobsen, Dennis A. 2001. *Doing Justice: Congregations and Community Organizing*. Minneapolis: Fortress.

Jacobsen presents advice about organizing community ministries based on his fourteen years of experience. The author combines biblical and theological authority with practical techniques and Saul Alinsky's organizational principles to promote justice in the public realm in support of the poor and disadvantaged.

Jarl, Ann-Cathrin. 2003. *In Justice: Women and Global Economics*. Minneapolis: Fortress.

Jarl explores the dangers of global economic trends and the meaning of economic justice, focusing particularly on the condition of women. Concentrating on feminist critiques of neoclassical economic theory, the author emphasizes meeting fundamental human needs as the basic measure of economic justice.

Jefferts Schori, Katharine. 2007. *A Wing and a Prayer: A Message of Faith and Hope.* **New York: Morehouse.**

Jefferts Schori, who was elected by the 2006 General Convention of the Episcopal Church as the first woman primate in the history of the Anglican Communion, presents her views on the need for reconciliation and peace. As the bishop of Nevada before her election as presiding bishop, Jefferts Schori flew her own plane to reach distant locations in the diocese.

Joh, Wonhee Anne. 2006. *Heart of the Cross: A Postcolonial Christology.* **Louisville, KY: Westminster John Knox.**

Although not abandoning entirely the notion of the cross's connection to pain and suffering, Joh uses postcolonial and feminist understandings of the world to emphasize love as the fundamental notion supporting Christianity. The author employs the Korean concept of *jeong* to refer to love and commitment.

Johnson, Ben Campbell, and Glenn McDonald. 1999. *Imagining a Church in the Spirit: A Task for Mainline Congregations.* **Grand Rapids, MI: W. B. Eerdmans.**

The authors argue that the crucial problem facing the mainline denominations is lack of vision rather than simply declining membership and changing social loyalties. They suggest ways in which pastors can reinvigorate their ministries based on an appropriate vision.

Jones, Alan. 2006. *Common Prayer on Common Ground: A Vision of Anglican Orthodoxy.* **Harrisburg, PA: Morehouse.**

Recognizing the divisions within the Episcopal Church and the Anglican Communion, especially over the issue of homosexuality, Jones explores an avenue for reconciliation through an orthodox perspective that he hopes can subdue the divisions within the denomination.

Kelly, David F. 2004. *Contemporary Catholic Health Care Ethics.* **Washington DC: Georgetown University Press.**

From the perspective of Catholic moral theology, Kelly examines the ethical and legal dilemmas found in the U.S. health care system. Among the topics covered is the dilemma of allocating finite health care resources.

Kennedy, Sheila Suess, and Wolfgang Bielefeld. 2006. *Charitable Choice at Work: Evaluating Faith-Based Job Programs in the States*. Washington DC: Georgetown University Press.

The authors investigate various aspects of faith-based initiatives, including the movement's historical development and the constitutional issues raised, especially the principle of separation of church and state. They analyze qualitative and quantitative data to assess the performance of faith-based initiatives compared to secular programs in Massachusetts, Indiana, and North Carolina.

Kew, Richard. 2001. *Brave New Church: What the Future Holds*. Harrisburg, PA: Morehouse.

Examining the status of the church at the beginning of the twenty-first century, Kew focuses on nine challenges, including accelerating globalization, the Internet, and demographic changes such as the "graying" of the church. The author explains how such challenges can become opportunities for the church.

Killen, Patricia O'Connell, and Mark Silk, eds. 2004. *Religion and Public Life in the Pacific Northwest: The None Zone*. Lanham, MD: Alta Mira.

In this region of the United States, a higher proportion of survey respondents than in any other part of the country state "none" when asked about religious affiliation. Various denominations, including Evangelicals, mainline Protestants, Catholics, and other groups share influence over the issues that concern the residents of the region.

Kirby, James E., Russel E. Richey, and Kenneth E. Rowe. 1996. *The Methodists*. Westport, CT: Greenwood.

The authors present various aspects of the Methodist church, including the denomination's origins in England and development in the United States to becoming the nation's largest Protestant group by the middle of the nineteenth century; its organization and leadership; and the controversies that occurred over such issues as race and the place of women in the church.

Killinger, John. 1995. *Preaching to a Church in Crisis: A Homiletic for the Last Days of the Mainline Church*. Lima, OH: CSS Publishing.

Recognizing that for many years the mainline churches formed the nation's political, social, and spiritual norms, Killinger asserts that these denominations now face a crisis resulting from major societal transformations. The author notes that the crisis, perhaps the greatest in Christianity since the Reformation, could have significant consequences for American society. In the last portion of the book, Killinger recommends ways in which mainline pastors still can preach effectively.

Kirk-Duggan, Cheryl A. 2000. *Refiner's Fire: A Religious Engagement with Violence*. Minneapolis: Fortress.

Kirk-Duggan investigates the role religion has played in either encouraging or ameliorating violence. The author examines biblical violence; the history of slavery; the civil rights movement; and current trends in violence, particularly among youth.

Kleiderer, John, Paula Minaert, and Mark Mossa, eds. 2005. *Just War, Lasting Peace: What Christian Traditions Can Teach Us*. Maryknoll, NY: Orbis.

This book is the outcome of a meeting among several theologians, peace activists, military persons, and public policy analysts who discussed just war doctrine and its application to current conflicts such as the violent conflict in Iraq. The participants presented their thoughts on the role that religion can play in bringing about peace.

Kosmin, Barry, and Ariela Keysar. 2006. *Religion in a Free Market: Religious and Non-Religious Americans—Who, What, Why and Where*. Ithaca, NY: Paramount Market Publishing.

Basing their analysis on the 2001 American Religious Identification Survey, the authors provide a detailed description of religious belief and affiliation in the United States and discuss religion in the context of such variables as economics, politics, and gender.

Krason, Stephen M. 2006. *Catholic Makers of America: Biographical Sketches of Catholic Statesmen and Political Thinkers in America's First Century, 1776–1876.* **Lanham, MD: University Press of America.**

Krason discusses several little-known Catholic figures in the first century of America. The author emphasizes these individuals' contributions to American politics and political thought.

Lagerquist, L. DeAne. 1999. *The Lutherans.* **Westport, CT: Greenwood.**

This volume traces the development of Lutheran churches from their origin in the sixteenth-century Reformation, describing the development of various Lutheran groups in America from colonial times to the establishment of the Evangelical Lutheran Church in America in 1988. The author provides biographical entries on key Lutheran leaders and a chronology of important dates.

Lindsey, William, and Mark Silk, eds. 2005. *Religion and Public Life in the Southern Crossroads: Showdown States.* **Lanham, MD: Alta Mira.**

The contributors to this volume describe the frequent religious conflicts called the culture wars that are characteristic of this region, composed of Arkansas, Louisiana, Missouri, Oklahoma, and Texas. The presence of significant numbers of Baptists, Methodists, Pentecostals, and Catholics, as well as various ethnic groups, contributes to confrontations over differing social agendas.

Linn, Jan G. 2006. *Big Christianity: What's Right with the Religious Left.* **Louisville, KY: Westminster John Knox.**

Linn, a Christian Church (Disciples of Christ) pastor, rejects the leadership of those on the religious right, opting instead for what she calls "big Christianity," a faith sufficiently large to include and accept all people. The author argues that the Christian faith cannot be limited to a particular nation, race, or social class.

Lippy, Charles H. 2006. *Faith in America: Changes, Challenges, New Directions.* **Westport, CT: Praeger.**

In this three-volume work, Lippy examines the status of organized religion in the United States; the issues, such as abortion, embryonic stem-cell research, and end-of-life decisions, that involve religious responses; and the important role that religious belief plays in individual lives and American culture

Lull, Timothy F. 2005. *On Being Lutheran: Reflection on Church, Theology, and Faith.* **Minneapolis: Augsburg Fortress.**

This collection of articles by Lull, which appeared over several years in *The Lutheran* magazine, deals with such topics as the confessional beliefs of Lutherans, the ability of Lutheranism over time to withstand adversity, what it means for Lutherans to be evangelical, reestablishing Lutheran piety, and the future prospects for Lutheranism in the United States.

Lynn, Barry W. 2006. *Piety and Politics: The Right-Wing Assault on Religious Freedom.* **New York: Crown.**

Lynn, a United Church of Christ minister and executive director of Americans United for Separation of Church and State, challenges the agenda of the religious right, arguing for an open marketplace for religious groups that is devoid of government involvement in order to maintain tolerance and religious freedom.

Maeker, Nancy E., and Peter Rogness. 2006. *Ending Poverty, A 20/20 Vision: A Guide for Individuals and Congregations.* **Minneapolis: Augsburg Fortress.**

The authors urge people of faith to investigate the issue of poverty and become committed to providing justice for those in poverty and those who are experiencing class prejudice. They employ specific examples to offer a definition of poverty, explore the dynamics of class, and help the reader to recognize that all people ultimately belong to one community.

Magnani, Laura, and Harmon L. Wray. 2006. *Beyond Prisons: A New Interfaith Paradigm to Our Failed Prison System.* **Minneapolis: Fortress.**

The authors examine the history and characteristics of the U.S. prison system, offering a critical moral evaluation of that system. They provide an alternative basis for a criminal justice system based on reconciliation and make several suggestions for immediate change.

Manuel, Paul Christopher, Lawrence C. Reardon, and Clyde Wilcox, eds. 2006. *The Catholic Church and the Nation-State: Comparative Perspectives.* **Washington, DC: Georgetown University Press.**

This work contains case studies from sixteen countries that portray the complex nature of Catholic Church involvement in and influence on diplomatic and political activity in various contexts.

Mapp Alf, Jr. 2005. *The Faith of Our Fathers: What America's Founders Really Believed.* **Lanham, MD: Rowman and Littlefield.**

Mapp describes the religious beliefs of eleven of the nation's founders, including Benjamin Franklin, Alexander Hamilton, Thomas Jefferson, James Madison, John Marshall, and George Washington. The author investigates the ways in which religious beliefs influenced the values, political understandings, and public acts of these men.

Marlin, George F. 2004. *The American Catholic Voter: Two Hundred Years of Political Impact.* **Fort Collins, CO: Ignatius.**

Marlin recounts the history of Catholic political and electoral participation from the founding of Maryland to the election of George W. Bush as president. The author emphasizes the significance of Catholic involvement in politics at the local, state, and national levels.

Marshall, Ellen Ott, ed. 2005. *Choosing Peace Through Daily Practices.* **Cleveland, OH: Pilgrim.**

The contributors to this volume, all of whom are on the faculty of Claremont School of Theology, suggest methods of achieving peace in a world filled with violence and injustice. They describe daily practices that individuals can employ in the work environment as well as in personal relationships to promote peace.

Martin, Dale B. 2006. *Sex and the Single Savior: Gender and Sexuality in Biblical Interpretation.* **Louisville, KY: Westminster John Knox.**

Investigating scripture to determine ancient conceptions of sexuality, Martin focuses especially on references to homosexuality in Paul's letters contained in the New Testament. The author concludes that the modern world's focus on what is appropriate in sexual relationships does not reflect the original gospel message.

Mathisen, Robert R., ed. 2006. *Critical Issues in American Religious History.* **2nd ed. Waco, TX: Baylor University Press.**

This extensive volume contains original documents and current essays on the history of religion in the United States. Chapters deal with such topics as religion in early America, the era of the Great Awakening, the influence of religious belief on the American Revolution, slavery and religion, the impact of religion on the Civil War, the religious response to scientific developments in the late nineteenth century, fundamentalism versus modernism in the Protestant denominations, and religious influences on the rise of the civil rights movement.

McKim, Donald K. 2003. *Presbyterian Beliefs: A Brief Introduction.* **Louisville, KY: Westminster John Knox.**

McKim, the academic and reference editor of Westminster John Knox Press, presents an introduction to the basic beliefs of the Presbyterian Church. The author arranges topics into three sections: "The God Who Reveals, Creates, and Guides," "The Christ Who Saves People Like Us," and "The Church Where Faith Begins, Is Nourished, and Grows."

McKim, Donald K. 2004. *Presbyterian Questions, Presbyterian Answers.* **Louisville, KY: Westminster John Knox.**

Intended primarily for Presbyterians who wish to gain a deeper knowledge of the denomination's theology and the Christian faith, this book contains answers to questions on such topics as the Presbyterian stance on the doctrine of predestination, the interpretation of the Bible, and the purpose of life for a Christian.

Meacham, John. 2006. *American Gospel: God, the Founding Fathers, and the Making of a Nation.* **New York: Random House.**

Meacham explores the place of religion in the history of U.S. public life, including the colonial era and the writing of the Constitution as well as more recent events such as the civil rights movement and the fight against terrorism. The author perceives a complementarity between the private sphere where individuals may exercise freedom of religion as they wish, and the public arena where religious belief has been a basic ingredient in the governing system.

Moe-Lobeda, Cynthia D. 2004. *Public Church: For the Life of the World.* **Minneapolis: Fortress.**

Moe-Lobeda examines the meaning of the Evangelical Lutheran Church in America's claim that the denomination plays a role in public life. The author explores the significance of being a public church; the advantages, obstacles, costs, and dangers of playing this role; and the possibilities for church members to provide public leadership.

Monsma, Stephen V., and J. Christopher Soper. 1997. *The Challenge of Pluralism: Church and State in Five Democracies.* **Lanham, MD: Rowman and Littlefield.**

The authors compare and analyze the status of church-state relations in the United States, the Netherlands, Australia, Germany, and England. They note that in the United States, emphasis on the establishment clause of the First Amendment denies faith-based organizations access to government assistance that other organizations enjoy.

Monsma, Stephen V., and J. Christopher Soper. 2006. *Faith, Hope, and Jobs: Welfare-to-Work in Los Angeles.* **Baltimore: Georgetown University Press.**

Monsma and Soper present the results of a study of seventeen welfare-to-work programs in Los Angeles County, including those operated by faith-based organizations. The authors examine the assessments clients made of the programs, the development of attitudes conducive to finding employment, and the actual success of gaining jobs. Monsma and Soper conclude with recommendations for public policy makers and social service organization managers.

Moore, Peter C., ed. 1998. *Can a Bishop Be Wrong? Ten Scholars Challenge John Shelby Spong.* **Harrisburg, PA: Morehouse.**

Ten Episcopal scholars and bishops respond to John Shelby Spong's writings that challenge church teachings on the authority of the Bible, the virgin birth of Jesus, Jesus's bodily resurrection, sexuality, and the nature of sin. Although respecting Spong's convictions, the authors offer defenses for the core beliefs of the Christian tradition.

Mount, Eric, Jr. 1999. *Covenant, Community, and the Common Good: An Interpretation of Christian Ethics.* **Cleveland, OH: Pilgrim.**

Mount discusses the positive effects that the notions of covenant and the common good can have on the renewal of various communities, including the family, the workplace, and the larger international realm. The author observes the need to initiate personal as well as more general social renewal.

Nessan, Craig L. 2003. *Give Us This Day: A Lutheran Proposal for Ending World Hunger.* **Minneapolis: Augsburg Fortress.**

Nessan focuses on the tradition of justice he sees expressed in the Bible, especially regarding care for the hungry. Referring to the Lord's Prayer ("Give us this day our daily bread"), the author notes that Jesus's teachings expressed concern for the hungry. With this biblical background, Nessan urges Christian churches to respond to the crisis and end world hunger.

Nessan, Craig L. 2003. *Many Members, Yet One Body: Committed Same-Gender Relationships and the Mission of the Church.* **Minneapolis: Fortress.**

In this brief book, Nessan discusses the controversial issues surrounding the church's stand on homosexuality and same-gender unions. The author's objective is to encourage discussion specifically in the Evangelical Lutheran Church in America and help to prevent the question from dividing the church.

Oden, Thomas C. 2003. *The Rebirth of Orthodoxy: Signs of New Life in Christianity.* **New York: Harper Collins.**

Perceiving lay church members who are rediscovering the ancient truths of the Christian faith, Oden claims that the mainline denominations and the Catholic Church, as well as evangelicals, are returning to orthodoxy. Oden describes his own move away from liberalism to orthodoxy and claims that such modern secular perspectives as Darwinism, communism, and psychoanalysis have failed and that Christians must look to their traditional roots for truth.

Oden, Thomas C. 2006. *Turning Around the Mainline: How Renewal Movements Are Changing the Church.* **Grand Rapids, MI: Baker.**

Oden presents the history of evangelical and orthodox renewal movements within mainline denominations. He details the difficulties that these denominations are facing, the basic beliefs and biblical teaching of the renewal movements, and the question of local church property ownership in mainline churches for congregations that may be contemplating separation from the central denomination.

Oldmixon, Elizabeth Anne. 2005. *Uncompromising Positions: God, Sex, and the U.S. House of Representatives.* **Washington DC: Georgetown University Press.**

Oldmixon investigates how legislators attempt to resolve policy conflicts, such as abortion, gay marriage, and prayer in the public schools, that have significant religious and cultural content. The author argues that participants in such cultural conflicts depend on religious values that tend to restrict the possibility of political compromise. Oldmixon recommends that House members cease resorting to the short-term temptation to appeal to ideological allies and instead focus on discovering workable solutions.

Olson, Carl E. 2003. *Will Catholics Be "Left Behind"?* **Fort Collins, CO: Ignatius.**

Olson provides a Catholic perspective on the fundamentalist notion of the rapture, that moment when Christ supposedly will return to take the righteous from the world before the "great tribulation" described in the Book of Revelation. The author discusses the biblical, theological, and historical bases of this notion that plays a crucial role in Tim LaHaye and Jerry Jenkins's *Left Behind* series of novels.

Ottati, Douglas F. 2006. *Theology for Liberal Presbyterians and Other Endangered Species.* **Louisville, KY: Geneva.**

Ottati presents an interpretation of the basics of liberal theological thought as an alternative to the conservative evangelical approach. Focusing on such issues as the ordination of homosexuals and the war on terrorism, the author urges liberal Protestants to engage in a revision of traditional beliefs in light of the realities of the contemporary world.

Patterson, Eric, ed. 2003. *The Christian Realists: Reassessing the Contributions of Niebuhr and His Contemporaries*. **Lanham, MD: University Press of America.**

The contributors to this volume discuss the contributions that theologian Reinhold Niebuhr and such public figures as John Foster Dulles, secretary of state under President Dwight D. Eisenhower, made to politics and political theory. Christian realists gained wide influence among U.S. government officials and the intellectual elite from the 1930s through the early era of nuclear weapons development.

Prendergast, William B. 1999. *The Catholic Voter in American Politics: The Passing of the Democratic Monolith*. **Washington DC: Georgetown University Press.**

Prendergast traces the voting behavior of American Catholics, focusing on the shift of many such voters from the Democratic party to the Republican Party in recent decades. Among the explanations for this change in partisan loyalties that the author entertains are the passing of first-generation immigrants, the effects of Vatican II, and the greater receptiveness to Catholics in the Republican Party.

Presbyterian Church (U.S.A.). 2006. *The Presbyterian Handbook*. **Louisville, KY: Westminster John Knox.**

This guide to the Presbyterian Church contains a historical account of the development of the church in the United States and a detailed explanation of Presbyterian beliefs and the denomination's understanding of the Christian life.

Prichard, Robert W. 1999. *History of the Episcopal Church*. **Revised ed. Harrisburg, PA: Morehouse.**

Prichard explores the 400-year history of the Episcopal Church, including the denomination's development during such major events as the Great Awakening of the early eighteenth century, the American Revolution, the Civil War, the First and Second World

Wars, and major social changes that occurred during the postwar era. The author treats the church's challenges during the 1990s, including the renewal movement involving dissenters within the denomination, the issue of homosexuality, and the alterations in leadership.

Ratzinger, Joseph. 2006. *Christianity and the Crisis of Cultures.* **Fort Collins, CO: Ignatius.**

Writing before his election to the papacy, Ratzinger discusses the crisis of culture he perceives in Europe and the rest of the Western world. Among the dangers he associates with this crisis are threats to security, poverty, and genetic engineering. Ratzinger argues that the solution to the nihilistic secularism of the West is not politics but spiritual renewal.

Ratzinger, Joseph. 2006. *Values in a Time of Upheaval.* **Fort Collins, CO: Ignatius.**

Ratzinger, who in 2005 became Pope Benedict XVI, discusses the relationship among religion, morality, culture, and politics in the contemporary world, defending the role that traditional Christian values still play in a multicultural era. The author covers such topics as morality in democratic societies, bioethics, and human rights and responsibilities.

Ratzinger, Joseph, and Marcello Pera. 2006. *Without Roots: The West, Relativism, Christianity, Islam.* **Fort Collins, CO: Ignatius.**

In this dialogue, Ratzinger and Pera, president of the Italian senate, discuss whether a civilization can survive without a sense of the sacred. In May 2004 Ratzinger addressed the Italian senate, and Pera presented a lecture at the Lateran Pontifical University. Both arrived at similar conclusions regarding the spiritual, cultural, and political crises confronting Western civilization.

Ray, Darby Kathleen. 2006. *Theology that Matters: Ecology, Economy, and God.* **Minneapolis: Fortress.**

Ray argues that Christianity can contribute to resolving the problems of an increasingly global economy. The author investigates topics relevant to Christians as they relate to an increasingly secularized world, the globalization of economic activity, and threats to the environment.

Ray, Stephen G., Jr. 2002. *Do No Harm: Social Sin and Christian Responsibility.* **Minneapolis: Fortress.**

Ray contends that Christians must recognize the possible evil that their own theologies may unintentionally encourage. According to the author, theologians may describe socially relevant sin in racist, sexist, or anti-Semitic ways, thus exposing the social evils in their own thought and language. He examines the work of such Christian thinkers as Reinhold Neibuhr, Martin Luther, and John Calvin to illustrate the strengths as well as the weaknesses of traditional theological approaches.

Reichley, A. James. 2002. *Faith in Politics.* **Washington DC: Brookings Institution.**

Reichley provides an excellent overview of religious belief and political action in the United States. Individual chapters deal with differing value systems, the intentions and expectations of the founders, interpretations of the free exercise and establishment clauses of the First Amendment, the political engagement of various religious groups in the nineteenth and twentieth centuries, and the significance of religion to a democratic state.

Rogers, Jack. 2006. *Jesus, the Bible, and Homosexuality: Explode the Myths, Heal the Church.* **Louisville, KY: Presbyterian Publishing Corporation.**

Rogers argues that the church should be willing to ordain gays and lesbians and that homosexuals in American society should have equal rights. The author claims that—just like women, people of color, and divorced people—gay, lesbian, bisexual, and transgender persons will gain a place within the church. Claiming that the Bible does not condemn homosexuality, Rogers notes that, just as the church once used the Bible to justify slavery and the subordination of women, some today employ the scriptures to deny equal rights to gays and lesbians.

Roof, Wade Clark, and Mark Silk, eds. 2005. *Religion and Public Life in the Pacific Region: Fluid Identities.* **Lanham, MD: Alta Mira.**

The contributors to this volume emphasize the religious diversity of the region, which encompasses California, Nevada, and Hawaii. California is the home of Robert H. Schuller's mega church, the Crystal Cathedral. Although affiliated with the Reformed Church in America, Schuller is perhaps more representative of the various innovative religious movements that characterize the region. Residents frequently shift religious affiliation, often combining varied religious identities.

Roustang, François. 2006. *Jesuit Missionaries to North America: Spiritual Writings and Biographical Sketches.* **Fort Collins, CO: Ignatius.**

Between 1632 and 1637, Jesuit missionaries arrived in North America, and for twenty years they brought the Catholic faith to the local population. Roustang provides accounts of eight men, presenting their backgrounds, personality traits, and missionary work, portraying them as heroes for withstanding the harsh conditions of eastern Canada.

Schaller, Lyle E. 2005. *A Mainline Turnaround: Strategies for Congregations and Denominations.* **Nashville, TN: Abingdon.**

Arguing that the structures of the mainline denominations were established for conditions that not longer exist, Schaller offers suggestions for these denominations to restructure themselves in order to respond to circumstances in a different era.

Sekulow, Jay Alan. 2005. *Witnessing Their Faith: Religious Influence on Supreme Court Justices and Their Opinions.* **Blue Ridge Summit, PA: Rowman and Littlefield.**

Sekulow, lead attorney for the American Center for Law and Justice, a conservative Christian legal advocacy group, investigates major Supreme Court cases that shaped the legal foundations of church-state relations, focusing on the religious beliefs and practices of the justices who ruled on each case.

Shattuck, Gardiner H. 2000. *Episcopalians and Race: Civil War to Civil Rights.* **Lexington: University Press of Kentucky.**

Shattuck investigates the post–Civil War relations between black communities and the white leadership of the Episcopal Church.

Focusing primarily on the 1950s and 1960s, the author discusses the effects of the civil rights movement on the denomination, especially in the Southern states, and contrasts the official position of the church hierarchy with actual practice.

Shipps, Jan, and Mark Silk, eds. 2004. *Religion and Public Life in the Mountain West: Sacred Landscapes in Transition.* Lanham, MD: Alta Mira.

The contributors to this volume note three fundamental religious influences in this region: Catholicism, Mormonism, and pluralism, each having dominance in a portion of the region. For instance, in Arizona and New Mexico, Catholicism dominates the public expression of religion, and in Utah, Mormonism prevails. In other parts of the region, no religious group holds sway.

Smidt, Corwin E. 2004. *Pulpit and Politics: Clergy in American Politics at the Advent of the Millennium.* Waco, TX: Baylor University Press.

Based on data collected from the 2000 election, Smidt explores religious beliefs and political activities of U.S. clergy, including mainline Protestant and Catholic clerics as well as religious leaders from African American, Baptist, and Jewish groups. The author investigates the reasons why religious leaders engage in political activity and how they do so.

Solomon, Lewis D. 2003. *In God We Trust? Faith-Based Organizations and the Quest to Solve America's Social Ills.* Lanham, MD: Lexington Books.

Solomon examines faith-based organizations, religious groups to which the George W. Bush administration is offering grants to conduct various social welfare programs. The author investigates the constitutional law questions that have arisen over separation of church and state, the effectiveness of such organizations, and methods of funding and staffing. He analyzes the arguments presented by opponents of faith-based funding.

Spong, John Shelby. 1998. *Why Christianity Must Change or Die: A Bishop Speaks to Believers in Exile.* New York: Harper San Francisco.

Spong presents a liberal Christian perspective on such topics as biblical interpretation, theism, understandings of Jesus, and morality. The author calls for critical thinking rather than blind faith and love rather than judgment as the necessary bases for a rejuvenated Christianity that can survive in the contemporary world.

Spong, John Shelby. 2005. *The Sins of Scripture: Exposing the Bible's Texts of Hate to Reveal the God of Love.* **New York: Harper San Francisco.**

Spong, the retired Episcopal bishop of Newark, New Jersey, and a longtime advocate of liberal Christian beliefs, discusses biblical passages that he notes have been used to condemn, oppress, and discriminate against others. For instance, Spong declares that the Bible was used to support the divine right of kings, slavery and ultimately segregation, treating women as second-class citizens, and currently discrimination against gay and lesbian people.

Spong, John Shelby. 2007. *Jesus for the Non-Religious.* **New York: Harper Collins.**

Spong continues his attempt to revise traditional Christian beliefs, arguing for an understanding of Jesus that he hopes will transcend narrow religious notions and appeal to people in differing cultural circumstances. The author rejects the accuracy of much of the biblical account of Jesus, including the miracle stories.

Steinfels, Peter. 2004. *A People Adrift: The Crisis of the Roman Catholic Church in America.* **New York: Simon and Schuster.**

A Catholic layman, Steinfels argues that the Catholic Church must institute fundamental reforms or else face serious decline. Pointing to well-known indicators such as the erosion of the number of priests and nuns, as well as the widespread sex abuse scandal, the author identifies a lack of strong leadership to maintain the church's vital public role and to initiate internal change.

Stewart, Carlyle Fielding, III. 2003. *Reclaiming What Was Lost: Unlocking Spiritual Vitality in the Mainline Church.* **Nashville, TN: Abingdon.**

Discussing the difficulties faced by mainline Protestant denominations, Stewart offers suggestions to congregations with regard to involving laypeople in leadership, extending the church's mission into the community, and presenting the biblical message to a skeptical population.

Strommen, Merton P. 2001. *The Church and Homosexuality: Searching for a Middle Ground.* **Minneapolis: Kirk House.**

Strommen suggests that churches adopt a compromise solution to the controversy over homosexuality in which individuals avoid extreme positions and instead engage in a discussion that both recognizes biblical authority and expresses love for those who have been discriminated against.

Swaine, Lucas. 2006. *The Liberal Conscience: Politics and Principle in a World of Religious Pluralism.* **New York: Columbia University Press.**

Focusing on the challenge that fundamentalist theocratic groups pose for liberal societies, Swaine attempts to demonstrate how such societies can develop political institutions that recognize the significance of freedom of conscience. The author suggests a legal standard that provides theocratic communities with a level of sovereignty within liberal democracies.

Taylor, Mark Lewis. 2001. *The Executed God: The Way of the Cross in Lockdown America.* **Minneapolis: Fortress.**

Noting that the prison population in the United States has increased to more than 2 million, Taylor decries the abuses and injustices he observes in the U.S. justice and prison system—including racism, capital punishment, prison rape, and coercive policing techniques—and calls for effective and compassionate Christian action to transform the system.

Thistlewaite, Susan, ed. 2001. *A Just Peace Church.* **Cleveland, OH: Pilgrim.**

This volume resulted from the work of the Peace Theology Team, a group commissioned by the General Synod of the United Church of Christ to investigate the theological, political, and practical foundations of becoming a church dedicated to peace. The contributors suggest ways in which the church can make the transformation.

Toulous, Mark G. 2006. *God in Public: Four Ways American Christianity and Public Life Relate.* **Louisville, KY: Westminster John Knox.**

Toulouse, a professor of American religious history at Brite Divinity School, Texas Christian University, has investigated religious periodical literature and key events in U.S. history to clarify the varied modes of interaction between Christianity and public life in the United States.

Townsend, Craig D. 2005. *Faith in Their Own Color: Black Episcopalians in Antebellum New York City.* **New York: Columbia University Press.**

Townsend presents the history of St. Philip's Church, the first African American Episcopal church in New York City. Founded in 1809, the church experienced the violence of antiabolitionists and the discrimination of the Episcopal Church before the congregation finally received official recognition from a reluctant Episcopal Diocese of New York convention in 1853.

Trent, Mary Alice, Trevor Grizzle, Margaret Sehorn, Andrew Lang, and Elsa Rogers, eds. 2006. *Religion, Culture, Curriculum, and Diversity in 21st Century America.* **Lanham, MD: University Press of America.**

The fifteen essays in this volume explore issues of policy making with regard to diversity, including race, ethnicity, and disabilities, at institutions of Christian higher education. The contributors examine hiring practices as well as recruitment and retention policies for minority students and faculty.

Trexler, Edgar. 2003. *High Expectations: Understanding the ELCA's Early Years, 1988–2002.* **Minneapolis: Augsburg Fortress.**

Trexler examines the first fourteen years of the Evangelical Lutheran Church in America, which was formed from the merger of three separate Lutheran bodies. Based on official church documents, personal interviews, and published materials, this book contains discussions of the church's efforts to establish its identity and to deal with such issues as ecumenism and sexuality.

Varacalli, Joseph A. 2006. *The Catholic Experience in America.* **Westport, CT: Greenwood.**

Varacalli provides an overview of the Catholic Church in the United States, including discussions of Catholic theology and formal organization; historical evolution of the church; difficulties, including the sex abuse scandal, that the church currently faces; the diverse groups within the denomination; and key events such as the Second Vatican Council, which met in Rome from 1962 to 1965. Appendixes include a glossary, a list of voluntary organizations, and a discussion and list of key church documents.

Wald, Kenneth D., and Allison Calhoun-Brown. 2006. *Religion and Politics in the United States*. 5th ed. Blue Ridge Summit, PA: Roman and Littlefield.

Wald analyzes the role religion plays in U.S. society and politics, detailing the relationship between religious beliefs and political issues, how religious groups and individuals have influenced the development of the so-called culture war, and how religious beliefs affect political values.

Walker, Randi J. 2005. *Evolution of a UCC Style*. Cleveland, OH: Pilgrim.

From the varied origins of the United Church of Christ, including the heritage of the Reformation, the Enlightenment, and pietist influences, Walker focuses on the guiding characteristics of the church as they have developed over time, as well as the tensions that remain.

Wall, John N. 2000. *A Dictionary for Episcopalians*. Revised ed. Cambridge, MA: Cowley.

This brief reference work includes explanations for the basic terminology associated with the Episcopal Church, including the traditional creeds, church structure, officials and leaders, governance, interdenominational relations, worship practices, Christian symbolism, and church year festivals.

Walsh, Andrew, and Mark Silk, eds. 2004. *Religion and Public Life in New England: Steady Habits, Changing Slowly*. Lanham, MD: Alta Mira.

The contributors to this volume focus primarily on the tensions between the Protestant establishment, which traces its roots back to the colonial era, and the present Catholic majority. Catholics began immigrating to the region in the 1840s and soon came to challenge the traditional Protestant dominance. The authors discuss the possible future evolution of religious affiliation in this region.

Webber, Christopher L. 1999. *Welcome to the Episcopal Church: An Introduction to Its History, Faith, and Worship.* **Harrisburg, PA: Morehouse.**

Webber, a parish priest in the Episcopal Church, presents a general introduction to the denomination, including the following topics: historical development, worship traditions, fundamental beliefs, the significance of scripture, the organizational structure of the church, and its mission and outreach activities.

Wee, Paul A. 2006. *American Destiny and the Calling of the Church.* **Minneapolis: Augsburg Fortress.**

Wee discusses the historical background to the church's contemporary role of criticizing the nation's ideological understanding of its global status. Recognizing that the United States has assumed world leadership following the end of the Cold War and the terrorist attacks of September 11, 2001, Wee argues that members of the church should provide an understanding of that role in the context of biblical and theological principles. The author focuses on the primary importance of the gospel, the role of the church in ministering to the world, and the need for the nation to act responsibly in the international realm.

Weigel, George. 2005. *The Cube and the Cathedral: Europe, America, and Politics Without God.* **New York: Basic Books.**

Weigel contrasts the traditional European civilization of the "cathedral" (represented by Notre Dame in Paris) with the modern secularized society represented by the "cube" (the Great Arch of La Défence, also in Paris). The future of European democracies is threatened by the lack of religious presence in the public square. The author contrasts the condition of the United States with Europe, but argues that Americans ultimately may face similar threats to democratic values.

Weigel, George. 2005. *God's Choice: Pope Benedict XVI and the Future of the Catholic Church.* **Fort Collins, CO: Ignatius.**

Weigel, biographer of Pope John Paul II, discusses the rise of Joseph Ratzinger as the new pontiff, Benedict XVI. Using interviews with those close to the new pope, he provides a personal account of Benedict and evaluates the status of the Catholic Church in the contemporary world and the role it will play in the future.

Welch, Sharon D. 2000. *A Feminist Ethic of Risk*. Revised ed. Minneapolis: Fortress.

Welch proposes a religious perspective for the attainment of social justice that can deal effectively with such problems as environmental degradation and racism. The author contrasts her approach of a feminist ethic to that of other current treatments of religious ethics.

West, Traci C. 2006. *Disruptive Christian Ethics: When Racism and Women's Lives Matter*. Louisville, KY: Westminster John Knox.

West discusses racism and sexual aggression against women as violations of ethical, moral, and theological principles. She maps a course to fundamental social change through a detailed intellectual examination of those principles. West provides concrete examples of women who have suffered prejudice and violation.

Westerhoff, John H., III. 2002. *A People Called Episcopalians: A Brief Introduction to Our Peculiar Way of Life*. Harrisburg, PA: Morehouse.

Westerhoff, an Episcopal priest, presents a short introduction to the Episcopal Church, explaining to Episcopalians themselves the nature of their denomination. The author investigates basic Episcopalian identity, including authority within the church, the Anglican Communion, spirituality, and the Episcopal political structure.

Wiehe, Philip. 2001. *Ten Dumb Things Churches Do and How to Avoid Them*. Harrisburg, PA: Morehouse.

Wiehe, an Episcopal priest for twenty-five years and subsequently a consultant to congregations, presents advice to local churches to assist them in becoming more effective representatives of the gospel message. The author focuses on ten "dumb things," or mistakes, that congregations can make, including failing to conduct strategic planning, making poor decisions, and allowing internal conflicts to arise.

Wilcox, David R. 2004. *God and Evolution: A Faith-Based Perspective.* **Valley Forge, PA: Judson.**

Wilcox argues that scripture and the natural world cannot conflict because both result from God's actions. The author claims that the strong disagreement over evolution results from neglecting the boundaries of science and theology, and that no one needs to choose between God and science. Instead, people of faith can accept science as part of God's divine plan for the universe.

Wilke, Richard B. 1986. *And Are We Yet Alive? The Future of the United Methodist Church.* **Nashville, TN: Abingdon.**

Citing loss of membership and a precipitous decline in church school attendance, Wilke claims that the United Methodist Church is a denomination in crisis. The author proposes steps that can be taken to reverse the trend, including examining the church's value system, instituting more long-term pastorates, and restructuring the denominational organization.

Williams, Rowan. 2004. *Anglican Identities.* **Cambridge, MA: Cowley.**

Archbishop of Canterbury Rowan Williams discusses the differing approaches to scripture, authority, and the Christian tradition of such Anglican figures as William Tyndale, Richard Hooker, George Herbert, and B. F. Westcott. Williams notes the rich diversity of these individuals, but also deals with the troubling question of when such differences lead to the serious divisions.

Wilson, Charles Reagan, and Mark Silk, eds. 2005. *Religion and Public Life in the South: In the Evangelical Mode.* **Lanham, MD: Alta Mira.**

In this region of the United States, Christian evangelicals and more conservative congregations of the mainline churches tend to dominate. From the mid-nineteenth century to the present, evangelicals, drawing from their interpretation of scripture, have often influenced public policy. Although other religious groups compete for political and social influence, the generally conservative nature of religious belief influences the public debate of political issues.

Wimberly, Edward P. 2006. *African American Pastoral Care and Counseling: The Politics of Oppression and Engagement.* **Cleveland, OH: Pilgrim.**

Wimberly, an ordained elder in the United Methodist Church, contends that African American pastoral care and counseling are inherently political activities. The author discusses engaging in such counseling as a means of liberating individuals to become better able to act more effectively in their personal lives and in politics.

Wink, Walter, ed. 1999. *Homosexuality and Christian Faith: Questions of Conscience for the Churches.* **Minneapolis: Fortress.**

Protestant and Catholic as well as evangelical and mainline church leaders contribute to this volume about fundamental moral questions regarding homosexuality. The contributors, including Paul Egertson, William Sloane Coffin, and James A. Forbes, Jr., discuss such issues as biblical authority and the nature of homosexuality.

Winter, Gibson. 1996. *America in Search of Its Soul.* **Harrisburg, PA: Morehouse.**

Concerned with the level of violence in the United States, Winter urges the church to play a role in saving young people from the dangers of violence. The author delves into the history of violence in the United States, including slavery, the treatment of Native Americans, and participation in various wars. Winter investigates the activities of several religious movements that have attempted to ameliorate the consequences of violence.

Witte, John, Jr., and Frank S. Alexander. 2005. *The Teachings of Modern Christianity on Law, Politics, and Human Nature.* **2 vols. New York: Columbia University Press.**

This volume contains the writings of twenty major Christian thinkers of the nineteenth and twentieth centuries—including Dorothy Day, Reinhold Niebuhr, Martin Luther King, Jr., and Pope John Paul II—and analyses of those writings. The editors have divided the work into three sections: the Roman Catholic tradition, the Protestant tradition, and the Orthodox tradition.

Wuthnow, Robert. 2005. *America and the Challenges of Religious Diversity.* **Princeton, NJ: Princeton University Press.**

Employing data from a nationwide survey, including many in-depth interviews, Wuthnow investigates the ways in which Christians are adapting to the new diversity in American society. The author identifies three orientations for Christian beliefs and practices: "spiritual shopping," involving the willingness to borrow from various traditions; "Christian inclusivism," maintaining Christian beliefs but respecting other religious traditions; and "Christian exclusivism," rejecting the validity of other religions.

Wuthnow, Robert, ed. 2006. *Encyclopedia of Politics and Religion.* **2 Volumes. Washington DC: CQ Press.**

This extensive two-volume work of more than 1,000 pages presents a wealth of information about the relationship between religion and politics in various cultures around the world. The entries examine the history of that relationship and contemporary topics such as creationism versus evolution, the conservative Christian movement in the United States, and European Islam. An appendix contains documents relevant to the relationship between religion and politics. The book is helpful in providing a context in which to study religion and politics in the United States.

Yamane, David. 2005. *The Catholic Church in State Politics: Negotiating Prophetic Demands and Political Realities.* **Blue Ridge Summit, PA: Rowman and Littlefield.**

Yamane examines the history of the political advocacy efforts of American Catholic bishops at the state and local levels. Focusing on thirty-three states and Washington DC, the author details the activities of Catholic organizations and the strains created between religious principles and the demands of secular politics.

Yrigoyen, Charles, Jr., and Susan E. Warrick, eds. 2005. *Historical Dictionary of Methodism.* **2nd ed. Lanham, MD: Scarecrow.**

This book contains more than 400 entries on various aspects of the Methodist denomination in the United States and around the world, including the social and charitable activities of the church and the denomination's involvement in the ecumenical movement.

Periodicals

The following periodicals primarily represent the communication between the mainline denomination organizations and the members. These publications offer information and articles regarding church activities, theological and biblical interpretation, Christian ethics, and issues of concern both within the denomination and in the society generally.

America
106 West 56th Street
New York, NY 10019-3803
(800) 627-9533
www.americamagazine.org
Weekly. $48.

This Catholic periodical contains current news stories on such topics as the activities of the pope, the continuing terrorist threat that Al Qaeda poses, and the debate over the use of torture. The magazine also includes articles on religious topics, editorials on current public policy, and reviews of books related to religion.

The Christian Century
104 S. Michigan Ave.
Suite 700
Chicago, IL 60603
(312) 263-7510
www.christiancentury.org
26 issues per year. $49.

Founded in 1884 as *The Christian Oracle*, a Disciples of Christ publication, and renamed in 1900, *The Christian Century* became an independent magazine supporting the progressive Christian perspective. Today the magazine remains the major nondenominational publication reflecting the views of mainline Protestant denominations. The magazine publishes articles on political and cultural topics as well as theology.

Church Herald
4500 60th Street SE
Grand Rapids, MI 49512
(616) 698-7071
www.herald@rca.org
11 times per year. $20.

The Reformed Church in America sends the *Church Herald* to each member household. The magazine reports on and promotes the ministries of the RCA, provides information to encourage Christian leadership and educate readers about the mission of the church, and offers a forum for discussion of the policies and actions of the RCA within the church and in the larger society.

Crisis
1814 ½ N Street NW
Washington DC 20036
(800) 852-9962
www.crisismagazine.com
10 issues per year. $24.97.

This magazine reports on and interprets contemporary political and cultural events from the perspective of the Catholic tradition and is dedicated to offering a Christian humanist answer to the problems of the modern world.

Disciples World
6325 North Guilford Avenue, Suite 213
Indianapolis, IN 46220
(317) 375-8849
www.disciplesworld.com
10 issues per year. $25.

A publication of the Christian Church (Disciples of Christ), this journal includes news items, opinion pieces, commentary on such topics as church history and current issues of faith, book reviews, and Bible study.

Ecumenical Courier
United States Conference for the World Council of Churches
475 Riverside Drive, Room 1371
New York, NY 10115

www.wcc-usa.org
Quarterly. Available online.

This publication of the United States Conference for the World Council of Churches provides information about the involvement of member denominations in the United States in the World Council of Churches, reporting on highlights of U.S. Conference meetings.

Episcopal Life
P.O. Box 2050
Voorhees, NJ 08043-8000
www.episcopal-life.org
Monthly. $18.

This publication of the Episcopal Church contains articles on the activities of various groups within the denomination, the church's mission in the United States and around the world, and plans for the future of the Episcopal Church.

First Things
P.O. Box 401
Mt. Morris, IL 61054
(877) 905-9920
www.firstthings.com
10 issues per year. $39.

This journal is published by the Institute on Religion and Public Life, a nondenominational and nonpartisan research institute dedicated to promoting a religiously oriented public philosophy relevant to a well-ordered society. The publication contains articles on such topics as immigration, international relations, and religious freedom.

Journal of the Academy of Religion
Oxford University Press
2001 Evans Road
Cary, NC 27513
www.jaar.oxfordjournals.org
Quarterly. $159.

Each issue of this journal contains scholarly articles on subjects dealing with various religions around the world. Recent articles have dealt with such topics as the Catholic Worker Movement, the Pledge of Allegiance, liberal humanism, and religion and violence.

The Lutheran
Augsburg Fortress Press
P.O. Box 1553
Minneapolis, MN 55440-8730
www.thelutheran.org
Monthly. $15.95.

This magazine, published by the Evangelical Lutheran Church in America, "nurtures awareness of Christ's presence in our lives and the world, shares stories of God's people living their faith, connects us with the global Christian community, provides an open forum for discussion, [and] challenges us to bring God's grace and care to all." Among the columns is a regular contribution by the ELCA presiding bishop.

Lutheran Partners
8765 West Higgins Road
Chicago, IL 60631
www.elca.org/lutheranpartners
Bimonthly. $12.50.

The Evangelical Lutheran Church in America publishes this magazine for the denomination's pastors and lay leaders. The magazine includes articles on such topics as methods of church outreach and evangelism, Christian education, and applying faith to the world. Also included are book and video reviews.

Lutheran Quarterly
www.lutheranquarterly.com
Four times per year. $30.

This journal of the Evangelical Lutheran Church offers discussions of historical and theological topics. Contributors focus on the Christian faith from the Lutheran perspective, apply Lutheran principles to the problems of society, and promote understanding between Lutherans and other Christian denominations.

National Catholic Register
www.ncregister.com
Biweekly. $24.95.

This periodical provides news reporting from a Catholic perspective. Stories covered have included the aftermath of Hurricane Katrina, the Terri Schiavo case in the context of the debate over euthanasia and assisted suicide, the U.S. invasion of Iraq, and homosexuality among Catholic priests. The magazine also contains reports on the arts and book reviews.

Presbyterians Today
Presbyterian Church (U.S.A.)
100 Witherspoon Street
Louisville, KY 40202
www.pcusa.org/today
Monthly. $19.95.

This publication of the Presbyterian Church (U.S.A.) contains articles on such topics as religious art, the activities of the church to alleviate the effects of hunger and violent conflict around the world, and ecumenical outreach. Also included are reports on church meetings and a question-and-answer column dealing with biblical and theological topics.

Prism
United Church Press
Cleveland, OH
www.unitedchurchpress.com
Twice each year. $12.

This periodical, issued by the United Church of Christ, provides a forum for discussing theological questions. Contributors offer diverse viewpoints on questions of faith and the mission and ministry of the denomination.

Religion in the News
Leonard E. Greenberg Center for the Study of Religion
in Public Life
Trinity College
300 Summit Street
Hartford, CT 06106
http://www.trincoll.edu/depts./csrpl/default.htm
Three times each year. Free on request.

This quarterly publication provides summaries of news accounts that have relevance to religious organizations and activities.

Authors present the views of news outlets on such recent topics as the controversy over the election of an openly gay bishop in the Episcopal Church and the election of Joseph Ratzinger as Pope Benedict XVI.

Review of Faith and International Affairs
Council on Faith and International Affairs
Institute for Global Engagement
P.O. Box 14477
Washington DC 20044
www.cfia.org
Quarterly. $25.

This journal is devoted to investigating the interrelationship between religion and international relations. Articles deal with such topics as the relevance of religious belief and values to foreign aid, liberal democracy, and peacemaking. The publication includes reviews of books on religion and foreign policy.

U.S. Catholic
205 West Monroe
Chicago, IL 60606
(800) 328-6515
www.uscatholic.claretians.org
Twelve issues per year. $12.

This magazine is published by the Claretians, a Catholic religious community of priests and brothers. The publication attempts to provide guidance to Catholics by discussing the religious tradition of the denomination in the context of the difficulties of contemporary life.

Audiotapes, Videotapes, CDs, and DVDs

Bill Moyers on Faith and Reason
Type: DVD
Length: 7 hrs.
Cost: $959.95
Date: 2006

Source: Films for the Humanities and Sciences
                   P.O. Box 2053
                   Princeton, NJ 08543-2053
                   (800) 257-5126
                   www.films.com

In this twelve-part presentation, Bill Moyers discusses the impact of religion on the contemporary world with such noted writers as Salman Rushdie, Colin McGinn, Jeanette Winterson, Margaret Atwood, Richard Rodriguez, and John Houghton.

Call Me Malcolm
Type: DVD
Length: 90 min.
Cost: $39
Date: 2004
Source: United Church Press
                 Cleveland, OH

This film explores the discovery of personal identity and transgender issues by presenting an account of Malcolm E. Himschoot, a United Church of Christ seminary student who struggles with his faith and gender identity.

Christianity in World History Series
Type: VHS
Length: 200 min.
Cost: $319.95
Date: 2002
Source: Teacher's Media Company
                 P.O. Box 9120
                 Plainview, NY 11803-9020
                 (800) 262-8837
                 www.teachersmediacompany.com

This series of eight videos explores the history of Christianity from its origins to the present. Individual tapes treat Christianity in medieval Europe; European developments from the Reformation to the twentieth century; and traditions in North America, Asia, and Africa.

Convictions: Prisoners of Conscience
Type: VHS
Length: 20 min.

Cost:	$14.95
Date:	2004
Source:	Maryknoll Productions
	Walsh Building, Box 308
	Maryknoll, NY 10545-0308
	(914) 941-7636, ext. 2558
	www.maryknollmall.org

This video presents the story of those who protested the Pentagon-supported School of the Americas during an annual vigil outside Fort Benning, Georgia, in November 2003. The protesters objected to U.S.-supported militarization in Latin America.

Dealing with Tough Issues as Christians

Type:	VHS
Length:	58 min.
Cost:	$19.95
Date:	2006
Source:	Augsburg Fortress
	P.O. Box 1209
	Minneapolis, MN 55440-1209
	(800) 328-4648
	www.augsburgfortress.org/store/item.asp?clsid =184396&productgroupid=0

This video is meant to encourage discussion of issues, such as abortion and homosexuality, about which congregation members are likely to disagree. The program is organized into four segments: sharing experiences, searching for common understanding, seeking biblical guidance, and acting on conclusions. Intended for use in small groups, the video includes a leader guide.

Faith and Community: Models of Metropolitan Ministry

Type:	VHS
Length:	N/A
Cost:	$34.95
Date:	2003
Source:	Augsburg Fortress
	P.O. Box 1209
	Minneapolis, MN 55440-1209
	(800) 328-4648
	www.augsburgfortress.org

This program explores the ways in which U.S. congregations are creating metropolitan networks in novel ways in cooperation with other congregations and organizations. Emphasis is placed on selecting the most appropriate model for specific circumstances.

Faith, Politics, and Tradition

Type:	DVD and VHS
Length:	26 min.
Cost:	$129.95
Date:	2003
Source:	Films for the Humanities and Sciences
	P.O. Box 2053
	Princeton, NJ 08543-2053
	(800) 257-5126
	www.films.com

This program explores the possibility of conforming religious belief with contemporary society. Archbishop of Canterbury Rowan Williams holds that religion must alter the mode of communicating its message in order to reach a modern audience, while conservative historian Jonathan Clark recommends opposing the trends of modernity. Shaykh Hamza Ysuf, Islamic adviser to President George W. Bush, contends that, despite Muslims' tolerance toward Christianity, the West refuses to accept Islam.

Faultlines: The Search for Political and Religious Links—U.S.A.

Type:	DVD
Length:	34 min.
Cost:	$159
Date:	2003
Source:	Insight Media
	2162 Broadway
	New York, NY 10024-0621
	(800) 233-9910
	www.insight-media.com

John McCarthy examines the relationship between religion and politics in the United States, focusing on such issues as faith-based initiatives and the establishment clause of the First Amendment.

Interfaith Listening Pilot Project

Type:	VHS
Length:	37 min.

Cost: $9.95
Date: 2002
Source: Presbyterian Church (U.S.A.) Multimedia
                   Resources
                   100 Witherspoon Street
                   Louisville, KY 40202
                   (888) 728-7228, ext. 5210
                   www.btrinkle@ctr.pcusa.org

This video recounts the 2002 Interfaith Listening Pilot Project, in which eighteen Christians and Muslims from around the world visited the United States to meet in two-member teams with U.S. congregations to hold discussions and encourage interfaith listening as a way of promoting peace.

Introduction to the Word Alone Network
Type: DVD, VHS
Length: 30 min.
Date: 2005
Cost: $10 (DVD); $8 (VHS)
Source: Word Alone Network
                   2299 Palmer Drive, Suite 220
                   New Brighton, MN 55112
                   (888) 551-7254
                   www.wordalone.org

Mark Chavez, an Evangelical Lutheran Church in America (ELCA) pastor and director of the Word Alone Network (WAN), explains why a group of Lutheran pastors decided to form the WAN. Chavez affirms that the purpose of the organization is to return the ELCA to the confessional Lutheran foundations of the sixteenth-century Reformation, which he considers threatened by more recent trends in the denomination, including the approval in 1999 of a full communion agreement with the Episcopal Church.

John Paul II: The Millennial Pope
Type: DVD, VHS
Length: 150 min.
Cost: $19.98 (DVD); $14.95 (VHS)
Date: 1999
Source: PBS Video
                   2100 Crystal Drive
                   Arlington, VA 22202-3785

(800) 344-3337
www.shopPBS.com

This program highlights the great influence that Pope John Paul II had over the Catholic Church and world leaders on human rights and social justice issues, tracing his life from the Second World War to the fall of communism (for which he is given some credit) and beyond.

One Lord, One Faith . . . Many Churches: The Search for Christian Unity

Type:	VHS
Length:	55 min.
Cost:	$39.95
Date:	N/A
Source:	Presbyterian Church (U.S.A.) Multimedia Resources
	100 Witherspoon Street
	Louisville, KY 40202
	(888) 728-7228, ext. 5210
	www.btrinkle@ctr.pcusa.org

Produced for adult study groups, this video, in five twelve-minute segments, examines how various denominations may come to agreement on the issues that continue to divide them. The video package includes a study guide containing an overview of the content and suggested discussion questions.

The Politics of Gay Marriage and Abortion Rights

Type:	DVD and VHS
Length:	22 min.
Cost:	$89.95
Date:	2004
Source:	Films for the Humanities and Sciences
	P.O. Box 2053
	Princeton, NJ 08543-2053
	(800) 257-5126
	www.films.com

Broadcast prior to the 2004 presidential election, this ABC News program investigates the controversy over same-gender marriage in Massachusetts and then reports on a Catholic bishop in Colorado who announced that anyone who votes for an abortion rights or gay marriage supporter should refrain from participating in the sacrament of communion.

Pope John Paul II: Builder of Bridges

Type:	VHS
Length:	58 min.
Cost:	$2.99
Date:	2005
Source:	The Video Collection
	P. O. Box 2284
	South Burlington, VT 05407-2284

The video recounts the many peacemaking trips that Pope John Paul II made in order to mend the conflicts between the Catholic Church and other Christian as well as non-Christian religions. The pontiff visited England to meet with Anglican Church leaders, traveled to Eastern Orthodox countries, entered a mosque to open a conversation with Muslims, and visited German concentration camps and the Wailing Wall in Jerusalem in order to improve Christian-Jewish relations.

The Presbyterians Part II: History and Tradition

Type:	VHS
Length:	55 min.
Cost:	$19.95
Date:	N/A
Source:	Presbyterian Church (U.S.A.) Multimedia
	Resources
	100 Witherspoon Street
	Louisville, KY 40202
	(888) 728-7228, ext. 5210
	www.btrinkle@ctr.pcusa.org

This second installment in a five-part series examines the origins and development of the PCUSA from immigration from Scotland to North America through the American Revolution and the creation of the United States to recent ecumenical efforts and challenges for the future.

The Presbyterians Part IV: Polity

Type:	VHS
Length:	17 min.
Cost:	$19.95

Date: N/A
Source: Presbyterian Church (U.S.A.) Multimedia
               Resources
               100 Witherspoon Street
               Louisville, KY 40202
               (888) 728-7228, ext. 5210
               www.btrinkle@ctr.pcusa.org

This video examines the governing structure and activities of
the PCUSA. Viewers are shown scenes from various denominational meetings, including the General Assembly, to demonstrate
how the church members interact and make decisions about the
PCUSA's mission.

Religion, War, and Violence: The Ethics of War and Peace
Type: DVD and VHS
Length: 91 min.
Cost: $159.95 (DVD); $169.95 (VHS); $79.98 (Digital
               On-Demand)
Date: 2002
Source: Films for the Humanities and Sciences
               P.O. Box 2053
               Princeton, NJ 08543-2053
               (800) 257-5126
               www.films.com

The segments in this program, selected from *Religion and Ethics
Newsweekly*, include discussions among scholars and religious
leaders from various religious communities on such topics as
terrorism and its causes, just war doctrine, holy war, and pacifism. Interspersed with the panel discussions is footage of actual
conflicts.

Sacred Covenants, Faithful Conversations
Type: DVD
Length: N/A
Cost: $20
Date: 2005
Source: United Church Press
               Cleveland, OH

Based on the resolution, "Equal Marriage Rights for All," passed
at the twenty-fifth General Synod of the United Church of Christ,

this presentation explores the meaning of Christian marriage, the role of the church and the state in marriage, and the blessing of unions of same-gender couples.

Shalom: A Study of the Biblical Concept of Peace

Type:	CD-ROM
Length:	N/A
Cost:	$19.95
Date:	2003
Source:	Augsburg Fortress
	P. O. Box 1209
	Minneapolis, MN 55440-1209
	www.augsburgfortress.org

Maintaining the primary importance of peacemaking for the church in the contemporary world, Old Testament scholar Donald E. Gowan explores the meanings of peace within a biblical context and the notion's relevance today. The program includes study guidelines, questions for discussion, and issues for further study.

So Send I You: A Mission Yearbook Video

Type:	DVD
Length:	20 min.
Cost:	$14.95
Date:	2006
Source:	Presbyterian Distribution Service
	100 Witherspoon Street
	Louisville, KY 40202
	(800) 524-2612
	www.pcusa.org/media/socialjustice.htm

Intended as a teaching tool about the mission of the Presbyterian Church (U.S.A.), this video documents the church's congregations, presbyteries, and synods, and General Assembly involvement in various assistance projects in the United States and around the world.

200 Years of Presbyterian Women

Type:	VHS
Length:	55 min.
Cost:	$19.95
Date:	N/A

Source: Presbyterian Church (U.S.A.) Multimedia
Resources
100 Witherspoon Street
Louisville, KY 40202
(888) 728-7228, ext. 5210
www.btrinkle@ctr.pcusa.org

This video offers an introduction to the history of women in the Presbyterian Church, beginning 200 years ago when Presbyterian women first met for prayer and to contribute money for church activities.

Wrap Up: General Synod 25
Type: DVD
Length: N/A
Cost: $19.95
Date: 2004
Source: United Church Press
Cleveland, OH

The program offers various views of the United Church of Christ's twenty-fifth General Synod meeting. Among the events treated are the plenary session discussion and vote on a marriage equality resolution and John Thomas's statement at a press conference following the session.

Internet Sources

Advocacy
www.elca.org/advocacy

The Web site, maintained by the Evangelical Lutheran Church in America, contains updated material regarding events and issues of concern to the denomination, such as immigration reform, efforts to end poverty, assistance to U.S. farmers, and the Arab-Israeli conflict. The site offers advice to congregations regarding political activities in which they lawfully can engage.

beliefnet
www.beliefnet.com

This site contains information for people of many faiths, including Christianity, Judaism, Islam, Buddhism, and Hinduism.

Information is provided about religious doctrine and practices, inspiration, news, interviews with public personalities, and advice about personal relationships.

The Catholic Goldmine
www.catholicgoldmine.com

The site provides links to many other Catholic-affiliated sites, including those dealing with pro-life advocacy, general news, history, education, and church affairs.

Catholic.net
www.catholic.net/index.phtml

This Web site contains various news accounts relevant to Catholics, including such topics as Pope Benedict's overtures to Muslim leaders, the mass media, the political activity of Catholics, and pro-life commitments.

Church Herald
www.herald.rca.org

The Reformed Church in America maintains the Church Herald Web site to communicate news that is of interest to RCA members and to provide the opportunity to discuss issues facing the church. The site provides an archive of articles from the print version of the magazine.

Evangelical Lutheran Church in America Electronic Bookshelf
www.elca.org/library/bookshelf/index.html

This site provides links to various Internet sites on such topics as Christian ethics, religious journals, creeds and confessions of various Christian denominations, sources of research on religion, and materials on the world religions.

For Denominations
www.forministry.com/profile/ChurchSearch.cfm

This site is a directory of various religious denominations in the United States, including the mainline churches.

Journal of Lutheran Ethics
www.elca.org/jle

This online publication of the Evangelical Lutheran Church in America is dedicated to the study and discussion of Christian ethics from a Lutheran perspective. Topics include the biblical and theological basis and history of ethics; contemporary ethical issues; the church's role in social witness; and living a life appropriate for a Christian calling as a family member, citizen, worker, and church member or pastor.

Lutheran Partners
www.elca.org/lutheranpartners/archives

This site contains archived articles from the periodical *Lutheran Partners*. Among the topics indexed are church history, death and dying, poverty and hunger ministries, sexuality, science and technology, community development, and sexual abuse prevention.

Official Denominational Web Sites–Hartford Institute for Religion Research
www.hirr.hartsem.edu/org/faith_denominations_homepages .html

This site contains an extensive list of denominations in the United States, with links to individual churches within each denomination.

Papal and Episcopal Documents Relating to Catholic Social Justice Teaching
www.justpeace.org/docu.htm

This site provides access to statements that popes, church councils, national bishops' conferences, and individual bishops have made on questions of social justice. Included are the speeches and encyclicals of Pope John Paul II.

Religion Databases
www.berkleycenter.georgetown.edu/database

These four databases (Religious Perspectives, Religion and Development, Faith 2008, and World Events) , made available through the Berkley Center for Religion, Peace, and World Affairs at Georgetown University, provide a wealth of sources on the ethical approaches of different religious traditions.

Religion On-Line
www.religion-online.org

This site provides access to more than 5,700 articles and book chapters on religion and its relation to the larger society. Among the topics listed are capitalism versus communism, ecology and the environment, pornography, public education, death and dying, ecumenism, abortion, economic justice, civil rights, and liberalism and conservatism.

Routledge Religion Resources
www.reference.routledge.com / public

The Taylor and Francis Group makes this resource available online for a base charge of $1,350. The site includes more than 14,000 entries included in encyclopedias on such topics as religion and war, ethics, religious freedom, Protestantism, the papacy, and African American religion.

UMNS Weekly Digest
www.umns.umc.org

The United Methodist News Service maintains this site to provide a digest of news items relevant to the members and clergy of the United Methodist Church. News stories treat such topics as ecumenical contacts between the UMC and other denominations, missionary activities in the United States and other parts of the world, and statements on public policy issues.

Virtual Religion Index
www.virtualreligion.net / vri

This resource provides a wealth of links to other Web sites on various topics relevant to the study of religion, including academic sites, religious organizations, ethics and moral values, the history of Christianity, philosophy and theology, and the psychology of religion.

Wabash Center Guide to Internet Resources
www.wabashcenter.wabash.edu / resources / guide_headings .aspx

This site provides an annotated guide to Internet resources for those engaged in the study of religion. Among the topics listed are religion and science; women and religion; various religions around the world; the history of Christianity; religion and politics; social issues such as abortion, capital punishment, violence, and the environment; and official Web sites of religious organizations.

Web Links, Department of Religious Studies, Saint Mary's College
www.saintmarys.edu/~incandel/funweb.html

This site offers links to various Catholic Web sites, including those focusing on Catholic beliefs, theology, religious education, the Vatican and papal encyclicals, and U.S. foreign policy in the Middle East.

Glossary

Anglican Communion The international group of churches that are associated with the Church of England under the spiritual guidance of the Archbishop of Canterbury. Every ten years, each member church sends representatives to the Lambeth Conference.

bioethics The ethical, moral, and theological evaluation of biological research and medical treatment in the context of personal as well as collective political and legal decision making. Mainline denominations have devoted attention to various aspects of medical research and procedure, including embryonic stem-cell research and its promise of providing treatments for debilitating and fatal diseases, abortion, euthanasia and physician-assisted suicide, and the best use of limited health care resources. An important question within such investigations is whether ethical questions can always be resolved or whether there can be ethical dilemmas in which no one morally best solution arises.

Called to Common Mission The agreement of full communion between the Evangelical Lutheran Church in America (ELCA) and the Episcopal Church, which went into effect in 1999. The two denominations reached accord on doctrines of faith, recognition of each other's churches and clergy, and sharing in the ordination of future bishops. Dissenters in the ELCA who opposed the agreement quickly formed the Word Alone Network to express their continuing dissent.

capital punishment Also referred to as the death penalty, this public policy involves the execution of a person convicted of certain serious crimes such as murder. Several mainline denominations have stated officially their opposition to capital punishment, although it appears that the rank-and-file membership of these churches are more divided on the issue, with greater proportions supporting the death penalty, particularly for especially heinous crimes. The United States Conference of Catholic Bishops, emphasizing the "seamless garment of life," opposes any action that devalues the worth of human life, and other mainline denomina-

317

tions support demonstrations against capital punishment at the time of scheduled executions.

catholic   This word, meaning "general" or "universal," when capitalized usually refers to the church governed spiritually by the pope in the Vatican. When not capitalized, the term refers to the notion of a universal Christian church. In mainline church creeds, such as the Apostle's Creed, reference is made to the "catholic church," which signifies what the church always has believed and should continue to believe.

celibacy   Within the Catholic Church, the vow taken by men and women entering professional church service as priests or nuns that they will refrain from marriage or sexual intercourse. In contrast, the mainline Protestant churches require that pastors limit sexual intimacy to marriage between one man and one woman, although some denominations have considered broadening this limitation to "committed relationships" that include two people of the same gender. Those Catholics critical of the celibacy rule note that it has reduced the pool of candidates, becoming the single most important variable determining who will enter the priesthood.

charismatic movement   A phenomenon in Catholic and mainline Protestant churches begun in the 1960s that emphasizes such divinely inspired gifts (charisms) as speaking in tongues and faith healing. Adherents believe that, like early Christians, God blesses believers today with these abilities, which are described in the New Testament (I Corinthians 12:4-11). Some in mainline denominations have frowned on these practices, saying that they can cause divisions within congregations between those who claim to have the gifts and those who do not.

civil disobedience   The public and nonviolent refusal to obey laws considered to be unjust or immoral. During the civil rights movement in the 1950s and 1960s, many mainline Protestant pastors, Catholic priests, and laypeople engaged in civil disobedience in the effort to bring an end to segregation and achieve equal treatment for all people. During the Vietnam War era many mainline church members engaged in protest demonstrations. Notable figures such as Daniel and Patrick Berrigan, both Catholic priests, and William Sloane Coffin, Jr., a Presbyterian minister and chaplain at Yale University, took part in such demonstrations, inviting arrest. These and other religious figures later became involved in a campaign against the production of nuclear weapons that involved civil disobedience. Following the Supreme Court decision *Roe v. Wade* (1973) legalizing abortion, many Catholics and evangelical Christians took part in demonstrations at abortion clinics and invited arrest.

civil religion   The term involves the use of religious symbolism to explain and justify national objectives and purpose. Civil religion in the

United States provides an overall set of values to people of varying beliefs that supports such goals as justice and equal regard for all. However, a nationalistic version of civil religion can involve identifying God with the country and hence provide support for intolerance of differing beliefs within the nation and aggressive actions internationally.

classis Originating in the Latin word for "fleet," a term used in the Reformed Church in America to refer to several churches in a geographic territory, each one containing at least one minister and one elder who have an equal vote in all deliberations. The classis has jurisdiction over the work of the church in its geographic boundary, including the calling and dismissing of ministers.

culture war The conflict over differing perceptions of American society beginning in the 1960s and intensifying in subsequent years. Disagreements, distinguished generally between more conservative and more liberal elements of society, revolved around such issues as feminism, how homosexuality is to be regarded, affirmative action policies, curriculum in the public schools and higher education, and political correctness. The culture war raged not only between mainline denominations and more conservative evangelical churches but within the mainline denominations over such issues as the blessing of same-gender unions; the ordination of women and gay pastors; and public policy positions on such issues as military spending, environmentalism, economic justice, and abortion.

diocese Within the Catholic and Episcopal churches, the geographical area consisting of several local parishes that constitutes the basic unit of church organization. A bishop oversees each diocese. In the Catholic Church, the pope appoints bishops, but in the Episcopal Church, a diocesan convention elects a bishop who is then ratified by vote at the General Convention, held every three years. In the Catholic Church, especially large or historically important dioceses are designated archdioceses and are headed by an archbishop.

double effect The doctrine that an action that brings about some harm, foreseen but not intended, is permissible as the consequence of achieving some good result. One example of the double effect is administering drugs to terminally ill patients that alleviate pain but that also hasten death. Theologians and philosophers have debated the adequacy of the principle in explaining why certain actions are considered permissible.

ecumenism Derived from the Greek word *oikoumene*, which means "inhabited world," this term refers to efforts, especially prevalent in the mainline denominations, to achieve greater unity of understanding and doctrine among Christian churches. The push toward ecumenism has resulted in several interdenominational organizations, including the World Council of Churches, founded in 1948; the National Council of

Churches, founded in 1950; and Christian Churches Together in the U.S.A., formed in 2006. More conservative churches tend to avoid engaging in ecumenical dialogue with other denominations.

embryonic stem cells Undifferentiated cells from fertilized embryos that have been donated from in vitro fertilization clinics to be used in medical research. Researchers are enthusiastic about the possibility that stem cells, which can develop into various types of cells in the human body, can be used in medical procedures, including the treatment of deadly and debilitating diseases. Mainline denominations have expressed concern about the use of embryonic stem cells in research because the embryos from which they are derived are destroyed. Although the Catholic Church, which believes that life begins at conception, considers the destruction of embryos as equivalent to taking a life, other denominations have decided that the potential benefits for human beings are significant enough to permit well-regulated use of stem cells in medical research.

encyclical A letter from the pope to all people in the Catholic Church communicating his thoughts and judgments on doctrine, morals, or discipline. Only since the late nineteenth century have popes frequently issued such letters. Examples are Pope John XXIII's *Pacem in Terris* (1963) stating the Catholic principle that government has the purpose of promoting the common good for the total person, body and soul, and Pope John Paul II's *Evangelium Vitae* (1994) calling on Catholics to promote life at all stages of the life cycle.

episcopal The Greek word for bishop, *episcopos* means "overseer." Hence, the name of the Episcopal Church refers to being governed by bishops.

euthanasia The practice of ending a person's life for reasons, including extreme pain or deformity, that are considered merciful. Mainline denominations hold that the value of human life prohibits euthanasia. However, some denominations have issued statements that recognize the appropriateness of withholding extraordinary medical treatment in cases of extreme suffering and imminent death.

evangelical Derived from the Greek word for "good news," this term originally was used to refer to Lutherans who stressed the authority of the Bible, especially the four gospels of the New Testament. In the nineteenth century in the United States, evangelicals tended to emphasize personal devoutness as well as social reform. Today, evangelical churches, generally distinguished from the mainline denominations, emphasize a personal conversion experience and take conservative stances on social issues, emphasizing personal responsibility rather than social transformation.

faith-based initiative A term used to refer to various proposals to permit religious organizations to receive federal funding in order to provide social services. Following his inauguration in January 2001, President

George W. Bush announced the creation of the White House Office of Faith-Based and Community Initiatives in five cabinet departments. Although mainline denominations expressed interest in participating in a program of faith-based funding, they also voiced concern for maintaining independence from secular government regulation.

fundamentalism   A term used to refer to those who adhere to what conservative Christians in the early twentieth century, responding to liberal trends within the church, identified as the essential beliefs, or fundamentals, of Christianity, including biblical inerrancy, the deity and virgin birth of Jesus, and the second coming of Christ. Today, the terms "fundamentalist," "evangelical," and "conservative Christian" are used interchangeably. Controversies still rage in the mainline denominations on such issues as the ordination of gay ministers and the blessing of same-gender unions between those who adhere to a more literal reading of scripture and those who contend that the Bible must be interpreted in the context of the present culture.

heterodoxy   A synonym for heresy, this term refers to any opinion or doctrine that departs from established beliefs or traditions. Conservative dissenters within the mainline denominations in effect are charging their leaders with failing to uphold fundamental Christian doctrine. Evangelical and fundamentalist churches demonstrate far less willingness than mainline denominations to engage in ecumenical associations for fear of compromising orthodox Christian beliefs.

higher criticism   The scholarly examination of the Bible with the use of information about the history and culture of the period in which specific books were written. For instance, retired Episcopal Bishop John Shelby Spong, in *The Sins of Scripture*, engaged in higher criticism, pointing to attitudes and behavior recounted in the Bible that people today would reject. Because this approach raises questions about the factualness of scripture as history and hence as an inerrant source of faith, conservative Christians have tended to reject higher criticism as a threat to the authority of the scriptures.

humanism   The belief that all human beings have basic worth, are able to distinguish between right and wrong, possess the ability to reason, and can improve their condition here on earth. Although conservative Christians consider humanism to be non- or antireligious, or a religious competitor to Christianity, referring to the philosophy as secular humanism, humanistic assumptions can be identified as well in traditional religious movements, including mainline denominations.

intelligent design   The belief that scientific theories of the physical world cannot provide an exhaustive explanation of the origins of the universe and of human beings. Some conservative Christians offer intelligent design as an alternative scientific theory to that of Darwinian evolution.

Mainline denominations have remained largely aloof from this contention. In 2006 the Vatican newspaper, *L'Osservatore Romano*, published an article by Fiorenzo Fachini, a professor of evolutionary biology at the University of Bologna, which stated that although human beings, beyond the empirical realm, are not the product of chance or necessity, intelligent design is not science and hence insisting on its teaching along with evolutionary theory can only create confusion.

just war doctrine   Among the traditional criteria for engaging in a war justly (*jus ad bellum*) are that only a legitimate authority may wage war, the cause must be just, there must be a sufficiently high probability of success, the good to be achieved must outweigh the destruction caused by the use of force, and all nonviolent alternatives must have been tried. With the development of nuclear weapons following the Second World War, many church leaders and theologians agonized over whether a just nuclear war could be fought. Prior to the U.S. invasion of Iraq, several mainline church leaders questioned whether preemptive military action could be defended on just war principles. Given the lack of evidence of weapons of mass destruction and extended fighting in Iraq, denominational leaders continued to express their ethical and theological reservations regarding continuing the conflict, which appeared to violate the principles of conducting a just war (*jus in bello*), in particular the principle of discrimination, which holds that force must target combatants and not innocent civilians.

Lambeth Conference   The meeting of bishops in the Anglican Communion, chaired by the Archbishop of Canterbury, which is held every ten years. The bishops gather at Lambeth Palace in London or at the University of Kent in Canterbury. The conference provides the opportunity for bishops to cultivate relationships among the various churches, to investigate issues of mutual concern, and to agree on policy.

liberation theology   A movement, largely within the Catholic Church, that flourished following the Second Vatican Council in the 1960s. Often considered a version of Christian socialism, it rejected traditional cooperation with the established authority, emphasizing instead the inevitability of political conflict in which the church must play a role in favor of the poor. This radical Catholic movement, concentrated primarily in Latin America, did not receive encouragement from the Vatican and in more recent years has declined. However, some liberal Protestant groups still consider it an important theology of social action.

mega churches   Religious institutions having 2,000 or more worshipers each week that provide members with the opportunity to take part in groups and engage in a wide variety of activities touching all aspects of their lives. In the United States, more than half of these large congregations are nondenominational, and approximately 20 percent are associated with the Southern Baptist Convention. One of the older mega churches is Robert Schuller's Crystal Cathedral in Garden Grove, California, which is nominally associated with the mainline denomination Reformed Church in America. Mega churches have the opportunity to exercise influence in the local community and to raise funds for activities outside the church.

modernism   The adaptation of traditional religious beliefs to contemporary cultural trends and the optimistic conviction that human beings are capable of improving their environment and social institutions in a progression toward a godly kingdom here on earth. This view differs from the conservative Christian belief that human beings, tainted by original sin, are basically depraved and incapable by themselves of improving their condition.

partial-birth abortion   An abortion procedure, technically termed dilation and extraction, in which the fetus is partially delivered before the fetus's head is punctured. Although many mainline denominations recognize circumstances in which abortion might be justified, they uniformly condemn this procedure in all cases except when the life of the mother is involved. In 2003 Congress passed and President George W. Bush signed legislation banning the procedure.

physician-assisted suicide   The provision to an individual by a medical doctor of equipment, medication, or information about the use of available means to end the person's life. Mainline denominations have uniformly rejected any positive actions that would bring about a person's death, whether or not the individual has requested such actions. Jack Kevorkian, a medical pathologist and avid advocate of the right to die, was convicted of second-degree murder and imprisoned in 1999 for helping a terminally ill patient poison himself. In 1997 Oregon enacted the Death with Dignity law, which permits terminally ill patients to end their lives through the self-administration of lethal drugs prescribed by a physician. The Oregon Department of Human Services reported that in 2006, 46 people used the law to end their lives, most of whom were cancer patients.

presbytery   The local organizational unit of the Presbyterian Church (U.S.A.). Each church is overseen by presbyters, or elders. Regional organizations of presbyters are called presbyteries.

primate   A term used in the Church of England and the Anglican Communion to refer to the chief bishop of a national church. In the United States, the primate of the Episcopal Church is referred to as the presiding bishop.

renewal movements   Organizations within mainline denominations that claim the church has fallen away from the traditional teachings of

Christianity. Members of these groups object to what they consider challenges to biblical authority and theological orthodoxy. Denominational leadership is considered to have wandered from the truths of Christianity and therefore the movements are geared to return the church to traditional beliefs and concerns.

schism   A contentious division or split in a religious denomination or movement. Although members of renewal movements state that their purpose is to provide a voice for those who disagree with the dominant trend within the organization, ultimately they may become divisive or schismatic, depending on whether a separation of some or all of the dissenters ultimately occurs.

school vouchers   A school funding system by which government provides financial aid to individual families rather than to public school districts. The families may then select either a public or private school for their children to attend and have the tuition paid. The Catholic Church stands to gain significantly from a broadening system of school vouchers. The number of parochial schools has declined significantly since the 1960s, given the decline in services available from sisters and priests and the decreasing ability of parishes to subsidize schools. Claiming that parish schools provide a major subsidy to the public school system, the Catholic Church argues that fairness requires financial assistance in the form of vouchers. Other mainline denominations and evangelical churches that provide educational services also would benefit from school voucher systems.

seamless garment of life   A reference to Jesus's garment, which was "seamless, woven in one piece from the top" (John 19:23), which the soldiers hesitated to tear. This expression has become a call, especially in the Catholic Church, for a consistent policy regarding the protection of human life that includes not only opposition to abortion but also to the death penalty, euthanasia, nuclear warfare, and the so-called culture of death in general. The phrase also involves support for programs to assist children, pregnant women, and the impoverished.

social gospel   A movement among American liberal Protestants beginning during the late nineteenth century that emphasized Christians' responsibility to ameliorate the social ills attributed to industrialization and urbanization. Proponents argued that the gospel included a message of social reform as well as personal redemption. Concerned about a neglect of personal responsibility and what they considered the true message of Christianity, many conservative Christians objected to the social gospel. The movement continues today in the various social welfare programs and public policy recommendations of mainline Protestant denominations.

social services   Various assistance programs for the needy provided by local, state, and federal government as well as private institutions, including foster care, housing, transportation, in-home care, food assistance, health care, day care for children, employment assistance, and disaster relief. Several mainline denominations traditionally have engaged in social service programs, supporting professional organizations (for instance, Catholic Charities and Lutheran Social Services) that receive government subsidies for their services.

subsidiarity   The Catholic doctrine, expressed by Pope Pius XI in the 1931 encyclical *Quadragesimo Anno*, that a good society should have intermediate social institutions by which citizens can engage in civil society and that decisions should be made at the most local level feasible. Such institutions prevent the monopolization of power by the state or other institution.

synod   Within the Lutheran tradition, an administrative region similar to a diocese. A bishop, who is elected by the synod assembly, oversees the operation of the synod.

INDEX

About the Author

Glenn H. Utter, professor and chair of the Political Science Department at Lamar University, was educated at Binghamton University, the University of Buffalo, and the University of London. Utter specializes in modern political theory and American political thought. He wrote *Encyclopedia of Gun Control and Gun Rights* (2000); coedited *American Political Scientists: A Dictionary* (1993, 2002); and cowrote *Campaign and Election Reform* (1997), *Religion and Politics* (2002), *Conservative Christians and Political Participation* (2004), and *The Religious Right* (1995, 2001, 2007). He has written several articles for political science journals and other scholarly publications.